Needs Analysis for Language Course Design

A holistic approach to ESP

*Marjatta Huhta, Karin Vogt,
Esko Johnson and Heikki Tulkki*

*edited and with an introduction
by David R Hall*

CAMBRIDGE
UNIVERSITY PRESS

CAMBRIDGE UNIVERSITY PRESS
Cambridge, New York, Melbourne, Madrid, Cape Town,
Singapore, São Paulo, Delhi, Mexico City

Cambridge University Press
The Edinburgh Building, Cambridge CB2 8RU, UK

www.cambridge.org
Information on this title: www.cambridge.org/9780521128148

First published 2013

Printed and bound in the United Kingdom by the MPG Books Group

A catalogue record for this publication is available from the British Library

Library of Congress Cataloging in Publication data
Huhta, Marjatta.
Needs analysis for language course design : a holistic approach to ESP /
Marjatta Huhta, Karin Vogt, Esko Johnson, and Heikki Tulkki ; edited and
with an introduction by David R Hall.
     pages   cm
Includes bibliographical references and index.
ISBN 978-0-521-12814-8 (pbk.)
1. English language–Study and teaching (Higher)–Foreign speakers.   2. English language–
Business English–Study and teaching.   3. English language–Technical English–Study and
teaching.   I. Vogt, Karin.   II. Johnson, Esko.   III. Tulkki, Heikki.   IV. Hall, David R.
(David Robert), 1947-   V. Title.

PE1128.A2H88 2013
428.0071'1–dc23   2012040141

ISBN 978-0-521-12814-8 Paperback

Contents

Thanks and acknowledgements

The author team would like to acknowledge several people who have helped us in creating the book, and also institutions that facilitated completing the title. We are grateful to our CEF Professional Profiles Project members who contributed to the project besides the author team: Rafal Glowacz, Anne Hannila, Leena Hämäläinen, Dr Cor Koster, Riitta Purokuru, Dr Zsofia Radnai, Hannu Ryynänen, Ivan Shotlekov and Penka Taneva. More information on the CEF Professional project (2005–7) is available in the CEF Professional Website Handbook at www.proflang.org.

Warm thanks go to Metropolia University of Applied Sciences students who trialled the simulations and activities and thus impacted on their quality.

This book would not have been feasible without the experts in numerous companies, hospitals, consultancies and universities who kindly gave their precious time for interviews and document checking.

We are also grateful to David R Hall, who devoted much time to improving the draft manuscript and who provided an introduction that clearly shows his expertise and knowledgeability.

We acknowledge that some of the activities in this book were derived from simulations published earlier in *Connections – Communication Guidelines for Engineers by* Marjatta Huhta.

Contributors

Authors

Marjatta Huhta, *Helsinki Metropolia University of Applied Sciences, Finland*

Marjatta Huhta coordinates the Master's Programme in Industrial Management and Services Business. She has researched work communication and published research reports on language and communication needs in business. She has taught professional communication and published coursebooks and material for business and technical communication (e.g. *Connections: Communication Guidelines for Engineers*, 2007). She has also designed and implemented corporate language training as Head of Language Department (Fintra).

Esko Johnson, *Centria University of Applied Sciences, Finland*

Esko Johnson has taught ESP technology since 1984. His research interests include teacher/professional growth and development, intercultural communication and learning, online teaching and learning, foreign language literacy and language programme evaluation.

Heikki Tulkki, *Helsinki Adult Education Centre, Finland*

Heikki Tulkki currently works as the Head of Languages at the Finnish Adult Education Centre in Helsinki. He has a teaching background in English, Swedish and German, both in secondary vocational education and in higher education. He has co-authored a number of textbooks on English, Swedish, German, intercultural communication and social sciences for course use in secondary vocational and tertiary education, as well as self-study. In addition, he has coordinated both national and international language and business projects.

Karin Vogt, *University of Education Heidelberg, Germany*

Karin Vogt has previously worked as a professor in the English department at the University of Education, Karlsruhe, Germany. She is a fully trained teacher with several years of teaching experience at different schools. Her research interests include Vocationally Oriented Language Learning (VOLL), intercultural communication and intercultural learning, and classroom-based testing and assessment. She has also published in these areas; her latest publication is a book on adapting descriptors of the CEFR for VOLL/ESP (*Fremdsprachliche Kompetenzprofile*, 2011).

Editor

David R Hall, *Macquarie University, Australia*

David Hall is Associate Dean International in the Faculty of Human Sciences at Macquarie University, Australia, following four years as Associate Dean for Higher Degree Research. He was Coordinator of International Relations for the Division of Linguistics and Psychology from 2006 to 2008, and was the elected Head of the Department of Linguistics from 2000 to 2005. He has taught curriculum innovation, management, and language for special purposes at masters level, and units on curriculum, leadership and linguistics research at doctoral level. He has also been a consultant for international aid agencies, educational bodies and state government departments. He is joint general editor, with Chris Candlin, of two international book series on Applied Linguistics. He has published widely on distance learning in language teacher education. He is also the co-author (with Sandra Kies) of a forthcoming book on *Language for Specific Purposes* (Palgrave).

CEF Professional Profiles Project needs analysts whose communication profiles are included in the appendices:

Bożena Górska-Poręcka, *Warsaw University, Poland*

Bożena Górska-Poręcka is a university teacher of English for general, academic, business and legal purposes. She has also taught courses in public speaking at Ball States University, Muncie, USA.

Katja Hämäläinen, *Helsinki Metropolia University of Applied Sciences, Finland*

Katja Hämäläinen is involved in testing new teaching methods and learning activities in practice as well as developing ways of teaching and testing the oral language skills of the L2 learners.

Mirja Järvinen, *Helsinki Metropolia University of Applied Sciences, Finland*

Mirja Järvinen has taught Swedish and English languages for healthcare students since 1989. In addition, she has also written many textbooks and materials in Swedish and English, including network-based language learning and testing.

Vanya Ivanova, *University of Plovdiv, Bulgaria*

Vanya Ivanova works as an assistant professor of English at the Faculty of Mathematics and Computer Science at Plovdiv University, Bulgaria, teaching General English and ESP, with over fifteen years of experience in the tertiary education sector. Her professional interests include intercultural studies, testing, translation theory and practice. She is an author of books with language testing in practice, and a co-author in a number of comparative studies of idioms across different languages (English, French, Russian and Bulgarian).

Introduction

David R. Hall, Macquarie University, Australia

A typical problem for new and experienced language teachers alike is that of having to design a course that is efficient, effective and relevant, and that is tailor-made to cater to learners' professional needs, but where there may be only a limited amount of preparation time. In professional and organisational contexts, the problem is compounded by most communication teachers' lack of experience of such contexts and by a degree of social and linguistic complexity, as well as heterogeneity, in the workplace that even teachers with professional and organisational experience cannot be expected to understand without a coherent analytical framework. As a solution to the problem, the Common European Framework (CEF) Professional Profiles presented in this book outline an evidence-based approach to needs analysis with detailed instructions on how to use the profiles for course planning and design. This is a practical manual on conducting a needs analysis in modern enterprises and organisations, but it is also much more than that, as it builds on past models of needs analysis to create a new, dynamic, collaborative and inclusive model for identifying and dealing with the demands of the increasingly complex discourse world of the modern workplace. The profiles will certainly help the novice teacher, whose understanding of workplace communication will be facilitated by making use of the framework and by conducting the kinds of activities outlined here, which are strongly learner-focused, valorising participants' own professional experience, knowledge and practices. The book's audience, however, is not confined to novice teachers. Experienced teachers, as well as workplace communication researchers, will find that the holistic approach and the solid analytical framework provided here will furnish them with a well-informed basis for their work.

Communication teaching for professional purposes, like all specific-purpose language teaching, takes as a point of departure the idea that something about the communication and the contexts for which it is needed can be identified and that course design can focus on precisely those elements. This book is designed to provide an analytical framework for teachers and course designers, to help in making the necessary identifications in a practical way and in using these identifications to form the basis for the design of professionally orientated courses and learning activities. The ultimate goal of the profile-based innovation is to create and promote professional communication competences needed in the working environment.

English for Specific Purposes (ESP), together with its early relative English for Science and Technology (EST), first sprang to prominence, at least in the modern era, in the late 1960s and early 1970s. The pioneering books of English for Science (e.g. Herbert 1965; Ewer and Latorre 1969; Swales 1971) had remained clearly within existing language-teaching traditions focusing on linguistic forms, whereas developments later in the 1970s coincided with the development of Communicative Language Teaching (CLT).

CLT privileged specific purpose and specific context, adding these to the existing range of practices of language teachers and course designers and to the activities of the language classroom, and the link between CLT and ESP (and later its more inclusive version Language for Specific Purposes, LSP) was established.

The need to identify what those specific purposes and specific contexts might be fell to the language teachers and course designers, who were often the same people, involved in designing materials for their own classes. This changing view of teachers as not just consumers of commercial textbooks but also materials writers, although it brought its own problems (see Swales 1980), meant that the LSP teacher necessarily also took on the role of researcher:

> the dividing lines in ESP between researchers and teachers, or curriculum designers, materials developers, and teachers, are frequently blurred. Since even the earliest days of ESP … practitioners have viewed assessment of specific needs as requiring research skills and creative approaches to novel situations.
>
> (Belcher 2006: 135)

Belcher's comment is particularly relevant to the present book as, despite the recognition of the dual researcher-teacher role within our own profession, it is unfortunately the case that teachers often operate within very restrictive time and funding constraints, and it is unrealistic for most people called upon to design and deliver a specific-purpose course to instigate a lengthy and in-depth investigation. There has to be a capacity for building on the experience of others. It is the aim of this book that the research carried out and the models developed as a consequence of that research should provide precisely such a platform for further building, as well as offering a template for the process of further investigation.

Even in the early stages of modern LSP, there was an awareness both that language competency alone was not the only desirable outcome of a special-purpose course and that artificial fragmentation of experience into teachable chunks did not reflect the challenges faced by learners in their workplaces and content studies. Teachers of courses for academic purposes, for example, soon discovered that for students of varied cultural and educational backgrounds and correspondingly varied expectations of appropriate and effective learner behaviour, it was not enough to have adequate language skills; they also needed guidance on a whole range of what were collectively known as study skills: note-taking, library skills, non-linear reading strategies, participating in tutorials, presenting papers, answering examination questions and so on.

Much of the development of LSP and study skills courses had been largely based on the teacher's intuitions, rather than any rigorous investigation of what actually happened when language-learners took their newly acquired linguistic and behavioural skills into the real-world situations that had been targeted in their courses. When John Munby's

Communicative Syllabus Design (1978) was published, it came, therefore, at an opportune time and was highly influential.

Munby took the individual learner as his starting point and outlined a comprehensive framework for analysing that learner's communication needs in the learner's targeted situations. The main part of the book was devoted to the Communication Needs Processor (CNP), which defined the features of communicative situations categorised under eight major headings (the first four primary data, the second dependent on the first four):

1. Purposive domain – the type of LSP, the purpose for which the language is needed
2. Setting – details of time, place, event
3. Interaction – the roles, relative status, relationships, etc. of the learner with other people
4. Instrumentality – the channel and mode of communication
5. Dialect – the language varieties that will be encountered
6. Target level – the level of proficiency that is needed for the learner in the target situation
7. Communicative event – what learners will need to be able to do with language in the target situation
8. Communicative key – similar to Halliday's **tenor**, including attitudes and levels of formality

This summary gives an idea of what major categories were covered but does not convey the template's impressive level of detail. Each of these parameters was exhaustively broken down into sub-components with often very delicate distinctions. The analysis overall resulted in a Profile of Needs for the individual learner.

The framework was seen as a definitive instrument for needs analysis. Its impact was later described in this way:

> With the development of the CNP it seemed as if ESP had come of age. The machinery for identifying the needs of any group of learners had been provided: all the course designers had to do was to operate it.
>
> (Hutchinson & Waters 1987: 54)

In practice, however, the framework was somewhat cumbersome and time-consuming (see Hall 2001a: 234). A definitive critique of the Munby approach appeared in a review by Richard Mead (1982), which neatly covers both the theoretical and the practical limitations of Munby's work. Among the more important limitations are that it does not involve the learner – it is very much an outsider's view of needs, collecting data about the learner, not from the learner – and that its subcategories are rather inconsistent and reliant on introspection. The Munby model does not propose a syllabus design process. It deals with the communicative needs of learners but does not propose how these should be turned into materials or methods, and it has no reference to logistical, administrative, motivational, pedagogical or procedural considerations.

If I have spent some time on Munby and the influence his book had on the development of needs analysis, it is because I believe that the present book embodies a similarly ambitious attempt to do for modern participant-focused, collaborative, process-based communication needs analysis and pedagogy what Munby attempted for the product-based, designer-focused, top-down paradigm of the 1970s. I also believe that it does so in a way that successfully avoids the shortcomings of Munby's approach as identified above. As we will see below, the writers of this book adopted a research and course design methodology that engages with the target learners' actual professional purposes, working in a plurilingual and pluricultural environment across a range of different workplace organisations. The model outlined here looks for inspiration much more towards sociological investigations of business and technical communication in the workplace than it does towards linguistic descriptions of the language.

This sociological and holistic approach is innovative, but can also be seen as consistent with developments in mainstream LSP since Munby, which have been characterised by two parallel threads: a focus on discourse, genres and communicative events and a more collaborative, bottom-up, socially engaged approach to needs analysis and course design.

Discourse analysis, where texts are analysed at a level beyond the sentence, has many theoretical and practical variations, and genre analysis, discourse analysis and their different schools of practice have been very influential in LSP, to the extent that **text-type** or **genre** is now a pervasive feature of syllabus specifications (see Freedman & Medway 1994; Johns 2002).

The move to an examination of language beyond the sentence has had possibly unforeseen but far-reaching consequences. Analysis of whole texts inevitably involves not simply the text as an isolated artefact but also the users of the text and the uses to which the text is put. This has resulted in practitioner-researcher attention being turned to macro-issues such as power and empowerment (e.g. Martin 1993; Berkenkotter & Huckin 1995; Fairclough 2001; Talbot et al. 2003; Blackledge 2005), identity (Norton 2000; Kiely et al. 2006), group membership (Lave & Wenger 1991; Swales 1998; Barton & Tusting 2005) and other considerations of what it means to be able to use language effectively in a whole variety of social, cultural, economic, political, professional, personal and institutional contexts. The communication perspective in the study of workplace communities demonstrates the central importance of communicative practices in constituting the organisation, and this perspective is now influential in the fields of organisational structure, management and organisational and institutional communication: 'The concept of language and discourse as both a mode of representation and as a tool for the construction of reality takes on a different meaning in institutional settings, in particular in determining whose construction of events and how such events are to be categorised, prevails' (Sarangi & Candlin 2011). Workplace communication practices are utilised to construct meaning within management systems (Jackson [2003] 2007), organisation cultures (Hatch 1997) and networks of stakeholders (Freeman & Reed 1983; Mendelow 1987: 177), form a key basis for learning in and by organisations

(Senge 1990; Argyris & Schön 1996; Argyris 2002) and are significant as a medium for decision-making in organisations (Hirokawa et al. 2004: 7).

Thus professional language and communication competences involve far more than traditional LSP. Language learning for professional communication embodies a much greater awareness of its own far-reaching complexity than might have been imagined in the days when the teaching of scientific language first separated itself from general language teaching.

Bazerman and Russell (2003) put a strongly argued case that the study of texts and how they are produced and understood is meaningless, unless we can look at what the text actually causes to be done in the real world:

> It is in the context of their activities that people consider texts and give meaning to texts. And it is in the organization of activities that people find the needs, stances, interactions, tasks that orient their attention toward texts they write and read. So to study text production, text reception, text meaning, text value apart from their animating activities is to miss the core of text's being.
>
> (Bazerman & Russell 2003)

Discourse analysts have themselves become aware that an outsider analysis of text is insufficient and potentially prone to errors of interpretation, so that collaborative analysis is now encouraged:

> Much recent criticism of discourse analysis has centred on [its] logocentric view of communication. Short pieces of transcribed language abstracted from their physical contexts, it is argued, cannot make claims to represent face-to-face communication with all its complex modes ... We need the wider context in which discourses are embedded if we are to understand them from an insider's perspective.
>
> (Roberts et al. 2001: 84)

One of the keys to understanding how an organisation works is to understand its systems of communication: who gets to say or write what to whom with what effect using what channels and modes, how different genres are used, abused or subverted, what the patterns of communication reveal about organisational structure, culture and decision-making processes. Orlikowski and Yates (1994) refer to the genre repertoire in an organisation, sometimes also referred to as a genre set or a genre collection. They outline how genres can be recognised in organisational contexts by looking at their purpose, their form or both. They also note the importance of looking at 'genre overlap' when trying to distinguish the communicative practices that make up an organisation. Most importantly, they discuss genre change and how genres are dynamic and can be changed, either deliberately or inadvertently. The centrality of variation and overlap has been noted by many writers on organisational communication (e.g. Kersten 1986; Broekstra 1998; Grant et al. 2001), including the key notions of intertextuality (Clarke 2002) and interdiscursivity (Candlin 2006) in the workplace, in which the interconnectedness of communicative events is paramount. Critical discourse analysts such as Ruth Wodak (1996; Wodak et al. 2000) have shown how the production and interpretation of individual texts cannot be understood without reference to the entire context, ultimately including not simply individual organisations but whole cultures. Gunnarsson (2000), for example, claims that discourse plays a crucial role in a company's success and even survival, that discourse helps to construct a company's self-image, that both professional and national cultures put constraints on what is possible, and that discourse reflects organisational cultures and ideas of leadership. For all of these reasons, any analysis of communication in context must involve multiple overlapping and often competing perspectives. Candlin (2006: 17 et seq.) and Crichton (2010: 15–17 and 20 et seq.), building on a multiperspectived research model developed by the sociologist Layder (1993, 1997) and outlining a range of challenges facing the communication researcher, emphasise the interdependence of the components in such a multiperspectived approach:

> What seems important to us is that the perspectives of this research are not prioritised: entry is possible in a variety of ways and drawing on different but complementary discourses of research. What is central is maintaining the mutuality and the integrity of the perspectives.
>
> (Candlin 2006: 19)

Candlin and Crichton (2010; Crichton 2010) have recently developed a five-perspective model of interdiscursivity, incorporating the text perspective, the participant perspective, the social and institutional perspective and the social action perspective, linked to a fifth, and complementary, perspective, that of the analyst (see also Sarangi & Candlin 2001; Sarangi 2005). This concept of five 'different but complementary' perspectives has proved particularly useful in informing the present study.

Insider knowledge is essential to understanding what kinds of communication take place and what their consequences are. As a result, needs analysis for LSP has often in more recent years been undertaken in a more collaborative and consultative spirit. Some have taken this a logical step further by making the needs analysis and course design participatory, so that the learners have some control over both processes and content of LSP courses. This approach owes much to ideas developed in the context of learner autonomy (Holec 1981; Dam 1995; Benson 2011) and to the strong version of CLT as presented by Breen and Candlin (1980). Holistic and participatory approaches to needs analysis have been implemented successfully (e.g. Savage & Storer 1992; Hall 2001b), taking account of the very much more complex picture we have of communication in context, but this has not been in quite such a systematic and wide-ranging way as is found in this book.

What kind of specificity can be achieved in an increasingly complex interconnected and hybridising world? In the workplace, in the professions and in the academic sphere, genres, styles and modes of communication are often as varied within the professional context as they are across contexts, thus apparently weakening the case for the traditional practice of languages for professional purposes: 'the situated talk and text in professional and institutional settings is increasingly characterised by *hybridity*. It is difficult to maintain an orderly discreteness and integrity in terms of which we have come to identify ideal text and interaction types' (Sarangi & Candlin 2011). In addition, the attitudes and goals of different stakeholders with different levels of power and ability to influence decisions and evaluate outcomes may be quite diverse. Many workplaces are multilingual, and workers may use a mixture of languages in their everyday working lives. Global business is plurilingual and pluricultural, meaning not that individuals are all multilingual and multicultural but that different linguistic and cultural practices are widespread in the workplace, that individuals deal with this variety as a matter of routine, and that such variability is seen as an advantage in the global marketplace. The multicultural group involved with this project saw clear evidence of this diversity in the project, taking in several different professions across several countries, and the holistic approach taken in the design of course activities is a consequence of the need to incorporate participants' contextualising knowledge and experience. It is not surprising to see that the current book had its genesis in a Council of Europe project, in a context where plurilingualism is extensive and there is wide appreciation of the role of language in the workplace and in education, but every area of the world has its particular linguistic complexity, so it should not be thought that the usefulness of the book will be confined to Europe.

When faced with the complexity of language use, individual aspirations, competing discourses, cultural differences and all the rest of the considerations covered above, it becomes obvious that the practices of 'classical' needs analysis will not suffice. We need a planning mechanism that does not simplify by omission, but that can incorporate all the contradictions and unresolved issues that constitute lived experience. The Common European Framework has provided a model and a set of benchmarks for a great deal of course development and evaluation, and it also enables a coherent needs analysis template that can accommodate different stakeholder perceptions and an analysis of needs from the macro- to the micro-level. The project which engendered much of the work described here was called the Common European Framework of Reference for Professional Language and Communication Competencies (abbreviated here to CEF Professional Profiles), and it acknowledges the sociological elements in the CEF, which have often been neglected amid the attention paid to banding scales and their descriptors. The framework described and exemplified in this book focuses on an action-oriented, task-based approach to needs analysis which goes well beyond traditional approaches and which can provide a way forward for professionals in language for professional purposes and LSP in a complex world.

In the comprehensive account of the CEF Professional Profiles Project that fills these pages, you will find in Chapter 1 an account of the genesis of the project, of the professional contexts in which it took place in various countries in Europe, and of the academic and practical considerations that framed the project, as well as an indication of the range of data-collection strategies that were used. Chapter 2 complements much of the historical account given in this introduction, outlining the academic and practical arguments in favour of or against different views of what constitutes needs analysis. A key concept here is that of 'communication situation', which is discussed at some length in this chapter and which underpins the framework presented in the book. Chapter 3 presents a fully detailed account of one specific case. Significantly for the purposes of the readership of this book (and in contrast to Munby 1978), Chapter 4 gives a meticulous account of how the profiles can be incorporated into the processes of professional communication course planning and can feed directly into classroom activities. In keeping with the insistence on authenticity, the activities are heavily influenced by task-based learning and activities that reproduce the discourses and actions of the workplace. Numerous detailed examples of classroom materials and procedures are given in this chapter. Finally, Chapter 5 outlines step-by-step procedures for developing your own profiles for your own purposes, with sample profiles and other useful documents made available in the appendices.

The theoretical underpinning of this book is predominantly sociological rather than linguistic or pedagogical. It conducts hands-on investigation of communication needs in companies in a spirit of participatory, holistic and workplace-embedded communication analysis.

One of the dilemmas of language teaching, in both academic and workplace contexts, is that resources are often limited and LSP becomes marginalised as an activity separate from the rest of daily workplace interaction. Teachers are only peripheral participants in the workplace community, with limited access to the practices and values of the professions they are dealing with. That is why the focus here is on Language and Communication for Professional Purposes (LCPP), providing hands-on assistance for effectively identifying the communication needs of a workplace and helping to devise realistic, motivating holistic activities usable in pre-service and in-service training.

The pair work, information gap activities and similar practices of traditional CLT are not sufficient for preparing the learner for the multi-participant, multi-professional, multi-location information exchanges of the modern workplace. Therefore the CEF Professional Profiles make an effort to describe the professional communities, their members, backgrounds and incorporated activities. This is done in a way which does not focus on functions and notions of communication but provides sufficient information for realistic workplace simulations in the classroom.

Communication is seen holistically as involving effective communication as a professional and to a professional standard (see Boswood 1999 for an indication of what this involves). This is the point of view that LCPP is concerned with: helping the professional to communicate in his or her discourse community. It involves varieties of genres and agendas interacting and competing in a way that is quite different from the clear-cut and fragmentary presentation common in coursebooks. The use of English as a lingua franca is now well documented internationally, but it is not the only language used in this way. Participants in communicative events are likely to use whatever shared resources they have to achieve effective communication. This project takes the plurilingual and pluricultural context as its point of departure, as it is such a pervasive feature of the workplaces that the author-researchers set out to investigate. The transnational collaboration evident in the writing of this book is itself indicative of the nature of our globalising world. It is my belief that the framework presented in this work, grounded as it is in careful research, is both of very practical benefit for the language practitioner for professional purposes and of significance in the advancement of the field of needs analysis in the teaching of language and communication.

1 Needs analysis and the CEF Professional Profiles in ESP

Chapter overview

In this chapter, we describe the methodology we have used to conduct needs analysis within the CEF Professional Profiles approach and how this relates to other approaches open to needs analysis in **English for Specific Purposes (ESP)**. We will:

- explain why needs analysis is integral to course design in ESP
- consider different ways in which needs analysis has been designed up to the present day
- provide an overview of how needs analysis in ESP has developed up to the present day
- explain the importance of **thick description** to the methodology used in our approach to needs analysis in the CEF Professional Profiles.

1.1 The need for needs analysis in ESP course design

Teaching ESP has always been characterised by a hands-on, **communicative approach** to language teaching. Learners are taught to accomplish tasks that they are familiar with from their professional environment in the foreign language. This kind of language teaching and learning brings the task to the forefront of the foreign language classroom (see e.g. Nunan 1989, 2004; Willis 1996; Ellis 2003).

However, the importance of tasks in language learning is not the exclusive preserve of ESP: it has also been highlighted by the **Council of Europe** in its groundbreaking and extremely successful document the *Common European Framework of Reference for Languages: Learning, Teaching, Assessment* (**CEFR**). The **action-oriented** approach adopted by the CEFR makes tasks central to language learning:

> A comprehensive, transparent and coherent frame of reference for language learning, teaching and assessment ... The approach adopted ... is an action-oriented one in so far as it views users and learners of a language primarily as 'social agents', i.e. members of society who have tasks ... to accomplish in a given set of circumstances, in a specific environment and within a particular field of action ... [L]anguage activities ... form part of a wider social context, which alone is able to give [these activities] their full meaning.

We speak of 'tasks' in so far as the actions are performed by one or more individuals strategically using their own specific competences to achieve a given result. The action-based approach therefore also takes into account the *cognitive*, *emotional* and *volitional resources* and the full range of abilities specific to and applied by the individual as a social agent ...

Language use, embracing language learning, comprises the actions performed by persons who as individuals and as social agents develop a range of *competences*, both *general* and in particular *communicative language competences*. They draw on the *competences* ... in various contexts under various *conditions* and under various constraints to engage in *language activities* involving *language processes* to produce and/or receive *texts* in relation to *themes* in specific *domains*, activating those *strategies* which seem most appropriate for carrying out the tasks to be accomplished.

(Council of Europe 2001: 9, emphasis added)

The main concern of an action-oriented approach to course design is therefore to enable our learners to use the foreign language to accomplish just those tasks that are of most relevance to them in their professional lives. Hence, the effectiveness of this approach to course design hinges on knowing which tasks are relevant to which professional situations. This leads us to a problem that course designers often face, namely, how to identify the tasks and situations (and the corresponding **functions** and **notions**; see e.g. Munby 1978; Wilkins 1976) that the learner typically has to face in the real world.

This is the point at which a **needs analysis** is called for, but this is a far less straightforward process than it might initially seem because first it is essential to establish *whose* needs we are interested in. This also involves consideration of not just one perspective or one context but multiple perspectives and multiple contexts. Needs may be investigated from the perspective of teachers, that of the learners or that of the employers who are funding the language course. Then within the learner group itself, perspectives on what can be learned, what should be learned and why will differ from learner to learner (Robinson 1991).

No learner group is ever homogeneous of course, but this is particularly true of the ESP[1] group. ESP learners vary, but more often than not they will be adults or mature adolescent learners, and they will have diverse learner biographies. Thus we often find ourselves dealing with heterogeneous groups regarding the age, proficiency in the foreign language and professional experience of the learners. The needs of the working professional with extensive experience are likely to be very different from those of the inexperienced trainee, who must come to terms not only with the workplace context but also with the institutional context of whichever educational facility he or she is attending. The demands placed on the trainee by both the educational and the professional contexts may contribute to the perception that the

---

[1] What is true of ESP here may also refer to learner groups in English for Academic Purposes (EAP), **Vocationally Oriented Language Learning** (**VOLL**) and **Language and Communication for Professional Purposes** (**LCPP**)

trainee has either additional needs or else a completely different set of needs from those of the experienced professional in the same field.

The number of potential **stakeholders** of which the analysis can take account, together with the variety of perspectives from which the context can be considered have, not surprisingly, produced in the literature a wide range of definitions of what actually constitutes a 'need'. Hutchinson and Waters (1987: 54) define needs as 'the ability to comprehend and/or produce the linguistic features of the target situation'. They make a distinction between *target needs* and *learning needs*, subdividing target needs further according to the perspective taken. Figure 1.1 illustrates this classification of needs.

Hutchinson and Waters's scheme demonstrates clearly how the different roles and positions each group of stakeholders occupies result in needs which may vary considerably. It goes without saying that this variety in needs could lead to different views as to what kind of course should be designed or even to a conflict of interests between one or more of the groups. Conflicts of interest can arise when a learner group of employees perceive their needs to be different from those of the company that employs them and is thus funding the course. The learner-employees might lack confidence in their oral communication and so be mainly interested in developing their fluency in spoken discourse, whereas the company's focus might be on developing written skills because there has been a massive increase in the use of email and other kinds of electronic communication.

In their attempts to classify needs, both Berwick (1989) and Brindley (1989) have gone further than Hutchinson and Waters in exploring different kinds of perspectives on the professional context for learning. Berwick (1989) discusses *felt needs* and *perceived needs*, the distinction here being made between a personal, inside perspective and a more objective, outside view of the professional learner and his or her professional context for learning. Brindley's description (1989: 65) also starts out with an inside/outside perspective, which he

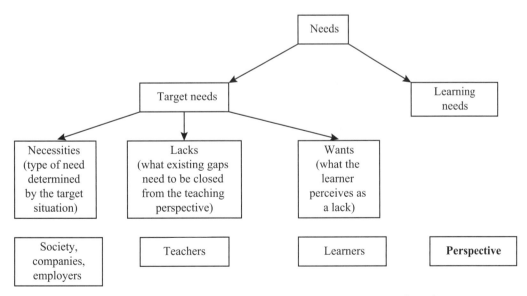

Figure 1.1: Classification of needs based on Hutchinson and Waters (1987)

refers to as *subjective* and *objective needs*. Here, objective needs tend to be based on facts and may be introduced from outside views, while subjective needs are those that involve the personal perspective of the learner as an individual. For instance, an objective need for a middle manager in the medical equipment industry might be *to be able to show visitors around*, but something like *to be more confident when dealing with visitors from abroad* would be representative of a subjective need.

However, Brindley then goes on to make a further distinction, between needs which are *process-oriented* and those which are *product-oriented*, where the former are concerned with how the learning is carried out, while the priority for the latter is the final outcome of the course. Taking the earlier example of the middle manager, a process-oriented view would consider how confidence in dealing with visitors can be gradually increased, and a product-oriented need would be defined as an ability to conduct a conversation with a visitor.

What these examples show is that needs analysis demands more than a straightforward process of one-to-one matching of means with objectives. Multiple stakeholders can have multiple perspectives resulting in a multitude of objectives and desired outcomes for the ESP course, some of which, as we have seen, may even be contradictory.

Consequently, the number of definitions for what can be considered 'needs' has led to a correspondingly wide range of definitions of needs analysis. Ellis gives us the rather straightforward definition of needs analysis as 'a procedure for establishing the specific needs of language learners' (2003: 345–6). While this is certainly true, it is far too general to be of much use to the course designer. A more complete view is given in Brown (2006), which takes into account the range of sources from which information can be gathered as well as the number of stakeholders for whom that analysis will be relevant:

> Needs analysis ... is ... the process of identifying the language forms that students ultimately will need to use in the target language. However, since the needs of the teachers, administrators, employers, institutions etc. also have some bearing on the language learning situation, many other types of quantitative and qualitative information of both objective and subjective types must be considered in order to understand both the situation and the language involved as well as information on the linguistic content and the learning processes. Needs analysis is the systematic collection and analysis of all subjective and objective information necessary to define and validate defensible curriculum purposes that satisfy the language learning requirements of students within the context of the particular institutions that influence the learning and teaching situation.
>
> (Brown 2006: 102)

Brown shows us just how essential a systematic and thorough-going approach to needs analysis is to ESP course design. While needs analysis can also make valuable contributions to the design of any language course, it is especially important to ESP because here the needs analyst has to consider the involvement of teachers, employees, the commercial interests of the employers, the standards of professional associations, the syllabi of regional/national vocational qualifications and so on. At any one time, each of these perspectives may either complement or contradict another.

As a starting point for needs analysis for the ESP course, Robinson (1991) views needs in ESP on three different levels: the *micro-*, the *meso-* and the *macro-levels* of need. Figure 1.2 illustrates these three levels with examples taken from the ESP context of the middle manager in the medical equipment industry discussed earlier.

As shown in Figure 1.2, micro-level needs are those that arise from the individual learner. In our example of the middle manager, at the micro-level is the perceived need to be more confident with visitors from abroad, which could include advanced small talk but also the necessity to 'talk shop'. Let us imagine that our middle manager now has to deal on a regular basis with new business partners based in Japan. Her encounters with the Japanese company have so far left her feeling clumsy in certain situations and so she now wants to improve her fluency.

The wider context of the workplace (or the institution providing the vocational training – in this case, a supplier of medical equipment) is considered at the meso-level. This level deals with those needs that are related to outcomes deemed desirable or necessary to an organisation, such as a private company or a government department. In our example, the key concern of the medical equipment suppliers will be to build and maintain a good business relationship with their Japanese partners. To that end, they will also need the middle

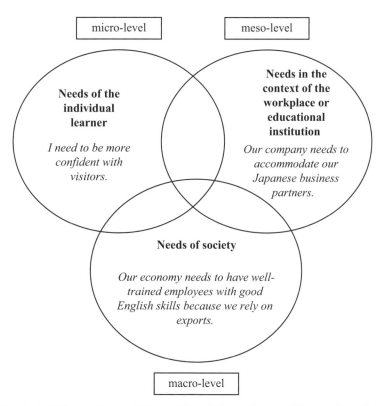

Figure 1.2: Needs in ESP on three different levels based on Robinson (1991)

manager to be confident in dealing with these important visitors, as she will need to attend to the Japanese delegation during visits. However, in order to accommodate the Japanese, it may also be necessary for her to be able to take part in business negotiations. We can see here how needs on the micro- and meso-levels overlap, but it is important to note that this will not necessarily be the case in other contexts or with other companies.

Finally, the needs of society as a whole are considered at the macro-level, making the concerns of this level the most abstract of the three. Needs at this level are related to questions of general importance to **language-in-education planning,** such as 'What languages should be known, learned and taught at all?', 'What is the objective in language teaching or learning?' or 'What methodology and what materials are employed over what duration?' (Baldauf & Kaplan 2005; van Els 2005). In the case of the example we have been considering here, a macro-level need might therefore concern vocational training on a national level, such as *We need a workforce which is proficient in English, as our national economy relies heavily on exports to North America.*

We have taken Robinson's (1991) description of needs, which can accommodate varied perspectives and sources of information, as our starting point for the main subject of this book: the CEF Professional Profiles Project. The approach in this project pays particular attention to meso- and macro-level needs, for it is from our investigation into these two levels of needs that the end product of our needs analysis, the *CEF Professional[2] Profiles*, derives. The basic aim of a CEF Professional Profile is to describe the language and communication needs of professionals at a level of detail sufficient to create an effective ESP workplace training programme or vocationally oriented language course. The profiles show how the CEFR, which focuses on general language use, relates to professional language needs.

Needs analysis for the creation of a profile begins with an investigation into what experienced professionals view as typical contexts, texts, communication situations, etc. in a particular professional field. We have particularly highlighted the meso-level because of the crucial role that the reality of workplace communication plays in the profiles. Each profile includes a focus on the typical contexts that professionals encounter in their working lives on a regular basis – in other words, routine situations. We refer to these 'slice-of-life' presentations of the particular professional fields as *snapshots.* However, we felt it was important not simply to stop at these snapshots but to include in the profiles those contexts which experienced professionals regard as a challenge. These were situations that were potentially more complex or that occurred less typically.

What the CEF Professional Profiles provide us with is a new approach to needs analysis in ESP, one which we refer to as **second generation needs analysis**. In contrast to the language-centred approaches of the first generation, which focus exclusively on functions and notions and on the four skills of speaking, listening, writing and reading (see Wilkins 1976; Munby 1978; Robinson 1991; Dudley-Evans & St John 1998), a second generation needs analysis requires a comprehensive task-based approach. We are not suggesting that there is a definite divide between the two generations of analyses, yet following Long (2005), we see

[2] 'Professional' is used here in its broadest sense and should be taken to include occupations other than law or medicine, such as hospitality, retail, facilities management, etc.

the task as the primary unit of needs analysis. However, we would like to go further than this, setting the task in the framework of one of the most important documents in language learning and teaching: the CEFR.

As we pointed out at the beginning of this chapter, the CEFR is an action-oriented approach which stresses the importance of tasks in all communication (Council of Europe 2001: 9, 43–56). One of the key features that interests us in the ESP context is the **professional discourse activity**. By this we mean a communicative task that is integral to the professional workplace context, but which is primarily fulfilled through the application of language and discourse skills (as opposed to, for example, workplace tasks that require specific technical expertise).

Professional discourse activities are tasks that engage the whole person of the learner. As a person, every learner is interwoven socially into diverse networks, each of which can be characterised by a different strand of social relationship. Not only is the learner a contributor to the learning experience of a group, he or she is also a family member, a stakeholder in local and national elections and, of course, a colleague in the workplace. The learner's participation in these various networks forms his or her identity as a person. This phenomenon is what the CEFR calls **social agency** (Council of Europe 2001: 1).

We can now see why a needs analysis which will take account of the goals, values and priorities of each of the stakeholders is clearly a necessity. This kind of needs analysis requires a **holistic** approach which will consider the person of the whole learner as that person appears in the context of his or her social group(s) (see Jaatinen 2001 on holism in foreign language education). In a holistic approach, dichotomies such as subjective and objective needs are no longer adequate because from the outset, the design and implementation of the ESP course need to accommodate the interplay of social, cognitive, emotional and volitional dimensions of learning. Again, what is of interest to us here is discussed by the Council of Europe in the CEFR as well as in the **European Language Portfolio (ELP)** (Kohonen 2001, 2005).

A holistic needs analysis, then, is one which takes account not just of the individual, but also of how that individual interacts in the contexts and situations of his or her field of action. The question to which we must now turn is: what types of data collection will be most appropriate to research in second generation needs analysis? The answer to this question is explored more fully in Section 1.3 below, but it should already be apparent from the foregoing that a second generation needs analysis will necessarily favour **qualitative research** methods over **quantitative** ones. Quantitative methods apply fixed categories to the research context and typically involve testing for gaps, looking for discrepancies or taking measurements of specific elements within the situation. We feel that to use only quantitative methods in needs analysis would be too blunt a tool to do real justice to the subtle complexities of stakeholder needs.

Second generation needs analysis is evaluative and therefore is fundamentally a qualitative approach. Personal narratives and/or biographical accounts are considered to be valid sources of data here, and the snapshot of routine tasks produced in the CEF Professional Profiles is an example of just such a method in action. In fact, in our view, qualitative inquiry (of the sort described in, e.g., Patton 1990) should be more widely accepted as a research method in needs analysis, and not only in the context of language education in workplace or vocational training contexts, but also more widely in the development of human resources in general (see Johnson 2006 and Luoma 2000 for a more general account of development in the area of human resources).

In Section 1.2, we present a typology of nine different research methods which are at the disposal of the needs analyst of ESP courses. After discussing the relative merits of each method, we finally look at how some of these methods have been applied in practice when carrying out needs analysis in three different areas of **LSP (Language for Specific Purposes)**: business management, electronics and electrical engineering, and the military.

1.2 Needs analysis: a typology of research methods in needs analysis

Long (2005: 24) notes that there is a 'paucity of information and of research on methodological options in [needs analysis]'. And indeed, needs analyses in professional contexts are quite often conducted somewhat casually, involving little more than the teacher setting a placement test for the learners and/or asking the professional client or vocational course administrator to provide a list of desired outcomes for the course. While it is true that these types of informal inquiries are quick and cost-effective, such investigations may reflect only a single perspective of only one group of stakeholders, for example that of the employers or learners. For that reason, they may lead to no more than a partial sketch of the professional context.

The first step to creating a more complete picture through needs analysis requires a more informed consideration of the research methods available to the teacher or course designer. This section presents a brief overview of nine of the most common methods used in needs analysis research, and then discusses the advantages and disadvantages of each. A summary of the main points is given in Table 1.1, below. We then go on to look at three case studies, each of which has used a so-called **mixed methodology** approach. This is an approach to needs analysis, which may also be referred to as a **triangulation** of data, in which the researcher has used a combination of qualitative and quantitative methods to identify the learning needs of the stakeholders. Finally, we consider the value of using mixed research methods in needs analysis for ESP, as this provides a useful background for presenting the methodology adopted in our own project, the CEF Professional Profiles. We argue that needs analysis for ESP should be evidence-based where the evidence is supported by a thick description of the professional workplace or training institute. A thick description is one which attempts to unpack the multiple factors that collectively determine a more accurate understanding of the context for each of the activities contributing to the professional discourse. As thick description acknowledges the importance of social agency, it is therefore an ideal complement to the view of language and action taken by the Council of Europe in its CEFR (2001).

Table 1.1: Overview of research methods in needs analysis (adapted from Long 2005: 23–45)

Method	Advantages	Disadvantages	Examples from the literature
Non-expert intuitions	• low-cost • low-effort	• unreliable • not evidence-based	*Not used in systematic approaches to research*
Expert practitioner intuitions	• low-cost • low-effort • access to domain-specific language	• unreliable • not evidence-based (informed by a single professional's intuitions)	*Not used in systematic approaches to research*
Unstructured interviews	• exploratory character means that interviews may include aspects the interviewer had not previously considered	• time-consuming • (usually) only a few interview subjects possible • risk of researcher influencing informant's views (interviewer bias) • narrative data can be difficult to analyse and it may be difficult to draw comparisons between informants • limited generalisability	Holme & Chalauisaeng (2006) Jasso-Aguilar (1999)
Structured interviews	• relatively low-cost • relatively low-effort • potential for a large number of informants to be approached • yield standardised data • low risk of interviewer bias • comparisons can be drawn between informants • results may be generalisable	• important aspects may be neglected as a result of standardisation • do not allow informants room to express own ideas and own answers	Matthes & Wordelmann (1995) Hecker (2000) Hall (2007)

Method	Advantages	Disadvantages	Examples from the literature
Surveys and questionnaires	• relatively low-cost • relatively low-effort • potential for a large number of informants to be approached • yield standardised data • low risk of interviewer bias • sizeable amounts of data can increase the reliability and validity of findings • comparisons can be drawn between informants • results may be generalisable • option of informant anonymity	• standardised • may neglect important aspects • response rates tend to be low, ESP especially with questionnaires mailed to subjects • range of responses limited	Weiß (1992) Schöpper-Grabe & Weiß (1998)
Language audits	• can produce deeper insights into the situation • institution is the unit of analysis, so potential to yield a complete picture (see Koster 2004c) • results are tailor-made to institution under review – provides a good overview of an institution's language needs	• potential difficulty to access data (confidentiality policy of institution) • publication of results may be restricted (confidential to the participating institution) • results specific to a single institution limit generalisability • time-consuming and requires effort • potentially expensive to conduct	Glowacz (2004)

Method	Advantages	Disadvantages	Examples from the literature
Observation	• allows direct, in-depth, contextualised study of participants' actions: valuable source of data	• time-consuming • only case studies possible • potentially difficult to access data	Schröder (1984) Louhiala-Salminen (2002)
Text-based analysis	• might yield important insights into potential materials for the classroom, i.e. relevant text-types, discourse-types	• is restricted to text, does not take into account the contextual and situational factors • neglects the task to be accomplished • tends to result in decontextualised structural items	Basturkmen (1999) Mauranen (2003)
Diaries, journals and logs	• personalised insights into learner and teacher needs • provide access to insider knowledge	• may be restricted to only one type of informant • time-consuming to write and analyse • potentially yield impressionistic and idiosyncratic data	Sešek (2007)

1.2.1 Non-expert intuitions and expert practitioner intuitions

The main advantage of these two approaches to needs analysis is that, informed as they are by intuition, they are naturally low-cost and do not require the investment of much time or effort. The key drawback is that both tend on the whole to be unreliable, primarily as a result of not being evidence-based.

Lacking in even personal experience of the professional context, non-expert intuitions are clearly more likely to be unreliable. Without any evidence as a basis or starting point for our assumptions about foreign language needs, the course designer has nothing more than intelligent guesses to work from. We might reasonably expect expert practitioner intuitions to be more reliable, but this is generally not the case. For while a needs analysis informed by experts can supply us with **domain-specific language** for a particular professional group, say, for example, the lexical items, functions and notions needed by fashion designers, that language is nevertheless still based for the most part on intuition. Consequently, this method may also be unreliable.

Neither of these methods appears in any studies which take more systematic approaches to data collection. In contrast to these intuitive methods, evidence-based approaches rely on data that has ideally been gathered from different sources employing various methods, both quantitative and qualitative in character. Different sources and methods lead to different viewpoints from which the object of investigation can be seen. When data is taken together in this way, we speak of 'triangulated data' (Denzin 1978), a term originally borrowed from land surveying and geodesy. As they take into account several perspectives, the results of triangulated data tend to be less biased and more reliable (Dörnyei 2007).

1.2.2 Interviews, surveys and questionnaires

Interviews may be structured or unstructured. Unstructured interviews are a qualitative method and are exploratory in character (Long 2005: 36). Typically, the interviewer will have either only a few or, perhaps, no pre-prepared questions for the subject and will instead let the interview develop out of the interaction. This less rigid and more open character allows for the possibility that the subject(s) may well introduce aspects of the situation that the interviewer simply had not considered previously. The flexibility of the unstructured interview is its primary attraction, although it is not without drawbacks. Firstly, the open-ended nature of such interviews means that they tend to be more extensive and rather time-consuming. Consequently, even if there are a number of informants who are willing and able to participate in a longer interview, the researcher will only be able to handle a few subjects. Secondly, there is a risk of introducing interviewer bias as the researcher may inadvertently slip in questions or comments which manipulate the informant's responses. Thirdly, even if interviewer bias can be avoided, the responses to unstructured interviews are narrative in character, which makes them challenging to analyse. Comparisons between the responses of different informants can be difficult to make, and this in turn will set limits on how far the researcher is able to make generalisations about the professional context under investigation.

So although the flexibility of the unstructured interview means that it certainly has a place in needs analysis research, it cannot be relied upon as the only method in a methodological framework. Unstructured interviews should be used to explore unfamiliar fields, and to help the researcher identify areas for further research and then select the most appropriate methods for systematic research in those areas.

Structured interviews, on the other hand, are predominantly quantitative and provide the researcher with standardised data. This means that, unlike unstructured interviews, a potentially much greater number of informants can be asked to participate as this kind of interview is much swifter to conduct (Long 2005: 36). Structured interviews facilitate comparisons between informant responses and, as a result, any generalisations about the professional context can be made by the researcher with more confidence. We need to be aware, however, that a significant drawback to standardised procedures is that important aspects of the situation will be missed if the researchers fail to take account of them in the design of their interviews. Furthermore, the rigid structure of this type of interview prevents informants from giving more personalised answers or additional comments, either of which might prove insightful to the research overall.

Despite these disadvantages, structured interviews are used in many studies on foreign language needs analysis, and in fact this method is not infrequently the main (or even the only) one used. Informants for structured interviews for ESP are commonly contact persons from human resources departments, from management or, less frequently, the professionals themselves. An example of a study using structured interviews can be found in Matthes and Wordelmann (1995) where as part of the authors' investigation into foreign language needs in workplace contexts, 34,000 respondents were contacted by phone. This study has since been replicated several times (see e.g. Hecker 2000; Hall 2007).

Surveys and questionnaires offer the researcher many of the same advantages found in structured interviews, though with the obvious further benefit that the researcher does not need to be physically available (either face-to-face or on the telephone) for the informants to respond. Given that it is relatively convenient and cheap for researchers to design, copy and distribute a few copied pages to potentially large numbers of people, surveys and questionnaires can produce large amounts of data and so increase the reliability and validity of findings. Generalisations are consequently also much easier to draw from the larger databases that this method makes possible. Surveys and questionnaires also share with structured interviews a lower risk of manipulation of the data on the part of the interviewer, and so interviewer bias is minimised. A further advantage of surveys and questionnaires is that they may be completed by respondents and returned to the researcher in complete anonymity. Anonymous informants may well feel less inhibited about answering questions on certain kinds of topics, allowing the researcher to access information on an individual or organisation that might usually be considered sensitive.

However, these very same potential assets of the use of surveys and questionnaires can also be their potential drawbacks. Again, as in the case of the structured interview, the higher the degree of standardisation, the less room there is for respondents to give us their own ideas and comments. This means that potentially important information of the kind that would be uncovered in a more comprehensive and thorough-going needs analysis is less likely to come to light. The reduction in the range of possible responses also means that the researcher needs to put a great deal of effort into designing the questionnaire and, above all, the questionnaire should always be piloted (Dörnyei 2003). Even assuming it were possible to create the perfect questionnaire for needs analysis, the fact that questionnaires can be so easy to distribute to large numbers of people does not result in greater inclination on the part of those people to respond. In fact, response rates are typically low, with 10% being generally considered an adequate return.

Nevertheless, we often find this method being used for large-scale needs analysis surveys. Weiß (1992), for example, used a questionnaire to survey 360 companies located in Germany. Interested in establishing foreign language needs for employees from the point of view of employers, he asked about the foreign language qualifications that are necessary for companies and the types of in-company foreign language training organised by them to meet those needs. Similarly, Schöpper-Grabe and Weiß (1998) had a sample of 663 small and medium-sized enterprises in their study. The aim of the latter study was to find out how present and future foreign language needs are addressed on in-company training schemes.

1.2.3 Language audits and observations

Language audits and observations share a similarity, in that they are both able to give the researcher a deep insight into their respective objects of study. Language audits represent a special type of needs analysis because they are typically carried out within a particular company or organisation and therefore focus on features that are institutionally specific. Koster (2004b: 5) defines a language audit as 'an investigation of the language needs of a particular organisation, with the findings of the audit providing the basis of a report outlining what action the organisation needs to undertake in order to increase the language competence of its employees and thereby improving contacts with foreign clients'. The primary objective of a language (or linguistic) audit is therefore 'to help the management of firms to identify the strengths and weaknesses of their organisation in terms of communication in foreign languages' (Reeves & Wright 1996: 5). A language audit may identify and analyse not only the current and actual foreign language needs of every employee and for every workplace context but also all potential future language needs, in a bid to maximise the efficiency of the organisation (Reeves & Wright 1996). Because a language audit takes an entire organisation as the unit of analysis, it becomes possible for the researcher to gain a more detailed and complete picture of its foreign language needs (Koster 2004c).

As attractive as this may sound, there are three main disadvantages to language audits to be considered. Firstly, while a company may agree to the language audit, it may at the same time be very reluctant to disclose sensitive consumer or customer data or, for that matter, secrets which competitors might find interesting! Consequently, either research into the company may be restricted (therefore giving a less complete picture) or else the final report may be considered confidential and access to it may be limited to company employees. Secondly, even if in cases where it is possible to publish the findings of the language audit for a wider audience, the results will not be generalisable as they apply to one organisation only. Finally, language audits represent a difficult undertaking: to be able to access data on all levels of the organisation and from all employees may prove to be not only prohibitively expensive but also (assuming funding has been secured) quite a challenge for the researcher to conduct. Nevertheless, since a language audit takes into consideration the structures of an organisation, it is useful for providing a good overview of the situation regarding foreign language needs in one single organisation (Long 2005: 41). A good example of a successful language audit is given in Glowacz (2004), which used scenario-based interviews with management, interviews with staff and an employee survey. Glowacz's language audit extended from diagnosis to recommendations for a language programme.

Observations provide the researcher with a source of rich data embedded in the professional contexts of the participant. Researchers usually accompany the professional for a certain period of time, for example a single working day or a whole week, during which they take note of the texts, discourse-types and situations the participant is faced with in the foreign language. It is easy to see how this method can lead researchers to an in-depth insight into the language needs of a given professional context. However, it should also be clear that such a method is not only rather time-consuming but somewhat limited, in that there are only so many professionals the researcher will be able to accompany. And so we tend to find that observations are used as a method for case studies only. With enough time and the right resources to hand, case studies of multiple participants are possible. For example, Schröder (1984) used observation as a method even though he had a substantial sample of 183 employees from the same chemicals company. The observations informed case studies which he then analysed to gain insight into the actual use of foreign languages within the workplace. As case studies provide information about a single participant, they are, however, inadequate for making generalisations about a given professional context. And as in the case of the language audit, observations are also potentially intrusive with the result that gaining full access to data may be difficult. Again, the company for which the professional participant works is likely to be reluctant to disclose any information which it considers sensitive or confidential.

1.2.4 Text-based analysis

In any professional context, large numbers of texts (in the broadest sense of the term, including spoken as well as written texts) are in use. Analysis of the texts for the purpose of evaluating foreign language needs can therefore give the researcher a lot of hints as to which text-types and possibly also which **discourse**-types (e.g. the preferred approach to negotiation) are most relevant to a given professional context. Text-based analysis of this kind can be particularly useful for pedagogic purposes, especially if the authentic texts which have been analysed can be included in the teaching materials for the ESP classroom. The following points need to be considered when using text-based analysis as an investigative method. Firstly, while a text-based analysis does give us information about the language, there is a risk that we will find ourselves with a list containing decontextualised structural items only (Long 2005: 23). For example, we might get a list of isolated phrases for negotiation but without embedded contextualised information on the task to be accomplished. And, in fact, a second issue to be considered in text-based analysis is that a study of the task which requires a given text-type to be completed is neglected here. To use only text-based analysis in order to determine the foreign language needs of a professional group also necessarily means that the wider contextual and situational factors contributing to the professional communication will be neglected. How, for instance, can the researcher know for certain that, say, the business culture in a particular company calls for a certain type of business negotiation? An audio recording of the negotiation as a discourse-type alone will not give us the information needed to answer this question. In short, text-based analysis is limited as a method because we need more information about the professional context and the situation of the negotiation.

1.2.5 Diaries, journals and logs

As useful as language audits, observations and text-based analyses may be, it should be recognised that the data which results from each of them necessarily represents an outsider's perspective on the professional context. Diaries, journals and logs, as Long (2005: 45) maintains, can be used to grant access to personalised, insider knowledge, and indeed we do get very detailed insights when, for example, a mechanical engineer in a company records instances of routine and challenging situations he or she encounters in a normal working day. These insights can be based on the perspective of the teacher or the learner or even, through the use of a class diary, a whole group. If, on the other hand, diaries, journals and logs are used to take into account the perspective of the learner only, the restriction to a single type of informant would consequently give us data that was heavily one-sided. There are certain drawbacks to the use of diaries, journals and logs, however. Firstly, this is a time-intensive method that requires a lot of effort both on the part of the participant who has agreed to compile the records and on the part of the researcher who has to read and analyse the results. Secondly, diaries, journals and logs by their nature are personal, and so they run the risk that the data yielded may be not only unobjective but also impressionistic or idiosyncratic. So diaries, journals and logs cannot be recommended as a single method in a systematic needs analysis research methodology.

1.2.6 Triangulation of sources and methods

As we have been arguing, an effective needs analysis should be one which includes a multiplicity of perspectives on the professional contexts. We therefore advocate the use of triangulated methods for needs analysis research. This entails combining different methods in order to arrive at a thick description of foreign language needs seen from a range of viewpoints. We are also strongly in favour of evidence-based research methods as opposed to those that rely on intuition or experience-based assumptions. We now outline three examples of studies, Huhta (1999), Louhiala-Salminen (2002) and Aho (2003), which are evidence-based and which use a triangulation of sources and methods.

Language/communication skills in industry and business

Huhta (1999) used a mixed methodology in the framework of the EU-funded Prolang project. The aim of this project, a forerunner to the CEF Professional Profiles Project, was to determine the foreign language needs of several different **professional domains** mostly connected with electronics and electrical engineering. In particular, Huhta (1999: 17) set out to provide foreign language instructors with the details of the communication situations of the professionals, which could then be used to make informed decisions about the curriculum when designing ESP courses. The study involved the participation of 169 informants with various organisational roles. A variety of methods was employed, including questionnaires, structured interviews and narrative accounts from the informants of their experiences of communicating in the foreign language in the workplace.

Personnel managers and employees were both included among the informants. The personnel managers were asked to give their perceptions of the foreign language needs of the company and then to give an assessment of their employees' competence in using foreign language skills. The personnel managers were also given a task in which they were presented with a series of workplace-based scenarios and then asked to comment on how relevant each was considered to be. For their part, the employees were questioned about their perceived foreign language needs and asked to give an assessment of their own competence in using the foreign language at work. Employees were also asked to provide detailed descriptions of workplace situations in which a foreign language was needed. This proved to be the most interesting aspect of the study as informants were asked to give details on more demanding communication situations as well as those considered to be routine and everyday, thus adding a qualitative element to the research methodology.

'The Fly's Perspective: Discourse in the Daily Routine of a Business Manager'

In her ethnographic study, 'The Fly's Perspective' (2002), Louhiala-Salminen used a combination of participant observations, interviews and also text-based analysis in order to gain insight into the communication activities of a business manager in a multinational corporation over the course of a single day. Communication situations were analysed or observed and recorded on tape. These data were then further supplemented by interviews with the participating manager. Using this combination of data-collection methods, Louhiala-Salminen was then able to describe the flow of communication activities and comment on the nature of different types of professional discourse. Her study highlighted the importance of the most varied forms of communication, the decisive role of email as a communication medium included, and concluded that knowledge of communication patterns and text-types is more essential than perfect language skills.

Systematic Language-in-Education Planning: The Finnish Defence Forces in Focus

Needs analysis has not only been used for curriculum development, but has also found its place in language-in-education planning as well. In this study, Aho (2003) explored ways of systematically developing language education at the Finnish National Defence College. Her research at the college was not primarily aimed at assessing the language needs of a particular cohort of military officers in order, for example, to achieve a more informed basis for specifying curricular objectives; rather, it was an attempt to produce a model for the systematic planning of pre-service and continuing language education in the Defence Forces. For this purpose, she used a combination of quantitative and qualitative data-gathering techniques: questionnaires on self-assessment and questions on self-perceived language needs; results from language proficiency tests; and interviews with senior officers. Aho (2003) suggests that by tapping the planning model and by merging the findings in a particular way, it is possible to evaluate how and where the current focus of teaching and learning should be put.

What these three examples point towards is that for an overall improvement in the quality of the results of needs analysis, the best approach is a triangulation of sources and methods. More specifically, this should involve a sequential or concurrent use of quantitative and qualitative methods. The reasons for this should be particularly obvious in the ESP context, and it comes as no surprise that arguments for the use of triangulated methods in research have been proposed by, among others, Tashakkori and Teddlie (1998), Creswell (2003) and Long (2005).

Foreign language needs analysis for professional communication situations has an exploratory character, and triangulation ensures that multiple sources and viewpoints are considered. When invited to participate as informants, experts from the professional domain and the teachers who instruct them in the foreign language will give the analysis greater breadth and depth. Varying the sources, for example by taking data from informants with different backgrounds, will lead to a rich description of the situation. Thus both a balanced and an evidence-based needs inquiry can be achieved.

In the following section, we show how the CEF Professional Profiles can themselves function as a foreign language needs analysis employing just this approach. We outline how the profiles were designed using a task-based approach as well as a triangulation of sources and methods. A full analysis of the CEFR for contexts and situations was integrated into the profiles.

1.3   Towards a more balanced, evidence-based needs inquiry in ESP: using the CEF Professional Profiles as instruments for needs analysis

1.3.1 Outline of the CEF Professional Profiles Project

The CEF Professional Profiles Project was developed between 2005 and 2007 with funding from the European Commission's Leonardo Da Vinci programme (LEONARDO DA VINCI, project no. FI-05-B-F-LA-160620). As a Europe-wide initiative, the CEF Professional Profiles Project partnership comprised partners from Bulgaria, Finland, Germany, Hungary, the Netherlands and Poland. The aim of the project was to devise professional, field-specific language proficiency profiles, called CEF Professional Profiles. The two primary outcomes of the two-year project consist of the CEF Professional Profiles and the guidelines for their application in ESP course design.

The professional fields studied during the project were technology, business, health and social care, and law. Three profiles were created within technology, two for business and one each for the domains of health and social care and law, with the last two of these profiles being designed with VOLL for (upper-) secondary students and ESP for students in tertiary education in mind. The domains were chosen because we attempted to cover as many occupations and fields as possible. Another reason for including healthcare and law was that they are typically under-represented in ESP. Each profile is the outcome of a needs analysis undertaken with, on the one hand, informant professionals from each of the respective fields and their language teachers and, on the other, reference to the task-oriented framework of the CEFR.

The profiles serve a twofold purpose: firstly, they can provide course designers with a solid empirical basis for curriculum planning in the secondary vocational education and tertiary education sectors; secondly, they can also serve as a foundation for tailor-made language courses in a given field. It is a commonplace in the ESP teaching context in particular that the number of classroom contact hours for a course as well as the availability of the learners themselves are often very limited. It is therefore essential for the ESP course to be designed with this economy of time in mind, and so language courses must focus very tightly on the specific learning needs of the respective target group of learners.

An important aspect of the CEF Professional Profiles Project has been to produce guidelines on how to apply the information in the profiles to ESP course design and curriculum planning. Two pilot seminars were held in 2007 with ESP teachers as part of the project, one in Finland and one in Germany. Participants were presented with exemplary profiles (in accordance with the areas in which teachers were teaching) and asked to evaluate them. Participants were also shown how the profiles could be practically applied. The profiles were additionally tried out on model courses. The model courses were designed for the tertiary business and law profiles. Owing to time constraints, only one course, the model course based on the Business Administration profile, was actually taught in Finland. The model course was piloted at a university of applied sciences and it focused on business communication as part of the degree programme of Business Administration with twenty contact hours.

1.3.2 The methodology used for creating the CEF Professional Profiles

The CEF Professional Profiles Project used a triangulation of sources and methods (for reasons outlined in Section 1.2.6). It was felt that using this methodology would provide something like an ethnographic approach to needs analysis. This approach was seen to be in opposition to a straightforward testing for gaps and wants (Long 2005) that assured the quality of the data.

In response to the need for an ethnographic approach described above, both quantitative and qualitative data were used for creating the profiles. Although the latter predominated, quantitative methods such as the use of structured questionnaires were included. A variety of qualitative methods was used, with the analysis of earlier work feeding into subsequent stages of the research. For example, text-based analyses were made on the content of different kinds of informational material related to the professional domain: job descriptions, curricula and syllabi for qualifications in the professional field. The analysis from the content of these texts was then used to inform a small number of in-depth informant interviews. The data collected from these interviews was subsequently used by the team to determine a set of core questions for use in a series of semi-structured interviews that formed the next step in the research (the core questions are given in Table 1.2 below).

The data gathered from informants' answers to these core questions during the second round of interviews was then used to inform the creation of the CEF Professional Profiles. From the profiles which resulted, it was possible to create a more general template which could be used as the basis for future research in other professional domains not covered by the CEF Professional Profiles Project. The general categories which make up the template for the profiles are shown in bold small capitals in Table 1.2. The template is discussed in more detail in Section 1.3.3.

It was not possible for the participating researchers in the six partner countries in the project to follow the procedure described here exactly. Some variation and flexibility was necessary as not all researchers had the same degree of access to the data and personnel in the professions and organisations that had agreed to take part in the project. For example, it was the policy of some companies not to allow interviews with their employee informants to be recorded. In these cases, only the researcher's field notes were available as a data source in place of a full transcription of the interview used elsewhere. However, we were primarily interested in obtaining results that were reliable and trustworthy, and the adopted measures we have described here helped to achieve that.

A possible weakness in the approach to research in the CEF Professional Profiles Project is that it was not possible to include **stratified random sampling** (Long 2005) of informants. This refers to a research method in which the subjects in the study are carefully chosen so as to be representative of the population of a whole community in miniature. This kind of sampling, however, would not have been possible in the project for two reasons. The first is a practical one: stratified random sampling can prove prohibitively expensive and the funding for this project could not have extended that far. Even if enough funding could have been freed up, the nature of a European project in which various contributions from different backgrounds came together meant that it was not possible to aim at a sample that was representative (even in stratified form) of a host of different cultures, business cultures included. This cultural aspect is not greatly represented in the CEFR, as shown by Risager (2007). In addition to being limited, it is pragmatic in an integrative way. The CEFR description of the relationships between language and culture is 'unclear and without theoretical foundation' (Risager 2007: 115, 143). However, the cultural aspect was clearly important on a project being carried out across six countries in northern, central and southern Europe. The influence of different cultures was taken up in the project by the shape of the interview questions. Table 1.2 shows the core interview questions that the project team agreed to use in the second round of interviews.

Table 1.2: Core interview questions in the CEF Professional Profiles Project

Background information
• What are some typical examples of professions/jobs/occupations for *X* professionals in your experience?
• What type of employers/organisations/companies employ *X* professionals?
• Let us go through a list of job descriptions these professionals typically do. Would you like to add something to this list?
• To what extent are foreign languages needed in your view? Which languages?
• Could you recommend persons or organisations that could give me more information about other aspects of *X* professionals' work? Are there associations that coordinate the *X* professionals? Websites?

Language-specific description: context information
• Which spoken communication situations are frequent in your view? PRIORITY
○ Here is a general list, based on the information available to us. SHOW COMMUNICATION SITUATIONS
• Which spoken communication situations are demanding in your view?
○ Here is a general list, based on the information available to us. SHOW COMMUNICATION SITUATIONS
• Where does this communication take place? LOCATION
• Which people would be involved? PERSONS, COMMUNITIES, COMPANIES, PARTNER INSTITUTIONS
• Can you see some other relevant situations that you see missing here? FOR WRITTEN TEXTS – SHOW YOUR PRELIMINARY LIST
• What kinds of texts/genres do *X* professionals need to write?
• Which of the texts/genres are common in your view?
• Who are these documents written for? TARGET GROUP
• What is the purpose/aim of such a document?
• What would make a really good *Y* text? BACKGROUND INFORMATION

Objectives of learning courses, materials, methods and assessment
• If you were to give *X* professionals a language course, what skills should it concentrate on, in your experience of how well *X* professionals communicate? AIM/OBJECTIVE
• Is foreign language needed more for oral or written skills? PROPORTION IN PER CENT
• What skills would be important components of oral performance or listening?
• What skills would be important in writing and reading?
• How important is terminology / specialist vocabulary in *X* professions?
• How important is the perfection of pronunciation in *X* professions?
• Is it possible in your field to get away with roundabout explanations?
• Can you think of methods that you would recommend for improving the skills you have described? LEARNING METHODS
• Can you think of authentic assignments you would give to the learners to improve the skills you described? LEARNING TASKS
• What would be the best ways of demonstrating the communication skills of *X* professionals? ASSESSMENT

General communication objectives

- Concerning general communication, what do you think are the most important general competencies/skills that *X* professionals should have? Can language practice improve some of the general competencies?
- What can you say about
  - social rank markers in your field?
  - dress code?
  - body language?
  - politeness practices?
  - respected qualities of *X* professionals?
  - values highly appreciated?
  - values not appreciated?

Note: The words in ʙᴏʟᴅ ꜱᴍᴀʟʟ ᴄᴀᴘɪᴛᴀʟꜱ refer to categories in the CEF Professional Profiles template (discussed in Section 1.3.3).

Also important for the approach to this project was the incorporation of the CEFR. As we pointed out at the beginning of this chapter, the action-oriented approach found in the CEFR is one in which tasks are central. And as we have also discussed here, a task-based approach to foreign language needs analysis is useful because it can be easily harmonised with **CBL** (**Content-Based Learning**) and other task-based methodologies found in second language teaching and learning (Long 2005: 22f.). CBL is, of course, of direct relevance to VOLL and ESP course design because the specific professional context of any given domain has an influence on the content and, in turn, on language use in those settings.

In the CEF Professional Profiles Project, the categories found in the CEFR were applied to the analysis of the situational factors and the communication situations of the VOLL and ESP contexts under review. Aspects used by the CEFR are particularly relevant to professional communication situations: the perspectives of the domain, of the context, of the text, the location and the participants in the situation are good examples (see Huhta 2007: 35). However, it was felt that the scales and descriptors found in the CEFR, for example 'Can find out and pass on straightforward factual information' (Council of Europe 2001: 81), would be too general to be able to describe a specifically professional communication situation adequately. Therefore, while the CEF Professional Profiles are explicitly based on categories in the framework, they avoid the scales and descriptors. The categories initially tried out were as follows: domain, tasks, strategies, texts and assignments, and assessment. However, while helpful, teachers found that there were too many categories to be useful for ESP course design. An adapted version was then developed which was designed to take account of the background information, general and communicative objectives, as well as specific course content related to the language. This version became the starting point for the CEF Professional Profiles Project in which researchers and practitioners developed field-specific language and communication descriptions for technology, business, health and social care, and law. The full profiles can be found in Appendix C of this book.

1.3.3 The structure of the CEF Professional Profiles

Each CEF Professional Profile is divided into the following six parts:

A. Target profession
B. Occupational information
C. Context information
D. The most frequent routine situations
E. The most demanding situations
F. Snapshots

Target profession

Part A of the profiles comprises background information on the profile. It outlines how data was gathered in order to put together this particular profile. General comments on the nature of the target profession are also included. For example, the training and qualifications necessary to enter the profession are given as well as what further training may be undertaken once employed, and what specialisations can be pursued by professionals in this domain.

Occupational information

Part B of the profiles provides general information, such as examples of occupations in the domain, typical organisations or companies in which such professionals can be found working, typical examples of job descriptions that relate to overall tasks in the domain, and finally the role that the foreign language usually plays in this job. The purpose of this part of the profile is to provide the novice language teacher and/or the teacher who does not yet have the specialised knowledge of the professional domain with relevant background information on the occupational field. This is why this section is rather general.

Context information

More language-related material is found in Part C. This is where the aforementioned adaptation of the CEFR categories can be found (see Section 1.3.2). The context information comprises aspects such as locations, persons, communities, companies and institutions, communicative situations (in terms of tasks to be accomplished) and texts, both for the work environment and for the prior training or study situation.

The most frequent situations and the most demanding situations

Parts D and E offer descriptions of professional communication situations in which communicative tasks have to be accomplished. It is important for the purposes of course design that the profiles do not limit themselves to describing only everyday events such as those given in Part D of the profile. Less frequent and more demanding situations represent critical moments for the professional (see Candlin 2005), and these too need to be described, as they are in Part E of the profile.

Snapshots

Finally, Part F of the profile offers the ESP course designer one or more 'day-in-the-life' narratives, or snapshots, of the professionals in the domain.

More details about the profiles and their possible uses will be discussed next in Chapter 2 of this book.

1.4 Conclusion

In this chapter, we have seen that systematic, evidence-based needs analysis is important to course design in the fields of ESP (including VOLL and LCPP). An effective needs analysis should specify what communicative tasks the learners have to accomplish and, secondly, what discourses they have to know in order to function in their profession or vocation. At the outset, the analyst should establish a clear definition of how a language need is to be understood. Ideally, this definition should be one which takes account of multiple perspectives, ranging from the individual learner and his or her teacher, through to the HR developer and institutional administrators as well as the needs of society in general. Successful curriculum development for ESP course design will need to prioritise and balance the needs resulting from these different perspectives when tailoring a foreign language course for a particular institution and group of learners.

We have also investigated crucial questions that the needs analyst should ask him- or herself, such as what sources of data should one then seek, and what research strategies and methods should be selected? We have shown how the widespread practice in ESP of simply relying on informally gathered data from learners and teachers lacks evidence and leads to insider bias. Using questionnaires alone has also been shown to be limiting and insufficient to give the course designer a contextualised description of professional language skills and types of discourse. Rather, our answer to the question of research methodologies has been to advocate a balanced, evidence-based needs inquiry: a triangulation of sources and methods to achieve high-quality data and inferences. As Long (2005) points out, it is the interaction of methods and sources that needs to be highlighted when specifying types of tasks and discourse.

The needs analysts of the CEF Professional Profiles Project have attempted to arrive at this kind of balanced, evidence-based needs analysis. Through the application of categories adapted from the action-oriented approach of the CEFR, they have also produced needs analyses which are particularly relevant to communicating in a foreign or second language. Each profile that the analysts produced for the project includes information about typical working-life organisations, professions/occupations and job descriptions in the field. The profile describes language tasks and the various roles that the foreign language plays in the job. The contextual information of the profile focuses on locations, persons (i.e. interlocutors), communities and companies. Communication situations describe the tasks to be accomplished and the salient discourses. The situations exemplified cover both frequent and demanding ones. Finally, a narrative account relates a day in the life of the professional, thus providing a thick description. Although strong in perspective and detail, as we have shown above, the profile may have a weakness in respect of its sampling of informants in the field. Therefore the applicability of each profile across teaching and learning contexts needs to be considered.

2   From teaching Language for Specific Purposes to teaching Language and Communication for Professional Purposes

---

Chapter overview

In this chapter, we explain the importance of contextual factors in workplace communication and how they led to the creation of the CEF Professional Profiles. We will:

- highlight the importance of contextual factors in workplace communication
- describe how contextual understanding of communication has evolved from previous needs analysis projects and communication theory
- develop the rationale and the background of the CEF Professional Profiles as a basis for ESP course development.

2.1   Introduction

In Chapter 1, we explained that evidence-based needs analysis provides a solid foundation for defining and validating a defensible curriculum to satisfy the language learning requirements of students (Brown 2006: 102).

The considerable interest in the practice of needs analysis over the last 40 years (see e.g. Long 2005; Huhta 2010) has provided some useful insights into language teaching, but the same cannot be said for course design, for which there remains little practical support. This chapter takes a closer look at the ESP teacher and his or her challenges in designing a course for learners with specific purposes for language learning. We will suggest ways in which the results gathered from the needs analysis of workplace communication can be represented in order to assist the teacher in identifying relevant course content and designing course activities. We will also show how knowledge of the contextual factors in communication can be combined with the CEF Professional Profiles in course design.

2.2   ESP revisited

English for Specific Purposes is applied widely, not only to English taught as a second language but to other languages that are taught as a second language. Strevens (1988b: 1) points out that despite the vastly greater demand for ESP, the characteristics linked to ESP are applicable to all courses for specific language purposes regardless of which language it is for. Courses in FSP (French for Specific Purposes), GSP (German for Specific Purposes) and RSP (Russian for Specific Purposes), amongst others, all exist and are constructed on the same basis as ESP. Thus, although we refer to ESP throughout this book, the CEF Professional Profiles are usable in any LSP context.

ESP has been defined using qualifying statements about its absolute and variable characteristics. The frequently quoted characteristics of ESP are consistent in respect of certain absolutes. The goal-directedness of ESP (Robinson 1991: 2) is seen as one of these absolute characteristics. The goals meet the needs of the learner (Strevens 1988b; Robinson 1991; Dudley-Evans & St John [1998] 2002). ESP applies the methodology and activities of the discipline it serves (Dudley-Evans & St John 2002). ESP is centred on the language, skills, discourse and genres appropriate for these activities (Dudley-Evans & St John [1998] 2002). An ESP course involves specialist language, especially terminology and content (Robinson 1991: 4–5). Strevens (1988b) sees ESP as being related in content (i.e. in its themes and topics) to particular disciplines, occupations and activities and centred on the language appropriate to those activities, in syntax, lexis, discourse, semantics, etc. ESP is generally designed for intermediate or advanced learners. Most ESP courses assume some basic knowledge of the language system, but it can also be used for beginners (Dudley-Evans & St John [1998] 2002). Several writers argue that ESP saves learning time or is less wasteful than General English (Strevens 1988b; Reeves and Wright 1996; Huhta [2000] 2002b; Koster 2004b). As for learner reception, ESP teaching is perceived as relevant by the learner, and ESP is contrasted with General English (Strevens 1988b).

While the choice of language is usually unproblematic (in that the context will normally determine which L2 (a second or foreign language) the learners need), the degree of specificity of the specific purpose(s) demands further scrutiny. In fact the ESP teacher will need to take a stand with regard to the question of what is 'specific' about the English he or she teaches. Koster (2004b) points out that the term 'special' has sometimes been defined as 'restricted', in reference to Mackay and Mountford (1978: 4f.), for example, which featured the limited linguistic needs of a dining-room waitress. This kind of restricted 'discourse' would not allow the speaker to communicate effectively outside the vocational environment (Koster 2004a: 41). Sometimes this may be the ESP teacher's only available option within a limited time frame of teaching. Hutchinson and Waters argue that:

> ESP is *not* a matter of teaching 'specialized varieties' of English. The fact that language is used for a specific purpose does *not* imply that it is a special form of the language, different in kind from other forms. Certainly, there are some features that can be identified as 'typical' of a particular context of use and which, therefore, the learner is more likely to meet in the target situation. But these differences should not obscure the far larger area of common ground that underlies all English use, and indeed, all language use.
>
> (1987: 18, emphasis in original)

In their article 'ESP at the Crossroads' (1980), Hutchinson and Waters lay down the main argument for the 'wide-angle' approach in ESP. They argue that specialised discourse should be left to those who know best, the specialist instructors of particular disciplines. Meanwhile, LSP teachers should occupy themselves teaching the 'underlying competence' that every student needs. Hyland (2002) discusses the specificity of ESP and argues that the ESP field has drifted away from specificity, becoming too generalised and diffuse. The 'wide-angle' perspective has become a necessity for classes that lack uniformity and focus, especially classes that are mixed. Hyland claims that generalised ESP 'has crept into our current thinking and practices' and is gaining ground in university language teaching programmes (Huckin 2003). Hyland lists four common reasons for this drift away from specificity: narrow-angle LSP (i) is too difficult for lower-level students, (ii) is too expensive and (iii) can only be taught by knowledgeable specialists; moreover, (iv) features of language and discourse are generic, not language specific. We may note that professional terminology is not even mentioned, the prerequisite in ESP being to teach English mainly in English without the support of the native language (L1). Huckin agrees with the first two points but claims that LSP scholars are needed to teach technical varieties of language based on the expertise they have gained through technical discourses. Discourses in different disciplines vary, but the functions of discourse elements remain the same (Huckin 2003: 8).

Both Hyland and Huckin agree that more specificity is needed and that the specificity of needs comes from the learner, not the teacher. This fairly recent discussion shows a common trend in ESP that calls for reconsideration. If ESP continues to foster more 'general underlying competencies' before the professional can learn to function in his or her discourse community, we need to think twice about the more cost-effective option of 'narrow focus'. Hutchinson and Waters claim that the narrow-angle approach is demotivating for students; therefore, students should be grouped for ESP classes across broad subject areas with materials drawing from topics in a number of different specialist areas, thus making students aware of the 'lack of specificity of their needs' (Hutchinson & Waters 1987: 166–7).

Bhatia (2004) sees disciplines identified in terms of their content and in part by the field of discourse. According to him, disciplines, in spite of overlap between registers, have their typical characteristics and are primarily understood in terms of the specific knowledge, methodologies and shared practices of community members (Bhatia 2004: 31–2).

We can now see, based on this discussion, that it is not clear whether ESP should focus on specifics or wide competencies. Our practical experience leads us to think that both elements are present in the contextual interpretation we are using in CEF Professional Profiles. A key factor in determining the difference between English for General Purposes (EGP) and ESP that has come to light in the course of carrying out our needs analyses is what Richards has identified as the 'delicacy of context' (1989: 215). We have also come to understand that what is specific about ESP is related not so much to domain-specific language – terminology, acronyms, neologisms and so on – as to what the professional requires in order to perform the duties of the role in context successfully. Data about the context of **situational communication** gathered during needs analyses for the CEF Professional Profiles Project proved to be especially useful in designing courses and classroom activities. Communication for professional purposes was taken to include gaining a mastery of the body of knowledge in the field, a mastery of skills, and also an understanding of, and a commitment to, the practice of professional ethics (Boswood 1999); in other words, an understanding of the responsible use of knowledge and skills in the field. The experiences gained during the studies undertaken in the framework of our work suggest that there are two further defining characteristics of ESP.

- *ESP is evidence-based.* As we have seen in Chapter 1, materials intended for professional purposes based on teacher/writer intuitions have been produced, but these have not always proved very reliable (Long 2005: 31–5). What courses and materials designed in this way lack is a solid knowledge base that responds to the needs of the learners on an ESP course. Such knowledge can be gained through an evidence-based needs analysis that provides insights from several perspectives. Multiple perspectives provide the ESP teacher with a 'thick description' of the professional context and bring to light the details of **communicative events** needed to design courses and on which to build activities. The profiles are a step in that direction.

- *ESP is specific to the professional context not the professional domain.* The specificity of ESP concerns the dynamic communication practices of particular **professional discourse communities** rather than the language associated with a particular professional group, such as accountants, nurses or software engineers. It is not enough to teach accountants language that is specific to accountancy if this group of accountants belongs to the professional discourse community of a multinational healthcare provider. The range of communication situations for any one discourse community incorporates many groups of specialists, related through a number of similar goals. For accountants working in healthcare provision, say, the design of the ESP course should address the real-world communication needs of the learners which may well (in fact probably will) extend beyond the limits of language specific to accountancy. Most obviously in this case, they will need language related to healthcare. The accountants will need to be aware of how their role relates to those of others in the same organisation. They will also need to have a grasp of how other staff – for example catering management or ward nurses – prioritise their needs. What we are saying here is that the specificity of ESP is more a question of **context reliance** than of occupation or profession. Therefore we propose to emphasise professional purposes and refer to the **professional community contexts** rather than specific purposes. In this sense, it would be more accurate to talk about teaching Language and Communication for Professional Purposes (LCPP), as the goal for this category of ESP focuses on communication in the professional setting. We will, though, for convenience and because the LCPP abbreviation does not yet have a wide currency, continue to refer to ESP in this book. Figure 2.1 shows how we see professional communication purposes as an ESP orientation.

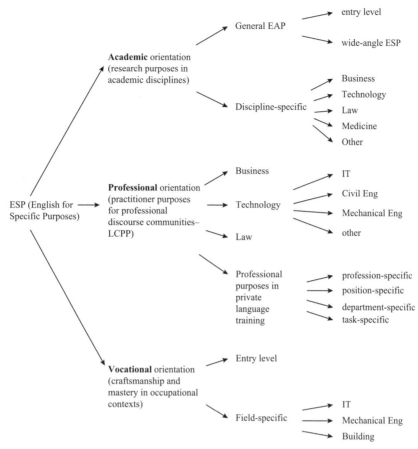

Figure 2.1: Orientations of LCPP within ESP (Huhta 2010: 17)

A defining characteristic of ESP is the teaching of a range of communication situations, from beginning to end, as that is how the user will encounter a foreign language in the workplace. In the next section we will see why.

2.3 The importance of situational aspects of communication

Communication situations (which may be written or spoken) are central to teaching LCPP. A communication situation should be thought of in very broad terms and could be defined as:

> a unified set of components [consisting of] the same general purpose of communication, the same general topic, and involving the same participants, generally using the same language variety, maintaining the same tone or key and the same rules for interaction, in the same setting.

(Saville-Troike [1982] 1989: 27)

Saville-Troike's definition is a useful starting point but should not be considered to be complete. To her set of components, we can also add more or less predictable event sequences, rhetoric, communication strategies, adequacy of role-taking and style, to name but a few.

We consider a broad definition of a communication situation necessary as it serves a practical purpose in the creation of a CEF Professional Profile. The professional respondents who take part in the needs analysis are, naturally enough, neither language teachers nor linguists, and as such they are likely to use a wide variety of ways to describe what happens in a given communication situation. A flexible definition is therefore very useful and the profile descriptions accordingly allow for several alternative ways of describing a communicative event.

Another useful concept of analysing communication situations is the concept of genre, as a communication situation often comprises one or more genres. A thorough examination of genre and the applications of genre analysis are given, for example, in Bhatia ([1993] 1998: 13–41, based on Swales 1990), but for our purposes here genre can be defined as:

> a recognizable communicative event characterized by a set of communicative purpose(s) identified and mutually understood by the members of the professional ... community in which it regularly occurs. More often it is highly structured and conventionalized with constraints on allowable contributions in terms of their intent, positioning, form and functional value. These constraints, however, are often exploited by the expert members of the discourse community to achieve private intentions within the framework of socially recognized purpose(s).

Genre analysis has proven its value to the practice of ESP teaching. Indeed, numerous genres have been examined for the benefit of language teaching, for example sales promotion letters (Bhatia [1993] 1998: 118), self-published résumés (Killoran 2006), meetings (Poncini 2002) and business correspondence, emails and faxes (Louhiala-Salminen 1999; Bhatia 2002; Kankaanranta 2005; Louhiala-Salminen & Kankaanranta 2005), abstracts in academic genres (Dudley-Evans 1994; Ventola, Shalom & Thompson 2002), to mention a few. This kind of research is necessary for gaining evidence-based knowledge on the teaching content.

However, an ESP teacher may still have a number of significant questions to raise concerning the limitations of genre. Bhatia ([1993] 1998: 18) has drawn attention to some of these limitations as follows:

> Is this pattern discovered by genre analysis true of all the genres in this particular variety? How do these linguistic features realize in social realities in a particular field of study or profession? Why do users use these features and not others? Does the use of these features represent specific conventions on a particular genre, and if they do, what happens if some practitioners take liberties with these conventions?

Candlin (2005) argues that there are serious limits as to the theory of genre, as it is people that achieve integrity in communication, not genre. Genre does not observe competing identities between institutional, professional and personal discourse choice (Sarangi &

Roberts 1999). Genre theory does not acknowledge 'motivational relevancies' of the researcher and the participant (Sarangi & Candlin 2001). Moreover, when discourse is in action, **multimodality** and **multisemiocity** are always present (Scollon 2001), and genre does not take this into account. Reality also recognises interactional and institutional orders that genre does not recognise, such as backstage and frontstage communication (Goffman 1959), for example how professionals communicate frontstage, with customers, and backstage, with colleagues and friends. Thus, genre theory can limit the understanding of professional communication as it occurs in real life, with special concerns arising in respect of how interdiscursivity in professional communication may be overlooked (Candlin 2006). For example, a team with an executive, a lawyer and a marketing consultant may have various discourse practices relating to each profession or genre, but in the mutual interaction of team members, it is difficult to predict which discourse practice is being applied and how. Interdiscursivity is still a little-researched area, as Candlin points out. Nevertheless, genre study has contributed greatly to the understanding of the discourse of academic, business and technical texts, and as a practical concept for the creation of CEF Professional Profiles.

When an ESP teacher considers the language content (discourse, lexis, syntax, intonation, etc.) of frequently occurring types of informal meeting or email found in the learner's professional context, he or she can be said to be considering the communication situation as an instance of genre. This kind of analysis in which content relevant to a given set of professional purposes is documented from a contextual and socio-cultural perspective is familiar to many ESP practitioners. However, it is worth remembering that this approach is a relatively recent development of the last 30 years or so.

Our knowledge about workplace communication has increased significantly as a result of evidence-based needs analysis practice. We have come to understand the context reliance of workplace communication and some of its implications with regard to language teaching. In the 1970s and 1980s, the aims of needs analysis were largely concerned with identifying potential language needs. The more recent needs analyses have moved towards the use of triangulated and mixed methods resulting in 'thick descriptions', where the communication of a discourse community, its professionals and interlocutors is explicitly documented for communication situations (for a review, see Huhta 2010: 56–7, 138–44). Descriptions such as CEF Professional Profiles help the ESP teacher to design content and plan activities.

The CEF Professional Profiles Project is based on a series of needs analyses for industry and business conducted and developed since 1989 in Finnish and European projects (Huhta 2010: 90–104). The focus in these analyses has been on the objective needs of professional work communities, mainly of industry and business, but also law, social services and healthcare, and culture. One of the evidence-based needs analyses is the Prolang project (Huhta 1999), referred to in Chapter 1 as a forerunner to the CEF Professional Profiles. This project was the first needs analysis to inquire into the contexts of communicative events within the total communication of an employee. Between 1997 and 1999, the Prolang study examined the language and communication practices of 197 individuals working in sixty-nine different companies.

The results of this study came out strongly in support of seeing language and communication as holistic *communication situations*. This view is summarised in the following five observations:

1. Communicative events occur in *integrated situations* involving many skills in the same event, thus increasing the complexity of learning. Therefore splitting the contents of learning into categories of sub-skills: reading, writing, listening, speaking and mediation is less helpful for workplace communication learning than an *integrated approach*.

2. Communication at work requires dealing with *complete communication events* from beginning to end, irrespective of what form it takes: reading, notes, telephone calls, consulting experts, appointments, documenting, and distribution to parties concerned, discussion. This is in contrast to more traditional models of ESP which have tended to focus on individual speech acts (functions and notions) or simplified interactions. While these functions may be thematically related to the professional domain, they can only fulfil one micro-need of the many functions found in the flow of a communication situation. The results of the needs analyses in the Prolang study suggested strongly that a more effective model for ESP course design is to look at the entire communication situation at the macro-level.

3. Some communicative events call for creative language/communication capacity, for example those of social situations, hosting visitors, solving problems. Others can be handled more formulaically, such as making telephone calls or writing memos. It thus seems that language and communication must be taught both as *education* (for broad, overall purposes) and *training* (closely targeted objectives of learning). Development of workplace communication often requires language training rather than language education.

4. *Translation and interpretation* represent important communicative events. Translation and interpretation have often been excluded from the design of ESP courses, but the results of needs analysis carried out for the Prolang study suggest that this is a significant oversight. Many professional communication situations call for some form of translation and interpretation, and so the need for this aspect of communication in ESP course design should clearly be investigated.

5. In order for workplace communication to be taught, it needs to be *authentic*. **Authenticity** relates to contents that are realistic, existing and meet the learning needs of the learner. Authenticity also relates to the language used in context ('chunks') in which learning takes place; separate functions and notions may produce useful language input, but the focal point itself will still need to be successful communication of holistic situations. Authenticity also

concerns the **ecological validity** (Cicourel 2007) of the curriculum content. In the context of classroom practice, ecological validity relates to the extent to which the teacher succeeds in organising learning activities that increment the competences required by the workplace in realistic units and contexts. In van Lier's terms (1996), authenticity goes beyond the usual domain of the term which he sees as authentic materials and authentic tasks. An understanding of authenticity based on the evidence of the Prolang project and on van Lier's thinking includes the process of engagement in the learning situation and the characteristics of the persons involved in learning. Authenticity relates to self-knowledge and to communication between learners, and between the teacher and the learner (van Lier 1996: 125). This kind of authenticity can be helped by learner empowerment and engagement of the workplace simulation.

Inauthentic, on the other hand, could be exemplified as language-manipulation exercises, such as finding matching synonyms or filling in gaps – elements that have been central in traditional language teaching approaches. In the context of course design, authentic tasks that are conducted in class are holistic: there may not even be a text, as proposed by Widdowson (1990), but only input that guides the learner to meaningful learning activities, relevant to professional communication. Widdowson admits that inauthentic language use behaviour may be effective language learning behaviour, but to call that 'authentic' seems to confuse the issue of authenticity (1990: 46–7). Agreement on the concept of authenticity appears to relate to authenticity as a process of validation or authentication (Widdowson 1990) conducted by the participants. It seems, based on van Lier, that 'it is easy to bring genuine pieces of language into the classroom, but to create authentic opportunities of language use on their basis appears to be quite another matter' (van Lier 1996: 126). One of the learnings of the Prolang project was that authenticity demands complexity in the language class, which involves introducing a variety of accents and misinterpretations of words and intentions, as happens in normal communication. Therefore simulations of workplace communication, despite their complexity, can promote empowered, engaged learning in the classroom.

   Using these five observations, the Prolang group then began to outline a system for describing communicative events thoroughly enough to allow for the planning of classroom activities. The result was a list of communication situations which could be used to form the basis of a written survey (Huhta 1999: 176). This original list, presented below, was built on the findings of previous needs analyses in industry and business carried out by Davidsson, Berggren and Mehtäläinen and expanded by the Prolang group of 23 teacher-researchers (Huhta 1997: 62).

LANGUAGE/COMMUNICATION SITUATIONS IN INDUSTRY AND BUSINESS

1. Talking about oneself and one's job

2. Travel

3. Social situations (e.g. introductions, small talk)

4. Routine telephone calls (e.g. taking messages, answering enquiries, making arrangements)

5. Client contacts (e.g. customer service, exhibitions, complaints by telephone, face-to-face)

6. Hosting visitors / Participating in visits

7. Solving computer problems

8. Explaining a process or a (working) method

9. Discussions concerning deliveries, installations, maintenance

10. Fault analysis, solving problems

11. Tutoring a new employee

12. Reading manuals, instructions, professional literature

13. Reading company documentation (memos, quotations, etc.)

14. Writing email messages, faxes; taking notes in a meeting

15. Writing memos, reports, documents

16. Giving a presentation (e.g. company profile, product presentation)

17. Meetings, negotiations

18. Other (interpretation, translation, projects abroad)

Needs Analysis for Language Course Design © Cambridge University Press 2013 **PHOTOCOPIABLE**

Each of the situation categories was expanded by asking respondents to describe a frequent and a demanding situation, including event name, location, interlocutors, details of process and points that made the communication successful or demanding. The Prolang group thus received 398 descriptions of communication events in total (Huhta 1999: 118–43). While the Prolang project was ongoing, information derived from it was also used in the process of designing the Finnish national vocational syllabus for secondary education in 1998. This situational approach to needs analysis, drawing upon contextual information, was innovative for its time.

The communication event and genre-based descriptions generated by the Prolang project turned out to be purposeful for syllabus design, but less useful for teaching than expected. The underlying objective of the syllabus in English was to prepare the learner to communicate in key workplace situations. The Prolang information on more detailed aspects of the professional situations was too cryptic, so while the Prolang surveys proved adequate for describing the general outline of the syllabus, they were not yet rich enough for planning classroom simulations based on realistic workplace scenarios. The contextual information should have been given on a more detailed level to provide necessary information for designing a learning simulation based on the data. For example, for a learner to simulate product presentation at a trade fair, the learner needs to know the company name, its field of operation and product specifics. The communication events described by the Prolang respondents were not given at that level of detail.

This suggested that there were limitations to using only written surveys and that future needs analysis should always take a mixed methods approach. Taking the results of the Prolang study and considering them within the comprehensive framework for languages of the CEFR as detailed in Section 1.1 above, we set out to create a 'thicker' description of the contexts for professional communication.

2.4 Evolving understandings of professional communication

This section highlights key understandings of professional communication, experienced in our evidence-based needs analysis practice, that are also prevalent in current language and communication theory. Firstly, we will look at the concept of 'communication', followed by what is understood as communication for 'professional' purposes.

In our definition of communication, the needs of learners are looked at in conjunction with the needs of the business or workplace in which the learner is based, which are, in turn, seen from the point of view of social institutions, held together by **communicative practices** (Sarangi & Roberts 1999: 1). Communication is purposeful human interaction typical of knowledge work of professionals. The communication includes the use of verbal and non-verbal communication as part of procedures of professional discourse community practice. Communication is utilised to construct meaning within management systems (Jackson [2003] 2007), **organisation cultures** (Hatch 1997) and networks of stakeholders (Freeman & Reed 1983; Mendelow 1987: 177). The purpose of knowledge work is learning (Senge 1990; Argyris & Schön 1996; Argyris 2002) in communities of practice (Lave & Wenger 1991) and in professions within society.

Communication is a medium of group interaction and therefore a channel for the effects of various factors on group decision-making and outcomes. Communication functions as a means for creating social reality in which decisions can be made (Hirokawa & Poole 2004). Communication occurs at workplaces, which are 'social institutions where resources are produced and regulated, problems are solved, identities are played out and professional knowledge is constituted' (Sarangi & Roberts 1999: 1). Cicourel argues that language communication and social practices are interwoven and cannot really be separated:

> If we do not invoke institutional and local socio-cultural details with which to identify the participants in conversation, the analysis of meaning becomes almost impossible. *Language and social practices are interdependent.* Knowing something about the ethnographic setting, the perception of and characteristics attributed to others, and broader and local social organisational conditions becomes imperative for an understanding of linguistic and non-linguistic aspects of communicative events.
>
> (Cicourel 1992: 292, emphasis added)

Because language and social practices are interdependent, knowledge of the institutional and local socio-culture is necessary for understanding the goals and objectives of communicative events in the workplace. Discourse practice differs between social domains (mobile communications, banking, law), each of which has its own discursive practice associated with a particular social domain or institution (Foucault 1982; Candlin 2005, 2006).

The messages conveyed in communication incorporate meanings. Communication can be more than just text (verbal); it may incorporate non-verbal elements such as tone of voice, gestures, use of space, clothing, tacit knowledge and behaviour, which are less centrally seen as part of ESP. In communication, **interlocutors** possess communication skills, which, in the linguistic tradition, have been classified into speaking, reading, listening, writing and mediation (Council of Europe 2001); however, in a professional setting they seldom occur separately, but rather as integrated clusters of sub-skills and clusters of source data in meaningful sequences. In Candlin and Maley's (1997: 203) words:

> Discourses are made internally viable by the incorporation of ... intertextual and interdiscursive elements. Such evolving discourses are thus intertextual in that they manifest a plurality of text sources. However, insofar as any characteristic text evokes a particular discoursal value, in that it is associated with some institutional and social meaning, such evolving discourses are at the same time interdiscursive.

National, cultural and subcultural factors influence communication in many ways. Therefore interferences and barriers (Hagen 1999; Risager 2006) are essentially part of communication. Interferences may relate, for example, to intercultural factors or to features such as social status, noise, gender, age, education, power or strategy (Huhta 2002a: 19–31). Specific fields of communication such as managerial communication, business communication and technical communication have established their own specific practices and research communities.

A few words need to be said about 'professional'[1] purposes. When we talk about professional communication, we deal with communication related to independent specialist work

---

[1] The term 'profession' is understood in 'a non-elitist sense which includes service and other occupations ... as well as the more prototypical categories of medicine, law, etc.' (Swales 1990: 103).

rather than, for example, manufacturing work. We will detail this kind of specialist work in line with Boswood's thinking.

Boswood (1999) maintains that professional communication involves two things: communicating *as a professional* and communicating *to a professional standard*. The expertise of a professional involves mastery of a body of knowledge, mastery of skills and the responsible use of this knowledge and these skills – i.e. understanding of, and commitment to, professional ethics. He details his definition with nine propositions describing professional discourse. According to Boswood (1999), a professional:

1. applies the body of knowledge by exercising a range of skills in an ethical manner;
2. is able to communicate within and across discourse boundaries;
3. is able to reflect critically on the workings of power through discourse;
4. has access to the technical, contextual and world knowledge necessary for communication within the communities concerned;
5. creatively uses the communicative resources of discourse communities to a standard that is recognised as exemplary;
6. applies knowledge and skills in accordance with codes of conduct which are recognised as ethical by communities;
7. is effective in reconciling and achieving multi-level purposes through communication;
8. can manage internal and external organisational communication by defining and implementing communication policy;
9. seeks to develop himself/herself through active reflection on performance.

In the professional context, communication serves numerous purposes. Hirokawa and Poole (2004: 12) mention six of them from *social information processing* to **rhetorical functions** such as persuasion, social influence and leadership that are used, for example, in the discourse of a job interview or negotiation.

We thus find that LCPP is far from a static research objective but is, rather, a highly dynamic phenomenon occurring in professional communities, influenced by several macro-factors, as referred to in the previous chapter. It is a major challenge to design communication courses that meet the demands of this set of standards. Based on this complexity of professional communication, the CEF Professional Profiles aim to incorporate some of these broader perspectives in the description of workplace communication.

The CEF Professional Profiles were developed to respond to the above workplace realities and the conclusions drawn from our needs analysis work (Huhta 1999; Huhta et al 2006) that multiple perspectives need to be included in a needs analysis to describe professional communication in a given field: occupation/position, location, typical job descriptions, contexts, participants, situation descriptions and texts. This was in line with developments in sociological and linguistic research. The sociologist Layder (1993, 1997) suggests four research elements in sociological investigation: *context, setting, situated activity* and *self*. Candlin (2002) proposes a four-perspective approach, incorporating *textual, social action, social/ institutional* and *participants'* perspectives. In our work, we have found that the concept of approaching our investigations from multiple complementary perspectives has proved very fruitful (see also Sarangi & Candlin 2001, Sarangi 2005). Bhatia (2004: 18 et seq.) uses what he terms a four-space model as the basis of his theoretical framework for analysing written discourse, with social, professional, tactical and textual spaces.

We consider that at least four categories of knowledge are needed to describe workplace communication adequately. In addition to the traditional *textual knowledge*, we need to consider the context carefully. In order to gain enough understanding about the context, we aimed to collect data on the *global, institutional and organisational* workplace setting, information about the *participant* and knowledge about the *social action* in the workplace.

In order to understand the context of communication in the workplace, the values and preferences of the activity need to be understood; for example, what is 'useful' to communicate relates to the values of the discourse system. A new member, our student, needs to become familiar with a culture of positive, neutral and negative communication in that particular discourse community. The communication teacher needs to supplement the more current information on the trends prevalent in global business in current publications or the Internet. There are focal themes in business domains that are currently prevalent, for example competitiveness, innovation, accountability, trust. Current trends or fads can fairly quickly influence what is positive and negative communication. For example, the focus on fast acceleration as a popular sales point in automotive advertisements has quickly changed to that of lower consumption and environmentally friendly fuel usage. This means that information about discourse community practice goals needs to be included in the profile. Almost all parts of the profile communicate some of the values and objectives of communication, especially the descriptions of frequent and demanding situations.

As for *institutional and organisational knowledge*, a variety of professional groups may operate and communicate at a single workplace, and these groups form communities of practice. Specialists of various areas work together in a number of professions, occupations and areas of expertise, both with in-group members (engineer to engineer; top manager to controller) or out-group members (project manager to supplier; project manager to potential client). The goals and aims of communication do not derive only from the social domain practice of international business but relate largely to the mission/vision or internal culture of specific organisations, and how these organisations wish to implement their mission through strategy and action. It is important to remember that institutions and their departments have differing organisation cultures, and the professional communication teacher therefore needs to consider the cultural factors (customs and procedures) that might affect communication.

The second category of knowledge about professional communication that the communication teacher needs is *participant knowledge*. A lot of communication is dependent on the communicating participants, for example their age, career, job profile, status and national culture. This is necessary knowledge about the participant and the mix of participants in various communication situations. Evidence-based needs analysis also documents the competence profile of the professional, including information on an individual's professional capabilities and the need for languages. Individual communication behaviour in an interaction is of course intrinsically variable and unpredictable, but it can help to know something about the character of the individual speaker. The decision about whether a person wishes to take a leadership role or an assisting duty, for example, often depends on the character. Interlocutors utilise communication strategies in accordance with their character and strategic goals.

The third category, *social action knowledge*, concerns a variety of issues. The interlocutor may decide to align or misalign with discourse community practice and assimilate or not adapt to intercultural differences. In some communication situations, implicit messaging may be favoured over verbal language, for example in situations of giving condolences. These are some of the contributing issues concerning what happens as social action in the communication event. In traditional ESP we tend to overlook other challenges besides language issues, such as cross-definition of aims, mismatching participants' intercultural differences, absence of a key participant, need for improvisation. In the social action perspective, non-verbal communication is an important part of language and communication as it affects communication greatly in the multicultural encounters of international business. In situations where language barriers exist between participants, the impact of non-verbal communication increases as verbal communication becomes more cryptic. Still, many business professionals report on successful deals done with little verbal interaction, as trust may have been created through solid credentials, reputation and respected hospitality.

The social action perspective emphasises the actual realisation of the communicative event in its immediate context as participants make sense of the status quo and communicate as best they can. Modular genres or typified communication situations may be far from the actual implementation that occurs in real life, but it is still important for ESP teachers to recognise them. The social action perspective is the most challenging element to document, as it depends to a great extent on the participant's own competences and interpretations of the communication event as well as the ability of the needs analyst to describe the complexity.

The fourth category concerns the familiar *text knowledge* perspective. The CEF Professional Profiles provide context information in communication situations, including a listing of *texts* that appear in those situations for teachers to include in the course. The profiles also reveal the location of the communication situations and the organisations that interlocutors come from. Additionally, the most frequent and demanding situations encompass the variety of crucial sites and critical moments to choose from in the course design (see Candlin 2006 for an explanation of how the components of social context link communities of practice to crucial sites and critical moments). Crucial sites are locations where the communication takes place, such as trade fair encounters or internal meetings. Critical moments occur in crucial sites (Candlin 1987) where the professional must succeed to perform well on the job, for example during audit visits or sales negotiations, as illustrated in the Mechanical Engineering profile in Chapter 3. Some of the critical moments are conducted in the native language, some in L2; some situations may be a mix of several languages, matching European language policies of plurilingualism and pluriculturalism (EU Language Policy). Language and the social activities involved are interdependent, so the domain and institution frame the ethnographic scene for the communication.

With the CEF Professional Profiles, we have broadened LCPP to include the socio-cultural environment of the domain – including interlocutors from a mix of professions and jobs, their communication objectives, specialist contents and discursive practices, which all materialise in communicative events through texts of various genres. In sum, workplace communication addresses all aspects of what it means to communicate professionally in a specific workplace for specific purposes – discourse communities of a workplace, working for established goals through interaction, both verbal and non-verbal, in the cultural setting of the community. When looking at language from this broader perspective of the workplace, signs, utterances and speech acts become micro-elements in the learning of language for professional purposes.

The need for *global, institutional and organisational knowledge* is addressed in the profiles by giving the professional communication teacher information on the social domain and field, including detail on the values and focal themes of the trade. Profiles give a long listing of typical organisations and communities where a graduate could typically be working in the future. This allows the learners to familiarise themselves with key organisations, be they suppliers, importers, standardisation bodies or professional associations. It also offers learners an opportunity to learn about the cultures of organisations. The CEF Professional Profile must provide data concerning institutions, locations and the professional groups involved, including information on whether they come from inside or outside the company.

Participant knowledge is given in the CEF Professional Profiles by the inclusion of lists of typical professions and occupations, such as designer of automation systems, project engineer and supervisory positions. These overall titles are substantiated in the profiles by lengthy job description lists, to provide expertise – and terminology – on various jobs such as product development, management and control systems (e.g. Enterprise Resource Planning – ERP), which teachers can incorporate in the course design. The naming of specifics helps the teacher in searching for relevant material on the Internet. It is worthwhile reading the descriptions of demanding situations in order to identify some typical communication challenges caused by the cultural differences and expectations of the other interlocutor. For example, one automation engineer went to validate his automation line design, expecting to meet his counterpart from another company, but ended up talking to a US Ministry of Agriculture representative, a hygienist who was interested not so much in discussing the actual design, but how the parts could be dismantled for reasons of hygiene. The engineer had to negotiate every day and then redesign the automation line at night to meet the Ministry standards. The thick descriptions of profiles, called snapshots, also feature stories of individuals that can be used as contextual knowledge and to plan simulations of professionals' lives. Many of these take the form of a description of a day in the working life of a professional. The language needs of the individual are also included in the profile, providing details of the various languages needed in work contexts and the level of competence required in each.

The *social action knowledge* of authentic communication is complex and challenging to document. Profiles do their best to describe the most frequent and the most demanding communication situations in such a way that it would be possible for another ESP teacher to use the documentation for devising learning activities. Snapshots – descriptions of employees' daily lives – also provide more in-depth explanations of events and their significance. The feedback from teachers who have trialled some profiles is mixed, with reports suggesting that the documentation within some of the profiles is detailed and good, while other profiles leave out too much background information to be of use in classroom activity design. This is clearly something that future profile writers should bear in mind as they look for still better ways of documenting authentic workplace communication.

Textual knowledge appears in profiles both as listings of communication situations, where for each situation the location, persons and organisations represented are also documented, and as listings of texts essential for the field, in the domain of both work and education.

Considerations of the four categories of knowledge appear in one or another part of the profile. To ensure the comprehensiveness of our description of the workplace communication contexts, the CEFR was used as a checklist in setting up the tools of the CEF Professional Profile. The use of CEFR is detailed in the next section.

2.5 CEFR used for CEF Professional Profile design

In 2001, it was agreed that the situational listing of Prolang ('Language/communication situations in industry and business', see Section 2.3) needed further refinement, and it was felt that the CEFR, as a widely accepted frame of reference, presented a comprehensive structure for this. While this focus on the analytic descriptions of sub-scales and the 'can do' statements in the CEFR has contributed to a mutual transparency of language levels that has undoubtedly been useful for the purposes of language assessment (for example, with the Cambridge First Certificate in English, the Diplôme d'Etudes de Langue Française (DELF) or the Goethe Institute's Zertifikat Deutsch für den Beruf), it has also meant that little attention has been paid to other factors in communication considered in the framework. We found that CEFR can also be used for professional purposes.

In particular, the CEFR clearly references the context in which communication occurs, taking account of exactly the kind of broader perspective of language and communication we discussed in the preceding section. The following pages from the CEFR (Council of Europe, 2001) have all been identified by Huhta (2007: 37) as matching the specialist content and the needs of English in the workplace:

- Domains where the learner communicates: personal, occupational, public, educational (pp. 80–5)
- Non-verbal communication (p. 88)
- Typical tasks performed in the occupation/profession for gaining results (pp. 86–90)
- Strategies and operations of the tasks needed to reach aims, e.g. interaction, mediation, listening (pp. 91–130)
- Texts/channel: oral or written products linked with specific areas of life, e.g. letter, email, dialogue (pp. 134–45; 201–2)

- General competences (pp. 146–81)
- Communicative language competences: skills required for receiving and producing messages (linguistic, socio-linguistic and pragmatic scripts/scenarios; individual/pair/group/social skills) (p. 33)
- Vocabulary (p. 208)
- Grammar (pp. 209–11)
- Pronunciation (pp. 211–12)
- Approach to mistakes and errors (pp. 214–15)
- Assignments (p. 229)
- Assessment (pp. 242–67)

The field-specific language and communication profiles which make up the CEF Professional Profiles Project were constructed using an extensive data-gathering process. Professionals working in companies and other organisations in various fields were interviewed, and language curricula of the institutes providing vocational and professional language and communication studies were analysed. Professionals were asked to give information on the situations in which they need languages in their workplace and the extent of that need, and on the most typical and the most demanding situations in which they are required to use the language. The results of the needs analyses were processed in a special format, namely, the CEF Professional Profiles. These profiles cover a wide range of contextual information on the communicative situations in the fields studied. For quality assurance, the profiles were evaluated by partner organisations and improved subsequently. Details on the data-collection methodology can be found in brief in Huhta (2010) and details of the CEF Professional Profiles Project can be found on the Proflang (Association of Languages for Professional Communication) website, http://www.proflang.org.

Each CEF Professional Profile consists of six parts. After the first part, which presents an overview of the professional field, each subsequent section provides a progressively more detailed description of the professional language and communication found in that domain. For convenience, the parts are labelled A–F:

- *Part A – Target profession* This specifies the target profession, professional field and relevant education. This in turn allows the teacher or course designer to see whether the profile matches his or her student needs fully or only partially.
- *Part B – Occupational information* This provides examples of relevant job titles together with some typical job descriptions for those posts and typical organisations in which the post-holders might be employed. This also allows the course designer to select roles for classroom activities that match student needs.
- *Part C – Context information* This gives information on the roles prevalent in the situation to facilitate the design of simulations that accurately reflect professional practices.
- *Part D – The most frequent situations* This part takes between three and five routine communication situations considered to be most common for the

professional field and describes the locations where the situations occur as well as the most likely sequence of events. The descriptions in Part D are an ideal basis for the design of classroom simulations.

- *Part E – The most demanding situations* In contrast to Part D, this part takes between three and five detailed descriptions of communication situations which require more complex responses and interactions. As with Part D, the descriptions in Part E also cover the location and the sequence of events but are explored in much more detail.
- *Part F – Snapshot* This final part provides a narrative of a day in the working life of a professional. The snapshot can take the form of a story detailing the events in a single working day or, alternatively, an inventory of all the most routine events in the current work of a professional. As is also the case in Parts C, D and E, Part F can provide a useful stimulus for designing simulations.

These are the different parts of the profile which were developed from a series of needs analyses and then matched against the comprehensive descriptions found in the CEFR.

2.6 **Summary**

This chapter has suggested the need for a shift in focus in our teaching of future and current professionals in two ways. Firstly, we conclude that ESP should be redirected away from foreign language education and towards training in communication for professional purposes in which the foreign language arises. The purposes themselves will be defined by the needs and demands of the specific workplace context in which specialists collaborate to achieve common goals. As argued in the foregoing, the ESP teacher can get to know the most relevant communication situations through building up a thick description in the needs analysis. The CEF Professional Profiles provide a framework for just such a thick description. Secondly, we suggest that the prevailing notion of specialisation in ESP, which has a tendency to consider professionals such as accountants, lawyers or engineers as discrete groups in isolation from one another, should be extended to consider the discourse communities in which the professionals are engaged. That is, the communication needs of an accountant working in a private law firm may well differ significantly from those of one who works in an engineering company. In other words, we should start to turn away from the idea of an English language which is particular to a specific purpose (ESP) and move towards the idea of LCPP, which is better suited to the fulfilment of the goals that members of the professional discourse community hold in common.

All this suggests once again that the content of the ESP course should be based on evidence, not teacher intuition. This is why *balanced, evidence-based needs analyses* work towards increasing teachers' knowledge base of the field and the authentic communication practices of the discourse communities in the field. Language learning times are shorter if the learner's language and communication needs are directly targeted (Huhta [2000] 2002b: 12–14) and combined skilfully with knowledge of these communication situations.

The CEF Professional Profiles provide teachers with substantial knowledge on the communication situations of various professions, by describing discourse communities and their communicative events that take into account the points mentioned in this chapter. In the next chapter, we present an example of a completed CEF Professional Profile based on a study of mechanical engineers in Finland. We also demonstrate a practical method for applying the information from the profile to course planning.

3 Sample profile and its application: mechanical engineers

Chapter overview

In this chapter, we present a completed sample of a CEF Professional Profile in full, before offering an approach to using the information in course design. The sample profile has been designed for university students of mechanical engineering. The target learner group consists of students and lecturers in higher education requiring English for the specific needs of mechanical engineering. This is a profession which requires a university degree, usually a Bachelor of Engineering. We will:

- show how to interpret the information in the profile
- present the full profile for mechanical engineering students specialising in machine automation
- describe each of the six parts of a CEF Professional Profile in more detail
- provide an example of how a profile can be applied to course design.

3.1 Understanding the CEF Professional Profile

In this section, we discuss each of the six parts of the Professional Profile (previously outlined in Chapter 2) in more detail and with specific reference to the complete profile given in Section 3.2.

3.1.1 Part A: Background information

The purpose of this section is to give general background information on the professional group for whom the ESP course is to be designed. In this case, we are looking at the *field* of mechanical engineering with a *specialisation* in machine automation (though of course any field is possible – see Appendix C for profiles for business, healthcare and law). *Qualifications* essential for entry into the professional group are also included in Part A. The profile was chosen from among the technology profiles (information and communications technology, mechanical engineering, metalwork and machinery, and structural engineering). Although it is technically impossible to cover all potential fields within the area of technology, we felt that by choosing four exemplary but very different fields, we would give an idea of the huge variety of professions within technology. The same has been done for the other areas (business, healthcare and law), always in line with the limited resources of the project.

Part A should also include background information on the research and construction of the profile itself. It is important to list this information, as it shows the course designer what kind of evidence has informed the profile and which methods have been used to gather it. This is useful for two reasons. Firstly, it will indicate to the course designer whether part (or potentially all) of this profile could be applicable to similar professional purposes in other circumstances, even if the mechanical engineering specialisation might not be precisely machine automation but, say, machine design. Secondly, it tells the course designer what further research could be undertaken so that the profile drawn up for mechanical engineers can be reformulated for use in an alternative context. The profiles are not static products but are flexible and open to adaptation.

In the profile in Section 3.2, two other types of informants were approached: firstly, employed professional mechanical engineers working at different levels and fulfilling different functions in the workplace, and secondly, the university lecturers in the subject. For drawing up the present profile, the following data-collection methods were used. To gain a global understanding of the business and field, information about the field in general was gathered from web sources such as Invest in Finland (http://www.investinfinland.fi), the Confederation of Finnish Industries (http://www.ek.fi/www/en/index.php) and Finpro (http://www.finpro.fi/en-US/About+Finpro/default.htm). This was complemented by information available on the occupation in general, for example from company websites, product information, company news and so on. Document analysis was conducted, based on documents provided by professionals in mechanical engineering and by lecturers in the field who had had a long experience in industry before entering university teaching. Job advertisements helped to provide an overview of the job market.

The most significant data for the profile came from semi-structured interviews. These were conducted with two types of informants: lecturers who had an industry background in mechanical engineering, and professionals currently working for companies. University lecturers (in this case specialists in mechanical engineering, mechatronics, machine automation and production engineering) were asked to describe communication situations which they had found demanding while working in industry. Although these lecturers are now removed from the day-to-day business of engineers, they could be said to have the 'bigger picture' of their educational institution (and maybe even of society) in mind, which enables them to contribute a different, somewhat more comprehensive, perspective to the profile creation.

The data yielded from interviews with teachers contributed to the information presented in Part C of the profile, and at times also to Parts D and E, focusing on the most frequent routine situations and the most demanding situations, respectively. Professionals, on the other hand, are rather closer to everyday business life and thus have a more immediate outlook on matters related to their profession, often based on the very distinct organisational perspective of a company. They draw on the personalised experience (past and present) that they themselves have gained on the job. Additionally, they usually have intimate knowledge of their particular company or organisation and of the different functions performed by engineers within the framework of that company. Business partners and other institutions that they regularly deal with represent another source of their knowledge. This level includes 'insider' knowledge about their industry or specialisation. In this way professionals as a second type of informant provide researchers with valuable data of a completely different type. This data mainly contributed to the drawing up of Parts D, E and F of the profile but also gave important ideas for Part C. After completing the first draft, the profile was given to other experts in the group who evaluated them. As a next step, profiles were thoroughly revised. Lastly, the profile trialled with a group of mechanical engineering students (n = 26). Students were asked to add their own experiences and to discuss the profiles accordingly. Feedback from the evaluation rounds was included in the final version of the profile.

By way of triangulated data from different sources and with variable data-collection methods, the context can be understood from multiple perspectives. This approach is essential for obtaining a thick description of a needs analysis (see the discussion in Chapter 1).

3.1.2 Part B: Occupational information

The purpose of this part of the profile is to provide general information about the occupation. The aim is to give the course designer an insight into the multiplicity of roles that working mechanical engineers can and do fulfil. For example, there is a variety of occupational roles within the specialisation of machine automation. Some mechanical engineers will be involved in design, and it is their responsibility to design automation systems according to the specifications of the company's clients. Others involved in programming the designed systems will be concerned with information technology. Mechanical engineers may also be responsible for the production and maintenance of a working automated system and may, for example, find themselves in charge of the ramp-up of an automation system of the kind typically found in automated packaging lines. As the engineers are employed by a company, they may also find themselves working in a supervisory or management capacity. Engineers in such roles may need to consider projects from a perspective beyond operations management. Another commercial role for a mechanical engineer would be working in sales, where an understanding of the field would be necessary for pitching to prospective clients.

Part B also describes the kinds of organisations in which mechanical engineers are typically found to be working. The industries associated with mechanical engineers include a variety of multinational companies as well as small and medium-sized companies (**SMEs**). Their employers may be major hydraulics importers such as Bosch-Rexroth, or paper machine design companies such as UPM, or ship design companies such as Metso. Or the employer may be a smaller company, specialising in plastics, food processing or machining operations. In the context of the particular profile given in Section 3.2, the students might end up working in the paper industry in factories or companies that function as subcontractors or partners.

An examination of the roles and responsibilities listed in typical job descriptions provides a useful overview of the field of activity of the professional target group. This would not include activities conducted in the foreign language alone, which is focused on in Part C. In our example, mechanical engineers design and program automated operations and systems in industrial production in general. They are also in charge of designing control systems for mobile machines, for example hoists and forklifts. They design related equipment as well. Overall, they are expected to find solutions to customers' problems and find steering solutions for programming, measurement and sensor technology, to name but a few.

Engineers can be found to assist in the full product cycle, ranging from developing a product to purchasing and sales operations. They monitor production operations, control and supervise engineering processes in plants, and assist and steer the project design and its implementation. Depending on their industry, part of their line of work includes planning, programming, commissioning, testing, as well as quality management. They are also involved in installation, service and maintenance, for example of machines.

On the business side of things, mechanical engineers are involved in corporate systems management and control. More precisely, this means being able to use enterprise resource planning systems, such as Enterprise Resource Planning (ERP), Standard Assessment Procedure (SAP), Manufacturing (MFG) and Distributed Generation (DG), through which the economic and financial status of the company can be monitored and controlled.

The foreign language needs of the professional target group are addressed in Part B, but only in very general terms. That is, this part of the profile specifies the extent to which the foreign language is needed by professionals working in this field. In our example, it is stated that a mechanical engineer cannot do without English as a foreign language. The reasons for this are also given: all text material is in English and English is the main language used for discourse with suppliers, subcontractors and clients. However, it is quite possible that, depending on the circumstances or professional field, English may be used mainly in reading or writing (for example, for reading annual reports or for communicating by email).

As is the case for most professions, career opportunities are better if the professional has a good command of English. However, engineers may find employment that does not require them to use English on the job at all. Apart from English, the other language that is important for mechanical engineers in the Finnish context is German as many German companies function as clients or suppliers of mechanical devices and their parts. It is important for the ESP course designer to be aware that the professional learners may be using more than one foreign language in their workplace.

3.1.3 Part C: Context information

The purpose of Part C is to inform the course designer about the core contents that arise from the foreign language needs analysis. The core contents constituting this context information are classified into four areas: *location*; *persons* (a category which also includes *communities*, *companies* and *institutions*); *communication situations*; and finally *text- and discourse-types*. These categories are clearly influenced by the framework of the CEFR. Context information in these four categories is further divided into *work contexts* and *study contexts*. This has been done to separate the activities and needs spelled out by the informants for communication in the workplace itself and for learning activities. While the aim of the learning activities (or learning tasks) is to simulate as much of the reality of the workplace communication as possible, there remain activities, such as 'reading study materials' or 'taking notes in class', that belong only to the study domain.

Location describes the settings in which the communication takes place and answers questions such as the following: What are the physical characteristics of the location (e.g. is the location a noisy trade fair hall or a quiet conference room; is it spacious or cramped, etc.)? Is the location likely to be familiar or unfamiliar (imagine the case of a project manager who is attached to a particular team or a sales person who regularly visits clients in their place of work)? Is the setting formal or informal? Does communication take place in an office, a conference room or in the competitive environment of a stand at a trade fair? In the work context of mechanical engineers, we find a variety of locations, reflecting the variety of roles and responsibilities for that professional group. Communication situations could take place at indoor locations, for example a performance review in the engineer's own office or a team meeting in a conference room (a place which may extend into virtual space via conference calls or video conferencing). Outdoor communication situations might include a discussion of technical issues which are best discussed on-site at the production facility of the engineer's company. An unfamiliar location for the same communication situation would be a visit to the production facility of a client, for example if some maintenance is required for the automated machine system or in advance of the installation of a new machine. Other communication situations could take place off-site, on more neutral ground, such as at a trade fair, at a restaurant or at a conference venue such as a hotel. In the study context, similar locations (offices, conference rooms, trade fairs, etc.) might be realistic for students who are completing a placement. In general, however, given that the particular target group in this case are mechanical engineering students in higher education, simulations of communication situations are most likely to take place in the lecture rooms of the institution.

Location is, of course, linked to any and all *persons* who might be involved in the communication situation. As noted briefly above, *persons* here refers not only to individuals but also to *communities* such as professional bodies (e.g. the UK's Institution of Mechanical Engineers, IMechE) or trade unions (which increasingly have transnational representation through organisations like the European Works Council). Knowledge of such communities relevant to the area is important for the course designer as such organisations commonly provide internet resources which can be used in materials development. For similar reasons, private sector *companies* and public sector *institutions* may also be considered as categories of persons in Part C. While companies may include competitors or clients, public sector institutions might be represented by a regulatory or a standardisation body, an example of which for Europe could be Machinery Directive 2006/42/EC, which 'provides the regulatory basis for the harmonisation of the essential health and safety requirements for machinery'.[1]

Specific examples of persons that our mechanical engineers might come across and interact with in the work context include subordinates, colleagues, managers, employers (internally) and clients, trade unions and professional bodies (externally). Groups that the engineer would face on a professional level would subsume suppliers of equipment and material, programming companies and sales companies. Regarding industries in Finland, companies specialising in plastics and paper are numerous. Also, domestic and global agents of multinational corporations from different fields of industry and commerce could be communication partners for mechanical engineers. On the public level, the engineers, at the client's request, may need to arrange an audit by members of a standardisation body. During such an audit, test-runs might be arranged for a new automated system in order to identify any potential deviations from the standard tolerances. Other examples of liaising with public organisations might include dealing with legal requirements set by ministries or other governmental agencies responsible for quality control or health and safety standards. In the study context, persons (communities, companies and institutions) with whom the engineer interacts would obviously include those from within the framework of higher education. Individuals whom student engineers might encounter in this context include overseas international students or else exchange students (such as those who might find a placement through the Erasmus programme, for example). The presence of guest speakers from outside the university or visiting lecturers is also a common feature of contemporary higher education. Professional and vocationally oriented degree programmes also frequently include placement in a company, where students may come across students from other universities or institutes. On a personal level, the placement represents an opportunity for the engineering student to meet and develop relationships with a prospective future employer, an experience which will be useful once job-hunting begins following graduation.

If *location* answers the question 'where?' and *persons* answers the question 'between whom?', the question 'what?' is answered in the description of the *communication situations*. A huge variety of events and activities can be classed as a communication situation. We can also think of a diversity of types of communication situations. Some situations will be scheduled in advance, will have an agreed agenda and so follow a more or less predictable sequence of events. For this type of situation – for example, departmental meetings, formal negotiations, product presentations – the engineer can prepare ahead of the event. However, there are clearly other events which are recognisable as commonly occurring communication situations that arise unexpectedly – for example, a phone call or a report of a fault which needs to be dealt with promptly. In the work context of our example for mechanical engineers, all of the following can be considered as instances of communication situations for

---

[1] http://ec.europa.eu/enterprise/sectors/mechanical/machinery/index_ en.htm

which the course designer might wish to incorporate material and activities into the syllabus. Starting with the production facilities of the engineer's plant (or at the premises of a client), a typical situation would be a discussion of technical specifications for the modernisation of an automated production line.

Alternatively, the engineer may be called upon to give a presentation of the operations facilities, describing to clients or partners the workings of the system and perhaps talking visitors through the key features and functionality of devices. This type of presentation would require the engineer to also be prepared to discuss the product's limitations as well as its potential. Other types of presentation may require the engineer not only to guide visitors through the operating system, but also to give information about the company, its history, its experience in this field, other products and existing clients. Presentations are a good illustration of why it is more accurate to think in terms of professional purposes than specific fields, as in such cases the mechanical engineer is clearly moving from a concern with production and machinery to an engagement in sales and promotion.

Project management is another (and complex) communication situation in which specialised domain knowledge (mechanical engineering) overlaps with organisational aspects of the business. Another area which blends business with specific knowledge is the provision of an after-sales service to existing clients where the mechanical engineer has to investigate any potential problems before negotiating viable ways of solving them in accordance with the client's needs. One of the tasks of a mechanical engineer may be to work with a business or sales expert at a trade fair to co-present a product (e.g. an automation line) or the solution to a general problem. Communication situations also involve discussing options or tailored solutions for prospective clients and solving the problems of existing clients. The course designer needs to acknowledge that meetings with clients will also entail engaging in small talk at the beginning or end of a meeting, or in the business socialising contexts of restaurants or hotels. Here engineers must display a skill for striking up and maintaining conversation on matters of topical and general interest. On the other hand, they need to have the linguistic flexibility to be able to get down to business and 'talk shop' at the right time. At more general venues such as conferences or seminars, engineers must be able to share information in order to keep in touch with the latest developments in the fields. As experts in the field, they may have to give a presentation themselves, either in the more academic context of a conference or a seminar, or during a meeting at a prospective client's company or organisation. In the office, much day-to-day work centres around gathering information from reference materials, for example from manuals or other sources of documentation, from network or internal sources.

Mediated communication through email or video conference is a feature of a mechanical engineer's everyday life, as is talking on the phone and managing business this way. Engineers must be able to use (and therefore understand) software such as AutoCAD or CATIA and deal with operations management systems such as Enterprise Resource Planning as well as systems for Manufacturing and Distributed Generation (commonly abbreviated in engineering circles as ERP, MFG and DG respectively, as already noted). In terms of writing, they need to formulate emails and compose instructions and specifications, for example for machines, as well as devise manuals, reports or memos. In a study context, learners read articles, study material, including web materials, in English. In the framework of their professional studies, they use extracts from books and technical articles to locate the best available knowledge. In the English class, they report orally, in groups, on texts they have read and interact with other learners in class, with final project workers and with project workers from abroad. Oral reports in class can include topics such as reporting on technologies used by current companies, or technologies under construction reported in popular technical magazines. In writing, they need to be able to draw up applications, such as for a traineeship or a student exchange, or even for their first job. They also, of course, need to be able to follow lectures and presentations that other learners make in class and to take notes in the foreign language.

The fourth consideration in Part C is that of *text- and discourse-types*. As will be obvious from our discussion in the previous paragraph of the sheer range of communication situations that mechanical engineers may encounter, they will come across many types of texts and discourses. Professional text-types for mechanical engineers would include articles in (online) trade journals, websites and other written material related to their work. Discourse types are equally varied and include presentations (of companies, products, details for solutions, etc.) but also more dialogic types such as telephone conversations, meetings, negotiations, process descriptions and so on. These types of discourse cross over into more generic business communication needs, but business correspondence has its own forms, such as enquiries, quotations, claims or adjustments to internal memos, project proposals, some or all of which might be needed in accomplishing an engineer's professional purposes. The study context for text- and discourse-types for mechanical engineers is equally varied. One notable addition which the course designer in this context might see good reason for including in the syllabus would be texts and discourses relevant to job applications: covering letters, curriculum vitae / résumés, online applications and job interviews.

3.1.4 Part D: The most frequent routine situations

The purpose of Part D is to outline the most frequent routine situations in the working life of a mechanical engineer in which use of the foreign language (e.g. English) is a prominent feature. The function of these descriptions is twofold. Firstly, they provide a deeper insight into a selection of frequently occurring activities in an engineer's typical working day. This is important for the learners as well as for the course designer and the teacher (who in ESP contexts are often one and the same person). As has been discussed, even in a group where all the learners are mechanical engineers, there can be a considerable variety of experience. For professionals, this is an opportunity to compare and contrast personal experience with the content of these descriptions. In the case of engineering students in higher education, it is quite possible that the learners themselves lack work experience, and so this is a way for them to learn about aspects of their future occupation. For course designers and teachers, it is an expedient way of learning more about the professional needs of the learners for whom the syllabus is being prepared and/or delivered. Secondly, the description of the situations in Part D informs the course designer and the teacher of the most relevant and suitable communication situations to include in the syllabus. The descriptions become a suitable basis for developing tasks and materials for the course. We will be returning to this point in more detail in Chapter 4, where a wide range of sample activities is provided.

The Mechanical Engineering profile in Section 3.2 describes six situations in detail.[2] Each situation is numbered and given a heading consisting of the primary text- and/or discourse-types involved. The particulars of the situation are prefaced by a summary of the context information drawn out of the analysis in Part C of the profile. So, for example, we have the *communication situation* (e.g. finding out about and fixing some changes in a drawing), the *location* (e.g. office) and *persons* (e.g. project manager, designer, engineer from the buyer company). These headings contextualise the situation for the course designer at a glance, providing him or her with a comprehensive picture of the situation. Before the details of the situation are given, a further heading, *critical success factors*, is given. This specifies what must be accomplished in order to achieve a successful outcome (e.g. clarity of the question, sufficient background details correct).

The six cases described in the sample profile are very much routine situations that learners in this field are likely to encounter themselves (either now or in the future) in a normal working day. This part of the profile is therefore particularly valuable for teaching, since it inspires the course designer to develop learning tasks that he or she knows are directly relevant to the learners.

In *Situation 1: Finding out about and fixing some changes in a drawing,* several options are possible for the course designer based on the situation presented: a manufacturer has queries on the design produced by the engineer (as the basis of the machine to be manufactured).

The details of the machine (in this case a web-dryer) presented by fax from the client give rise to several questions, such as a request that the engineer (who has designed the machinery) check and alter some of the measurements of the drawing or an enquiry about whether a part can be manufactured by a different company. In this way, the situation can serve as a basis for several learning tasks.

Situation 2: Finding out some details concerning quality of material deals with a different but equally frequent situation involving an engineer who has designed a bearing cover that is now to be manufactured. The workshop informs the engineer that the tolerance of the material is not given in the drawing provided. This is why they now have to enquire about the tolerance to be used for the bearing covers. This is done by telephone, and the engineer is able to help out fairly quickly in this way.

Situation 3: Finding out about and fixing some changes in a drawing describes another telephone conversation with the same engineer who has produced a drawing for a bearing

---

[2] There are normally between three and six frequent situations given for sample situations in a profile.

cover. The drawing lacks detailed information on one aspect of the bearing cover, the bracket, so the workshop calls the engineer to find out the exact diameter of the hole.

Situation 4: Invitation to tender gives the conditions of the tender, starting with the situation of a regional manager of an engineering company who is invited to join a tender. An invitation to tender is a typical activity of businesses and also of engineering companies. The ensuing discussion between the project manager, the designer from the manufacturer and the engineer from the buyer company takes place on the telephone.

Situation 5: Sorting out a problem concerning the signalling requirements of a processing line describes an example of electronic communication when a maintenance manager asks for a quotation for a change in the processing line that an engineer has designed. This type of communication typically involves not only the engineer and the buyer, but also the supplier, who must be contacted too.

Finally, *Situation 6: Scheduling dates for installation work* involves a negotiation of a date and time for an installation to be made on the client's premises, a slaughterhouse. The engineer is employed with the buyer company and has to confirm dates and times with the designer at the manufacturing company (also an engineer) and his or her project manager.

3.1.5 Part E: The most demanding situations

The purpose of Part E is to provide the course designer with a small range of situations which the informants of the needs analysis find, for different reasons, to be most demanding. These communication situations present a useful counterpoint to the most frequent routine situations. As with the communication situations described in Part D, the situations here give the professional trainee learners and the course designer/teacher access to the lived experience of the workplace. They also provide the basis for learning tasks and activities, especially for more advanced learners (those assessed at B2+ on the CEFR scale) and/or for those learners with extensive knowledge of the professional domain. The challenges presented by tasks and activities based on these communication situations can prove to be particularly stimulating. Furthermore, as learners gain in their own workplace experience, they may even be able to contribute to the profile through reflection upon their work and the situations that they have found most difficult.

In the case of our mechanical engineers, the most demanding situations were mainly those which involved reaching a consensus view. A problem arises, the complexities of which must first be communicated clearly to all relevant parties, where the solution can only be reached through negotiation. The presentation of the situations in the profile follows almost the same format as the routine situations found in Part D, that is, information about the *text-* or *discourse-type*, the *communication situation*, the *location* and the *persons* involved. Information about the specific *challenge factors* is given, with each factor being matched to the specific reasons why the situation was a demanding experience for the informant.

The first demanding situation described concerns the sales activities that an engineer can be involved in. While giving a presentation on a product, in this case a robotics line, the engineer has to bear in mind two particular things. First of all, he or she has to make a favourable impression in general in order to sell the product well. Secondly, he or she has to act professionally and competently when being asked particular questions. Some of these questions might concern organisational aspects such as delivery times, some might involve financial aspects such as how the payment can be made. Other details to be coordinated might be the number of days needed to install the robotics line at the client's premises, how much space is needed, etc. Problems arising from the previous arrangements for installation, for example a shortage of mechanics, have to be solved in the process by the engineer.

Situation 2 deals with solving problems as well. Apart from the situation itself, the need to alter the design for a manufacturing cheese line to conform to hygiene regulations, here the language aspect made the situation challenging. The engineer has to communicate with a non-specialist, a hygienist, who is a representative of an authority, the US Ministry of Agriculture, and who has the power to approve or ask for amendments to be made to the drawings. In the latter case, there is a risk that the deal would not be struck. The engineer not only has to detail the altered drawings to a non-specialist, but also has to be careful to achieve his or her objective and convince the hygienist. All of this has to be done under considerable time pressure.

Situation 3 is much more comprehensive, as it involves the preparation of an auditing visit. Auditing is a prerequisite for a business deal with the petrochemical company, a client to whom the engineering company has sold valve combinations. Random samples of these have to be tested, often under time pressure and in the midst of many other tests being conducted. This may cause delays in the schedule, which must then be rearranged by the project manager. The engineer must see to it that the documentation of the tests conducted is complete, even though the tests may take several days.

3.1.6 Part F: Snapshot

The purpose of the final part of the profile, Part F, is to give the course designer an insight into the personalised experience of a professional. Although information in the snapshot can be used as a springboard for tasks and activities, the primary function of the snapshots is to bring the content from different types of data together and present them in an easily digestible narrative form. As such, the snapshots are based on information gathered about the informant of the needs analysis as opposed to data supplied by them.

In Section 3.2, the snapshots in the sample are based on the normal working day of Esa Karila, a project manager in a waste management company, whose routines we feel are fairly representative of a mechanical engineer. The snapshot conveys the impression that Esa is shadowed during the day, giving comprehensive information on everything he does during that (typical) day, starting with logging on to the computer and finishing on the commuter train. In the second part, some typical tasks of a project manager are illustrated and described in more detail so that a comprehensive picture is given again, albeit not in a table as in the context information in Part C, but as a narrative.

3.2 Sample profile: mechanical engineers

CEF PROFESSIONAL PROFILE
TECHNOLOGY – MECHANICAL ENGINEERING – HIGHER EDUCATION

A. BACKGROUND INFORMATION

Field	Mechanical engineering
Education/Programme	Degree in Mechanical Engineering
Specialisation(s)	Machine automation
Degree/Qualification/Occupation	BEng (Machine Automation)
Language	English
Drawn up by	Marjatta Huhta
Date / City and country / Organisation	28 February–14 May 2006, Helsinki, Finland, Helsinki Metropolia University of Applied Sciences
Methods used for collecting the information (methods, persons, dates)	Sources: description by an experienced English teacher of machine automation students CEF Professional Profile draft by Marjatta Huhta, English teacher of machine automation students Website analysis of a variety of websites: • General industrial knowledge such as High Technology (http://www.hightechfinland.com/direct.as px?area=htf&prm1=391&prm2=article), Invest in Finland (www.investinfinland.fi), Confederation of Finnish Industries (http://www.ek.fi/www/en/index.php) and Finpro (http://www.finpro.fi/en-US/ About+Finpro/default.htm) • Specific companies in the field such as Rocla, UPM-Kymmene, M-Real, Valmet, VR, Finnair, Kone, Rautaruukki, ABB, Metso, Sencorp Corporation, Wärtsilä, Metso Automation, Metso Drives, VTI Hamlin, Vaisala, Componenta (gears), Elcoteq, Perlos, Eimo Muovi (plastics corporations) Semi-structured interviews with: • Head of Mechanical Engineering, 27 January 2006 • Senior Lecturer of Machine Automation, 27 January 2006 • Design, Consulting and Engineering Company • Regional Manager, Consulting and Engineering Company • Project Manager, Engineering Company Evaluation of first draft by one other project member Trialling with n=26 undergraduate students of mechanical engineering

B.   OCCUPATIONAL INFORMATION

Typical examples of professions/occupations/jobs	Designer and programmer of automation systems Project engineer Project manager Designer Sales engineer Management positions up to top management level Production engineer
Typical organisations, companies, communities to be employed in	Mechanical engineering companies, e.g. Kone, Rocla, Valmet, VR, Rautaruukki, ABB, Wärtsilä, Metso, Metso Automation, Metso Drives, Componenta (gears); design engineering companies for paper machine design (Metso), ship design (Aker Yards) Electronics and other, e.g. Nokia (for programming positions, production operations), Finnair (airline), Sencorp Corporation, VTI Hamlin, Vaisala, Elcoteq Food-processing industry, e.g. Valio, Atria Hydraulics, e.g. importers such as Festo, Bosch-Rexroth (own half of Germany's hospitals) Pneumatics, e.g. SMC (Japanese importer of pneumatics) Plastics, e.g. Perlos, Eimo Muovi Paper industry: factories, subcontractors, partners, e.g. UPM, M-Real Waste management, e.g. L&T (Lassila & Tikanoja)
Typical job descriptions	Designing and programming of automated operations and systems in industrial production Designing control systems for mobile machines such as hoists and forklifts Designing equipment and systems Tailoring solutions to customer's problems Developing steering solutions: programming, measurement, sensor technology Commissioning/ramp-up and maintenance operations Group leadership, supervisory or management positions Product development Production operations Control and supervision engineering in plants Project design and implementation Planning, programming, commissioning/ramp-up, testing, quality management, production, installation, service, maintenance Corporate management and control systems (ERP, SAP, MFG, DG) Purchasing and sales operations

To what extent foreign languages are needed	A mechanical engineer cannot cope without English as all new text material is in English, as are discussions with suppliers, subcontractors and clients. Also, communication with a possible principal from abroad occurs only in English. Some mainly read and write email in English. Those with a three-year technician education may be able to cope somewhere orally without English. In other positions, oral English is a necessity. If a graduate has English skills, career opportunities are wider. Mechanical engineers should also know German.

C. CONTEXT INFORMATION

	LOCATION	PERSONS, COMMUNITIES, COMPANIES, INSTITUTIONS	COMMUNICATION SITUATIONS	TEXT- AND DISCOURSE-TYPES
Work context	Office facilities at the employer's, conference rooms Production facilities The client's or partner's premises Trade fair locations Restaurants, hotels and travel targets during client visits Conference venues, seminars, working groups, video conferences Office	**Individual:** clients, employers/employees, managers, colleagues, subordinates **Professional:** suppliers of equipment and material, programming companies, sales companies; paper companies (manufacturing and processing), companies in plastics; domestic and global agents of global corporations from different fields of industry and commerce	Dealing with expert and client contacts in meetings and negotiations, including unexpected face-to-face interactions Participating in client and expert discussions on technical specifications, project design, project management, change of detail, amendments, project monitoring and follow-up Presenting operations facilities and guiding tours around the premises, giving information about the company, product/tailored solution and its functionality, solutions and limitations Presenting a product / solution / an automation line, discussing options of tailored solutions; solving problems of current clients Using small talk; talking about issues of general interest, e.g. current events, news and local knowledge, alongside business discussion	Company presentation Discussion about industry (fields, products, corporate operations) Interaction situations: • Trade fairs • Meetings • Interviews • Negotiations • Process descriptions Business letters and emails: • Enquiry • Quotation • Job application • Claim • Adjustment

	Public: standardisation bodies (CAN-CiA – CAN in Automation, ODVA, ISO) and other expert organisations producing statutes, directives and standards; external auditors; ministries and other governmental agencies	Sharing information, interacting or giving presentations in seminars, working groups or conferences Utilising information from reference materials such as manuals, network sources, instructions and documentation, professional sources Communicating through email and the Internet Managing business by telephone – undistracted understanding of speech Using computer programs, e.g. AutoCAD, CATIA, Excel	Articles, websites, marketing texts and text analysis Product presentations Negotiations and meetings Telephone contacts Social situations (e.g. functioning as a host) Dialogue (telephone: enquiry, fault analysis, feedback, appointments) Presentations (technical presentation, introduction of a plan)
Study context	International guests and guest lecturers, exchange students and trainees, final project workers, students in the Virtual Product Development (VPD) and CATIA project Search for job or traineeship	Dealing with operations management systems, e.g. DG, MFG Writing emails, instructions, specifications, manuals, reports, memos Reading articles, study materials and web materials in English Interacting in class and with final project workers and project workers from abroad Oral reporting Describing personal strengths and challenges Discussing family relations, living conditions Drawing up applications for traineeship or student exchange Taking notes in class	Report, memo Service instructions **Texts:** • Description (educational and work experience; procedures) • Presentations • CV and cover letter or web application • Job interview • Report • Abstract • Email • Note-taking tools • Small talk
	Lecture rooms, laboratories, at trade fairs and exhibitions, the Web, at the workplace/ company as a trainee/employee		

D. THE MOST FREQUENT ROUTINE SITUATIONS

Situation 1: Finding out about and fixing some changes in a drawing

Communication situation: finding out about and fixing some changes in a drawing

Location: office

Persons: project manager, designer (from the manufacturer), engineer from the buyer company

Critical success factors: clarity of the question, sufficient and correct background details

Details: A client from a Swedish machining workshop contacts the project manager of an engineering company to find out who has designed the equipment for web-dryers. The project manager forwards the call to the designer who receives a fax from the Swedish company with the following information:

Client: FPM Paper

Product number: VL-13 – equipment for web-dryers (equipment for drying paper)

Year/week: 2006/20

Project number: 328

Revision number: 02 (number of the version in question)

Designed by: SAA-EM (initials of the designer)

Checked by: SAA-EM

Approved by: CEM-SA

Program: CATIA (computer program used for designing the equipment)

Filed in: S/webdryers/EM (where the document can be found in SAA-EM's folders on the company's server)

A telephone call may be required to deal with the following:

• A Swedish subcontractor wishes to check some of the measurements for the above drawing for manufacturing as some measurements do not seem to match (diameter/width) or

• The manufacturer cannot supply them with a particular component and the workshop enquires whether the component assigned by the seller can be replaced by another manufacturer's corresponding component

A follow-up fax is sent to confirm the changes made.

Situation 2: Finding out some details concerning quality of material

Communication situation: finding out some details concerning tolerance of material

Location: office

Persons: project manager, designer (from the manufacturer), engineer (from the buyer company)

Critical success factors: finding the right person who knows all the details, obtaining sufficient background information

Details: The problem – The designer has made an instructional drawing for installing a bearing cover. The workshop informs the designer that the material is too smooth: the tolerance is not marked in the drawing. The workshop calls to enquire about the tolerance (= how many millimetres of free space is required; tolerance classes are such as J, H, K). The approved tolerance for the support could be H7/h6.

Situation 3: Finding out about and fixing some changes in a drawing

Communication situation: finding out about and fixing some changes in a drawing

Location: office

Persons: project manager, designer (from the manufacturer), engineer (from the buyer company)

Critical success factors: finding the person who knows the details, having sufficiently detailed documents, knowing the work processes/persons doing each phase

Details: The problem – The designer has made an instructional drawing for installing a bearing cover. A bracket is to be designed by a machining workshop. The drawing does not indicate the diameter of the hole. What is it? The information needs to be given to the subcontractor. Again, the changes are confirmed by fax.

Situation 4: Invitation to tender

Communication situation: looking for more detailed information in order to draw up a tender

Location: office

Persons: project manager, designer (from the manufacturer), engineer (from the buyer company)

Critical success factors: asking for enough detail to be able to draw up a tender

Details: A regional manager from a design engineering company is contacted to join a tender for designing a crane by a shipbuilding company. Size of the crane: 150 x 105 metres. Height: 40 metres. The strength of the material will be calculated in the Jyväskylä unit of the engineering company. The estimated design time is 7,000–8,000 hours. The hourly rate varied €30–60 (2006). For shipbuilding, all documentation must be in English. More information about engineering companies www.skol.ry.fi (SKOL Suomen Konsulttitoimistojen liitto)

Situation 5: Sorting out a problem concerning the signalling requirements of a processing line

Communication situation: sorting out a problem concerning signalling of a processing line

Location: office

Persons: maintenance manager of the client, project manager (from the manufacturer)

Critical success factors: acknowledging the problem, willingness to solve the problem

Details: The maintenance manager from Maple Leaf Pharm, a poultry-processing plant from Chicago, enquires about a change in the contents of a delivery of a newly installed processing line. The red light push-button indication signal for the 'GO' of the processing line must be changed to green, as red in the USA indicates NO. The engineer will check with the supplier to see if they or some other party can provide this option and draw up a quotation for having it changed. There is no hurry to do this in the morning as people in the USA are in bed until 3–4 pm Finnish time.

Situation 6: Scheduling dates for installation work

Communication situation: sorting out/timing the dates for installation work

Location: office

Persons: project manager, designer (of the manufacturer), engineer (from the buyer company)

Critical success factors: flexibility in serving the client's needs

Details: A client of a vacuum conveying process manufacturer confirms the dates for installations in the slaughterhouse. The installations must be done at night as production cannot be interrupted during the daytime. The slaughterhouse will have its own mechanics to do the work, but supervision is provided by the supplier. After confirming with the supervisor, the project manager informs the client that the supervisor will be present on the agreed dates.

E.   THE MOST DEMANDING SITUATIONS

Situation 1: Giving a presentation to a potential buyer group from Korea

Communication situation: giving a persuasive presentation about a potential robotics line

Location: office

Persons: project engineer, group of potential buyers

Challenge factors: new experience, attitudes of the listeners, presenting in a foreign language; similar deals had been made in the USA before, and therefore the engineer expected a predictable outcome to the negotiation

Details: In this case, the engineer was selling a project. Sometimes, when sorting out problems such as the scheduling and detailing of contents (what has been sold), unexpected issues arise.
The interviewee worked as a sales engineer in a company called Cimcorp, which delivered robotics and production lines internationally, including to Korea. In this case a delegation from a Korean company was attending the pitch meeting in the role of a potential buyer of a palletising robot for a production line.

The interviewee was doing pre-commercial work: presenting the company's products and solutions to production-line technology. A group of Koreans, including production management and departmental management (4–5 persons), were listening. A factory tour was organised and premises inspected. A palletising robot was needed in the production line for handling the motor blocks based on a turnkey project, tested and commissioned on-site. The price range was within €200,000–300,000. In Korea, the Letter of Credit is often the primary payment mechanism for a transaction, or perhaps some percentage advance payment, say 30%, including bank guarantee. As soon as the customer accepts the quotation, the advance payment is effected. An instalment of 30–40% may be paid after the trial round, and 20–30% after acceptance. Once the product has been documented, payment of the remaining 10% can be effected. At the meeting the product and its functionalities were presented by the engineer. During a brief question-and-answer session, some detailed questions came from the prospective buyers. The questions had to be addressed in such a way that there were solutions to all potential problems that might arise. In other words, the engineer had to manage to present the product in a very favourable light. After the discussion of the product itself, the conditions of a potential deal had to be hammered out, but in a non-obtrusive way. A Letter of Credit payment does not reflect too much trust in the business partner, so this has to be communicated to the delegation in such a way that nobody loses face.

Situation 2: Negotiating with public authorities

Communication situation: unexpected negotiations content because of different legislation in the USA; giving a US Ministry of Agriculture representative a persuasive presentation about a potential robotics line

Location: client's premises

Persons: project engineer, group of potential buyers, US Ministry of Agriculture representative

Challenge factors: The situation was demanding for the following reasons:

- The counterpart was not an engineer, but a hygienist > you must be careful with terminology.
- The counterpart/representative of the US Ministry of Agriculture had the power to approve or reject the plans > you cannot afford hard feelings or irritation.
- The schedule was tight; the inspector had reserved a week for going through the plans > no chance for any extra time.

Details: The engineer is sent by a manufacturing company to the USA to propose the design of an automation line to a client. The company manufactures three kinds of equipment, one being an automatic cheese-manufacturing line. A whole cheese production line was offered in Michigan, USA. The first visits involved getting familiar with the manufacturing of the local Emmental cheese. The outcome was that an order for a production line was placed by the cheese manufacturer. BUT if a company in the USA wishes to sell the product to the army or to schools, stringent hygiene requirements must be met and equipment approved by public authorities. The dairy had a need for this. The interviewee contacted the US Ministry of Agriculture. First, information was sent about the production line; later some information had to be presented on site. The negotiator was not an engineer, but a hygienist. Several problems were discovered. During a one-week process, negotiations were conducted (full cheese-making line for Emmental cheese) during the daytime, and new drawings were made at the hotel during the night. A lot of drawings were involved.

The problem was that all parts that were in contact with the product had to be made such that they could be dismantled and washed regularly for hygiene reasons. The dairy workers responsible for cleaning the parts of the machinery would need training. All parts in contact with the food product (cheese containers, piping, mixer, cutters, filters used for the curd, masses pivoted into moulds, mass pressed into cheese) had to become easy to dismantle, clean and reassemble. The collected mass is salted (in salt water), after which the cheese ripens on shelves for 3–12 months. For reasons of hygiene, all holes or gutters in the production line must be avoided.

The Ministry approved the plans; manufacturing of the production line was started. The lines were commissioned in Michigan. An inspector from the USA came to Finland to check that everything had been done in accordance with the agreement. The spirit was positive and constructive. During the visit the inspector presented the principles of establishing long-term hygienic requirements. During the process he focused on the principles and was pleased to find the solutions adequate as the product drawings were being improved. The installation on-site lasted three months. Ten professionals were needed (welders, mechanics, automation engineers) to complete the installation.

Situation 3: Organising an auditing visit

Communication situation: organising an auditing visit
Location: telephone, email, letter, actual audit programme
Persons present/involved: Italian client, project manager, British inspector
Challenge factors: new experience, an audit can cause unexpected problems, a native speaker speaking fast

Details: An Italian client ordered some valve combinations. Because their clients were all petrochemical plants, a three-party, objective external audit was required. The project manager had to organise this. The inspector had been invited from Britain (e.g. Lloyd's). First the product and the documents were inspected and some tests conducted at the manufacturer's site. For example, if a100 valves were ordered, a random sample of them would be tested. If everything was OK, Lloyd's would send a test report and approve the standard. If there were deviations, a report would be written and the project manager would have to fix an appointment for a new review.

The problem during testing days like this was that there were delays in the schedule (e.g. setting up test systems for large valves), so organising a schedule with a valid programme was challenging. The location was a negotiations room: 20 tests in three days. Sometimes there may be many tests during the same week. With such a tight schedule, it was sometimes difficult to maintain motivation. The most frequent deviations were missing elements in the documentation, such as when the client delivered the documents straight to the inspector and only the new versions drawn up by the manufacturer included the final details.

F.   SNAPSHOT

Snapshot 1: A working day

Esa, the project manager in a waste management company, arrived at work between 7 am and 8 am. He logged into the computer to find 5–10 emails in English. These emails pertain to changes in the contents of a delivery, schedule changes, requests for additional offers, confirmations, etc. After reading the emails, Esa went to get coffee from the hallway and returned to his desk.

Esa continued ongoing work, typically searching for information needed to prepare for a tender (see Situation 4 in Part D of this profile). He sent an enquiry to the factory. He went back to an order from the previous day, an order from a slaughterhouse in Denmark for a vacuum conveying system with two machines. They needed seven suction points. The total value of the deal is €450,000. Delivery time is nine weeks.

Esa met the production manager to discuss how the order can be placed in the production schedule. He had another meeting with the purchasing manager in order to arrange for the purchase of the required materials. Esa input the order information into the quality system according to the agreed quality management manual.

On returning to his desk, Esa sent an email to the Danish client to inform the company how the order had been processed further. Distractions kept occurring. A colleague arrived and wanted a second opinion on a rescheduling plan in the production. After lunch Esa received an email confirming that the factory could provide the green lights as requested by the American client (see Situation 5). He then had to process the information and put it into a quotation to be sent off to the American client for consideration.

An enquiry arrived through a Dutch sales outlet concerning the possibility of designing and delivering a special solution for delivering a heating jacket for controlling the temperature of waste in winter conditions to prevent freezing. The Taifun system was built by the Dutch to be located outside, where the temperature goes below zero.

On the commute home (which takes a long time), Esa phoned American and western European clients, e.g. in Italy, as the time difference means that these contacts were only now in the office.

Snapshot 2: Project manager's work

The project manager's tasks concerning the acquisition of equipment are as follows: the project manager is having a discussion with the designers, who draw up specifications, drawings, calculations and instructions on how the equipment will be built, based on the contracted deal.

If the machining workshop is part of a company, the project manager will visit production to see if anything needs to be done differently from any standard procedure solution. His or her task is also to see that the products are manufactured on time. Schedules are based on accepted details of the contract. All project managers compete for the same production capacity. A typical assignment is to initiate the purchasing of outsourced components, agree terms with the client and then supervise the project to ensure that the components arrive on schedule. Contacts with the end client and other contractors on the same site are also part of the project manager's job description. These similar jobs keep repeating themselves, only the object of the project changes.

There may be several (up to three) projects ongoing at the same time. The responsibility stays with the project manager until the project is finished and the production line is up and running. The project manager is in charge during the minimum of the guarantee time (e.g. two years), but often even after that. If the project is large, the manager controls only one at a time. Often, when the project is about to end, the project manager is asked to participate in a new bidding round.

There are critical moments/points, especially in production: some other project may take precedence and the manager's project will be delayed. He or she must contact the production manager in charge of production. Negotiations are conducted between project managers to minimise problems. The sales unit may often have promised too tight a schedule and as a result the delivery may be late. Supply may also be delayed. Other unexpected disturbances may occur. The project manager needs to be strong as a person as the job is challenging. If he or she gets upset, then this may indicate that control of the project has already been lost. Good nerves and an understanding of human psychology and different cultures are all assets. For example, the concept of 'saving face' is very important in some Asian cultures, and it is therefore important when problems occur to make a point in a way that does not challenge the other party's sense of prestige.

Orders for cheese-manufacturing lines may arrive, for example from Germany, which is full of small cheese-making factories. A Finnish company may have delivered a partial delivery for cheese manufacturing, for example a single mass press unit. The project manager may also be a designer, who besides designing also deals with other work in the project, such as acquiring materials and components, doing trial runs and dealing with the commissioning in Germany. Other cheese-manufacturing equipment may include post-treatment equipment such as cutting or packaging operations.

3.3   Exploiting the sample profile in course design

In this section, we look ahead to the content of the next chapter and discuss the ways in which the information in a CEF Professional Profile, such as the profile for mechanical engineers operating in southern Finland in the previous section, can be utilised by a course designer or the teacher of ESP.

As a first step, we wish to see how the information found in the profile can be translated into language and communication practices in the workplace. To do this, we can think of language and communication as existing at different levels of increasing specificity and detail. At one end of the spectrum, we can think of language and communication at the social and political level – in terms of the wider society of the nation-state, of international communities, such as the EU, and in terms of global economic and financial flows. Conversely, the focus at the other end of the spectrum is on smaller units of language, such as words within a framework of language and communication practices in the workplace. For convenience, we have placed these levels on a scale from 8 (the level dealing with the largest units of society and politics) to 1 (the smallest units we will deal with are words). Viewing the situation from 8 down to 1 would be to take a top-down approach, while the reverse, a bottom-up approach, would involve a movement from level 1 through to 8, as has been done in Huhta (2010). We have put this information into Table 3.1. As can be seen, the first column indicates the level (on a scale of 1–8); the second column then describes the language and communication practices associated with each level on the scale; the third and final column then illustrates each level with examples for mechanical engineers with reference to specific parts of the profile where relevant.

Table 3.1 can show the course designer what language and communication information the future mechanical engineer will need in this particular context. The second column shows the course designer potential areas of focus for language study, while the third column gives some examples of the language and communication contexts of a mechanical engineer who needs a foreign language (L2), English, in the profession, at the workplace with other professionals, with international clients abroad and at home, and following the developments of business and technology globally.

While the information in the profiles is clearly most concerned with levels of language and communication in the upper mid-range (levels 6, 5 and 4 in the table), we will now look at all eight of the levels in our discussion of how each can best serve the ESP course designer or teacher.

Level 8: Wide horizons

For mechanical engineers, wide horizons occur in the utilitarian global business environment. Information on this level is not included in the profile as this is an environment characterised by rapid change, sometimes unexpected and turbulent. Sources of information about this level would be the trade press, newspapers, news websites and so on. Language and communication is less useful to the course designer (who as a rule must plan the syllabus some time in advance of the delivery of the course) but can be introduced to the classroom

Table 3.1: Overview of the contexts of language and communication for the professional purposes of mechanical engineers

Focus of study	Language and communication at work	Contexts of language and communication for a mechanical engineer
	Top-down approach ⇓	
8	Wide horizons	Global business, economics, EU, country, education
7	Society and culture(s)	Industry and business
6	Communication practice in the context of the field	• Organisations of the field (e.g. equipment and material suppliers, paper companies, plastics companies) (Part C) • Organisational communication (e.g. companies and workshops; international manufacturers whose products are sold in Finland; importers of hydraulics, pneumatics; paper machine and ship design; automated systems for food-processing industry) (Part B) • Inter-professional contexts (e.g. business experts, accountants) (Parts D, E and F)
5	Range of communication situations	• In-group professional contexts for the discourse community would be all forms of internal interaction – note that in global corporations, it is not uncommon for the internal language of the business to be conducted in English (regardless of the geographical location of certain branches) • Out-group professional contexts: expert and client contacts in meetings and negotiations, project design etc. (Part C)
4	Communication situations	Discourse of genres: company presentations, trade fairs, meetings, negotiations, process descriptions, etc. (Part C; examples in Parts D, E and F)
3	Speech act	Communication strategies, politeness
2	Utterance	Grammar, vocabulary, pronunciation, stress (Parts A–F represent the vocabulary of central concerns)
1	Sign	Words
	⇑ *Bottom-up approach*	

by the ESP teacher to show an awareness of contemporary developments that are relevant to the field. In the case of the sample, Finland offers a competitive environment for industrial operation and investment. EU directives regulate many areas of operation.

Level 7: Society and culture(s)

The mechanical engineering *industry* is historically deeply rooted in Finland in numerous small and medium-sized enterprises (SMEs) and machining workshops which started to conduct export operations first and later on turned to global *business*. Major companies in the field operate in the paper and shipbuilding industries, producing elevators, hoists, metal and steel, gears, machine elements, forest machines and engines, or are involved in design engineering, automated systems (for a listing see Part B of the profile).

Level 7, as with level 8, encompasses so many possibilities that it is not efficient to include it in the profiles. Again, information at this level is unlikely to have an influence on course design, though again the ESP teacher may use current information taken from news media, journals and the Internet as a way of engaging learners in discussion about trends and possible future directions in the field.

Level 6: Communication practice in the context of the field

Level 6 is the first of the larger units on the scale for which the profile provides extensive information. Communication practice in the field is related to the professional discourse communities of the learners and would incorporate information on the practices of both in- and out-group members. Part B of the sample profile tells us that mechanical engineers in the Finnish context typically work in a variety of roles, such as designers and programmers of automation systems or as project managers. We also learn that while much of the work may be conducted in the mother tongue (Finnish or Swedish in the sample), the foreign language (primarily English but German is also a possibility) will be used extensively if the company operates globally. In fact, English may even be used as the internal working language of the business. The *external context of communication* for the mechanical engineer occurs in collaboration with equipment and material suppliers, paper companies, plastics companies (e.g. for automation of packaging lines) and customers.

As noted, some mechanical engineers have a need to communicate in foreign languages other than English. German is fairly common (and may be required in the context of work with a company like Bosch-Rexroth), but Japanese is another possibility, as in the example of certain equipment manufacturers. External contexts of communication may also include contact with a standardisation body (such as CAN-CiA-CAN in automation and ISO, which are common standardisation bodies for mechanical engineering) as part of an auditing procedure (Part C). In *internal communication* (which is often in English) systems information such as ERP and SAP needs to be communicated to corporate management (Part C).

In course design this means that the teacher has to consider in what context the planned learning activity is to take place. Tasks that consider external communication contexts, for example communication with standardisation bodies, will be completed using a different language from that used in internal communication, for example during an informal departmental meeting in the company. Here, the notion of appropriateness of the language used in the communication situation in the particular context plays a vital role and can be dealt with in the course, for example by discussing the impact of formal vs informal language in a given communication context.

Level 5: Range of communication situations

The range of communication situations is information that should also be found in the profile. The range of situations relevant to mechanical engineers, as the profile shows, is quite considerable. A course designer with little experience of mechanical engineering may anticipate discussions dealing with technical specifications, project design, changes to details of a design and scheduling events. The profile shows that fairly informal face-to-face meetings with experts and clients also feature as does the need to host visits, which may include business socialising, making small talk and light conversation on (non-controversial) topics of general interest. Email, internet communication and the use of printed sources of information, as might be expected, are needed on a daily basis, considering the time differences between locations (Part C). At this level, the course designer and the ESP teacher can find out who speaks to whom on what issue and what the outcome of the communication might be (Part C).

Part C illustrates the range of possible communication situations that are relevant in the everyday life of a mechanical engineer. While the details on situations, text-types, persons and locations provide an overview for the reader, they can also function as a starting point for course design. They would, for example, shed light on the question of whether a task such as a simulated presentation of an automation line at a trade fair stand would represent a realistic communication situation in the everyday life of a mechanical engineer. However, the comparable wealth of information with key words only will probably be more helpful for experienced teachers because the detailed situations themselves will have to be thought up or researched by the course designers. For novice teachers or teachers with little background in the field, the situations in Parts D and E might be valuable since they have been spelled out completely. Part C of the profile provides many potential starting points for designing classroom activities.

Taking an interest in mechanical engineers in terms of a discourse community is useful as it is the community which regulates the norms of communication practices ('this is how we do things around here'). By considering the routine situations and demanding situations at work, a course designer or ESP teacher lacking experience in the field can soon get an idea of what needs to be taught in terms of communication for professional purposes and language relevant to the learner needs.

Level 4: Communication situations

A frequent situation that can easily be simulated in class, and so incorporated in the design of the course, is a telephone call. In Situation 1 in Part D of the profile, for example, details are given of a common daily telephone call in the working life of a mechanical engineer. The mechanical engineer receives a phone call from a project manager of a Swedish company wanting to find out further details about a web-dryer they are buying. They have been unable to obtain a part required by the manufacturer, and they are asking whether they could use a replacement component. The communication includes a thorough identification of the precise deal, including product number, revision number and designer name initials.

All the details are communicated in the profile (Part D) for activity planning purposes. The solution of using a replacement component is discussed, and the mechanical engineer wishes to know more details. These will be communicated by fax or email. This task can be varied in many ways, as detailed in Part D. Students may forget to simulate the initial parts of communication as self-evident and hasten to a quick outcome to the call. Reality here, based on needs analysis respondents, emphasises the initial stages of communication. It is vital to start a telephone call by identifying the speaker and checking that he or she is the correct person to deal with the particular problem, in line with approved company processes. This is also a good example of integrated communication, including speaking, listening, writing and reading. Common practice is that changes such as the one described are not accepted unless written confirmation is conducted, in this case by fax or email. The sample profile includes six examples of frequent situations which an innovative teacher can easily vary.

Part E of the profile can be used to create tasks and activities with an increased level of challenge (both professionally and linguistically). A good example of this would be Situation 2, in which the engineers were required to use English not only in dealing with the client but where it was also necessary to work with authorities from the US government. The description of this situation should provide enough information for the course designer (or the ESP teacher) to prepare an extended simulation of the negotiation process:

- Giving personal introductions; engaging in small talk; active listening (i.e. acknowledging interest in the interlocutor)
- Drafting a presentation of the proposed production-line system in English; anticipating client questions/objections
- Presenting the proposed system to the client
- Discussing the design, identifying problems, recognising and responding to criticism, exploring alternative solutions
- Taking written notes, writing minutes, preparing an agenda for subsequent meetings.

In fact, the course designer or teacher may use this set-up for any number of tasks based on different phases of the situation. The situation could be further extended. For instance, as the simulation is based on a real incident reported by a professional informant, it might be possible to ask the students to send questionnaires to (or even telephone interview) the US-based cheese manufacturers about the current use of the production line. Learners could then write up a report on their findings.

The lower levels (1–3)

The levels of signs, utterances and speech acts (levels 1–3) are not detailed in the profile, as they are left to the teacher's diagnostic competence with regard to the learner group. Each teacher will gauge the level of students and can teach points of grammar or vocabulary as they arise in the context of the professional language and communication situations.

3.4 **On learner needs and the CEF Professional Profile**

Adult learners on any language course tend to have high expectations of the outcomes, and this is equally true in professional contexts regardless of whether the learners are in-service or pre-service professionals. Experienced teachers and course designers know that two important elements of a successful course are creating a good working atmosphere in the classroom and motivating the learners to use the foreign language freely, both inside and outside the language classroom. This may be especially challenging where learners share the same first language.

There are a number of information sources that a teacher may use for putting together an ESP course. Depending on the context, the following sources may be applicable:

- Institutional curricula (frequently expressed in short, summarising statements that give only generic information such as relevant communication situations in the field)
- Knowledge from prior teachers having taught similar target groups
- Earlier needs analysis results
- A CEF Professional Profile.

Some CEF Professional Profiles have been published online (http://www.proflang.org). Many teachers do not receive information on the course participants before a course, and in these cases the established information on the field must take precedence over group-specific considerations.

With the available information at hand, the teacher still receives a unique group of participants. Where students are organised in homogeneous groups according to profession (e.g. design engineers), position (e.g. accounting), department (e.g. R&D) or language level (Huhta 2010: 191), the planning of classroom activities presents the teacher with less of a challenge, as prior knowledge of target settings means that activities can be tailored to suit the specific needs of each group. However, when the group is a diverse mix of students from different disciplines, with different language levels or educational backgrounds, the challenge to the teacher is far greater. Many universities cannot afford to differentiate students by field and may sometimes place students from diverse faculties on the same language courses. This becomes a major challenge for the ESP teacher. But the consolation of our contextual professional approach is that workplace communication situations are still under the same categories of communication situations mentioned in Table 3.1, and by including workplace communication situations in the course the teacher can still make the course into a field-specific experience.

Adult learners, whether in-service or pre-service professionals, have distinctive learner biographies. Learners' previous experience, their beliefs about language and how it is learned, and their perceptions of their own aptitude for learning languages are important considerations for the teacher or course designer, especially if one of the intended aims is to enable the learners to use the foreign language with more confidence. Innovative use of the foreign language is more easily encouraged in a 'safe' classroom environment. However, if the learners have previously learned the foreign language in a climate where strict accuracy has been prioritised and where errors should be avoided at all costs, then they might speak or write only if they are positive that what they are producing is linguistically flawless. As we have shown in the profile for mechanical engineers, effective workplace communication requires the development of appropriate discourse skills in different kinds of communication situations. It is therefore important to make learners become active participants and partners in their own learning – and to encourage them to communicate without fear of embarrassing themselves in front of the class. These two elements can be dealt with through the appropriate selection of programme content and by adopting a liberal stance on accuracy. In effect, the aim is for learners to focus on the content to such an extent that their engagement with meaning overcomes their concern about making mistakes.

3.5 Selecting content from the profile

Since the overall aim of the course is to prepare learners for actual workplace communication, activity design should aim to mirror real-life practice as closely as possible. This can be achieved if the objectives are related to the content of the professional domain (van Lier 1996) and if the situation is modelled on one which is actually (or possibly) occurring in the lives of the professional. Part D (*The most frequent routine situations*), Part E (*The most demanding situations*) and Part F (*Snapshot*) of a CEF Professional Profile provide the course designer with the information needed to create realistic workplace-based activities. The designer then needs to identify participant roles and their objectives for the communication situation. From this, he or she can predict the extent to which the learners in the group will need language support in coping with the linguistic challenges of the text- or discourse-type(s) required by the situation (e.g. email, telephone, etc.).

Whatever professional domain the profile targets, the key to successful course design is to be flexible enough to accommodate the views of the learner group. Adult learners are more likely to be committed to a language course if they have been consulted by the course designer or teacher and have then actively participated in the selection of content. Prior to or at the very beginning of the course, learners can be presented with the list of communication situations and the list of text- and discourse-types (found in Part C of the profile) and be asked to prioritise the areas they feel are most important for them. The use of this information from the profile should further motivate learners. In-service professionals should be able to describe from their own experiences the content of communication events directly relevant to their needs.

The most demanding situations (Part E) form a part of the profile that can be used for more complex simulations comprising more than one communication situation. Complexity should be thought about not just in terms of the level of proficiency in the foreign language but also in terms of the situation itself, including the social action elements of unexpectedness and interdisciplinary interaction. In Situation 2 of the Mechanical Engineer's profile (pp. 71-2), for example, we saw an instance of the element of unexpectedness with an engineer having to negotiate with a hygienist from the US Ministry of Agriculture as opposed to a fellow engineer. This situation involves dealing with a public official from another country and having to cope with a discussion on an unfamiliar topic (hygiene in food processing) with its own repertoire of specialist English terms.

A number of other factors also contribute to the complexity of a situation. Firstly, the duration or extent of an interaction, a lengthy meeting or negotiation, for instance, can make it difficult to concentrate, resulting in a stressful experience (Huhta 1999: 108). Secondly, demanding communication situations seldom involve just two participants but tend to be group-to-group or one-to-group encounters (Huhta 1999: 114). Complexity may also be a result of interdiscursive communication if participants follow different work community practices, and this is even more likely to be the case where a number of the participants come from one or more different national or cultural backgrounds.

In other words, there may be a number of complex and overlapping discourses (Gee 1996) and identities (Norton 2000) based on membership of different workplace, national, cultural and other communities. This social action perspective causes unpredictability in the interactions of crucial sites. This aspect of complexity needs to be represented in the activities encountered on a professional communication course, through the inclusion of group-to-group activities as well as pair work. Presentation activities in many classrooms tend to focus on the role of the speaker, but it is essential that listeners are given an active role in the listening. For instance, listeners may be given different role cards before hearing the presentation. By following the role cards, listeners will have a specific but different motivation for listening to their fellow learner's presentation. Feedback will focus as much on the different perspectives and responses of the listeners as on the performance of the speaker. Such an approach reflects an authentic workplace experience by working opportunities for unpredictable events into classroom activities. Thirdly, demanding situations call on all four skills together (that is, speaking, listening, writing and reading). A meeting consists not only of spoken interaction but also of the production of written documentation in the form of agendas, preparatory reports and the writing of memos or minutes. Presentations involve the preparation of visuals and written handouts. Professional communication rarely separates out the four skills as traditional coursebook exercises may. Learning activities should therefore incorporate multiple skills and aims in order to be faithful to the procedures of the professional discourse community. The *challenge factors* of Part E of the profile are those that the interviewees have mentioned as the most important ones in their experience of this particular situation. It is clear that other challenge factors also exist, but the mentioned factors reflect upon the interviewees' experience of the demanding situation and its challenges.

The CEF Professional Profile provides the course designer or teacher with essential information about the target profession and communication within that field. However, the design of learner activities for the ESP course will additionally require a knowledge of more generic aspects of language and communication. Some of these aspects were discussed in Sections 2.2 to 2.5 of Chapter 2.

In the next chapter, we will explain in more detail how the CEF Professional Profiles can be used in the design of courses, again using the sample profile in Section 3.2.

4 From profiles to course activities: mechanical engineers

Chapter overview

Creating motivation for language learning is a key point for engineering students – as it is for all learners. The motivation of engineering students seldom arises from a keen interest in linguistics or the English language but rather from the need to work out what is appealing about the English language and the urge to communicate interesting content to another person. Packaging the language work into professionally relevant learning projects is a major challenge for a language teacher who may not be equally familiar with organisational communication practice in the field. For this reason this chapter will describe not only the suggested language work but also the professional challenges of the suggested activity as well as its communication challenges for the (future) engineer.

From the teacher's point of view, we will be demonstrating a practical application of Professional Profiles to course design and the development of practical classroom activities, using the example of mechanical engineers from the previous chapter (see Section 3.2 on pp. 64ff.), built on foreign language needs analysis. The majority of the activities are suitable only for learners who are at least low intermediate (B1+), though several activities are suitable only for stronger learners (B2–C1).

This chapter will help you:

- utilise the needs analysis results and contextual knowledge of CEF Professional Profiles
- construct learning activities and simulations for the target profession and the relevant professional communities involved
- familiarise learners with the target discourse community practice
- motivate and empower learners to build their professional identity and the language skills needed.

The rich data of the profile helps practitioners to accommodate the communication needs of the workplace more efficiently. We will start by showing how the suggested activities and their description link with the language and communication theory described in Chapter 2 (4.1). This is followed by reporting how the profile information is used to construct the activities (4.2). The learning activities in Section 4.3 are sequenced into six groups, focusing on some of the essential challenges of engineering communication. We start with learner analysis, keeping the focus of attention on the learner. Then we move on to activities that increase the learners' knowledge of their professional field and establish and develop their professional communication identity. We also take some activities that focus on an engineer's capability to differentiate and use suitable genres for appropriate purposes. Many communication events in engineering are normal, routine exchanges, and some of these are built in to activities as more specialised tasks. Later, more comprehensive simulations integrating several different communicative events are illustrated with examples found in the Mechanical Engineer's profile. Finally, this chapter concludes with suggestions for learner assessment and evaluation.

Links between activities and language and communication theory

Although the profile has been developed collaboratively with practitioners, the profile and its parts happily match with sociolinguistic theories of discourse and discourse communities.

The profile-based contextual and discursive information about the practices of workplace communities and communicators in the target setting is supported by sociolinguistic and ethnographic research. We categorised the four necessary elements for communication description in Chapter 2 as *global, institutional and organisational knowledge*, the competence-based *participant knowledge*, *social action knowledge*, and the linguistically familiar *textual knowledge*.

The texts to be deployed are included in the profile (Part C), familiar ground for linguists. The knowledge of typical professions and typical job descriptions (Part B) is necessary for interpreting participant knowledge in language training, so that the participant can imagine himself or herself communicating for specific purposes in specific situations. The CEF Professional Profile also includes global, social and institutional knowledge by describing the target field (Part A), typical employer organisations (Part B), locations, where the participant's communications occur and institutions (Part C) involved in the communication. This helps to envision the social context of a professional. The social action perspective is the most challenging of the four perspectives, and in their current state of development, profiles can only partially describe their complexity. The lists of communication situations (Part C) are brief and provide little information on social action, while the profile information of institution and participants (C) give little help about the contextual setting. However, the descriptions of frequent (Part D) and demanding (Part E) situations and snapshots (Part F) are much richer on the three aspects of social action, institutional and participant knowledge. The descriptions in profiles vary, and their quality depends on the willingness of interviewees to report detail and the ability of the recordkeeper to communicate the richness of factors. A lot of significant communication elements such as discourse community and cultural knowledge stay, unfortunately, unrecorded. The same applies to non-verbal and visual communication. However, professional profiles are a practical tool for bringing the ESP teacher closer to authentic workplace communication than before.

In the illustrative examples that follow, we make frequent use of simulation, since we believe that well-designed simulations are motivating, engaging and necessarily bring in many of the beyond-text features. A possible disadvantage of simulations is that if they do not fully engage the learner, they can become mere exercises, with no real investment in the outcome of the simulated event. It is important, therefore, to make simulations as near to real-life situations, as analysed through the needs analysis, as possible, and to exploit as much personal motivation (e.g. by using elements of the learners' own experience) as is achievable.

Learning activities for the classroom

This section now suggests activities based on the profile that make an effort to comply with the theoretical considerations of good professional communication practice, as well as the needs of the field. There are six points that the ESP teacher could consider when designing a language course that meets the needs of the field and the professional working in the field. These six categories of communication practice could be expressed in six guidelines for designing a relevant professional communication course. The six categories are shown in Figure 4.1.

As indicated in Figure 4.1, we first wish to involve the learner as an equal partner in learning, and the activities give the participant true agency and autonomy in his or her own learning. To this end we suggest activities for identifying participant language needs (4.1). This is particularly important for adult learners, not only to address generically important issues but to focus on their personal communication needs. Secondly, it is important to start fostering a professional communication identity (4.2) for the discourse communities in the field; therefore our second category suggests activities to this end. The career of pre-service learners in the new field may yet be covered in a haze of guesses and misconceptions. This is why we are suggesting activities that aim to familiarise the participant with the field, its organisations and work done in the field. These activities focus on professional field knowledge (4.3). Federations of engineers in different countries pose ethical standards and community practice to engineers. Fourthly, engineers are increasingly involved in communication using increasing varieties of genres. This is why we have suggestions for activities that help engineers differentiate between different genres and become confident about when to use one and not the other, and when combinations of genres are applicable. This fourth category therefore focuses on differentiation of professional genres (4.4). The fifth kind of activity concerns one-to-one routine activities (4.5) that the profile of mechanical engineering includes. This, as we found in the needs analysis work, is essential as a professional likes to feel confident in everyday frequent activities, and even though these routines may not be difficult, rich practice around routines contributed greatly to the confidence of both experienced and inexperienced learners. Finally, we propose a set of complex simulations (4.6), which take up several sessions of class time and help learners reflect upon the complexity of workplace com-

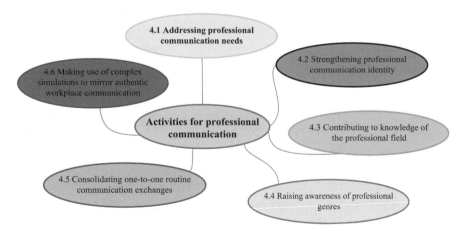

Figure 4.1: Activities for professional communication

munication. These, from experience, are often the activities that, after the course, participants mention as having been the most beneficial aspect of their learning.

The activities or simulations in this chapter have been designed for the mechanical engineers using the profile information (see Chapter 3, pp. 64ff.). It is worth mentioning that since the professional context is essential, other professionals collaborating in these contexts, such as business, health or legal experts, will also find the activities equally relevant for their communication needs (see Table 4.1). For those designing ESP courses for other professions and vocations, the activities in this section provide models which can be reproduced within contexts relevant to other professions. Appendix C provides CEF Professional Profiles for clerical workers in export sales, nurses, lawyers and IT professionals. Where the needs of the target group are significantly different from the information in the profiles in this book, Chapter 5 gives advice on creating a completely new profile.

Table 4.1: Activities based on the CEF Professional Profile in mechanical engineering

Activity	Derived from the CEF Professional Profile (mechanical engineering)					
Focus on	Part A Target profession	Part C Context information	Part D The most frequent situations	Part E The most demanding situations	Part F Snapshot
4.1 Addressing participant communication needs		X	X	X	
4.2 Strengthening professional communication identity	X				X
4.3 Contributing to knowledge of the professional field	X	X	X	X	X
4.4 Raising awareness of professional genres		X			
4.5 Consolidating one-to-one routine communication exchanges			X		
4.6 Making use of complex simulations to mirror authentic workplace communication		X		X	

4.1 **Addressing participant communication needs**

Based on existing institutional curricula, established practice and possibly profiles made for the field, the teacher may be quite sure at the start of the course about what to include. For motivation and agency reasons, however, it is vital to allow course participants to be co-designers of their course – and their own learning. The first activity is designed to this end.

Activity 4.1.1 Participant communication needs

Learning activity description	Participant communication needs
Professional challenge	This activity helps (future) professionals become aware of their roles as significant contributors to the organisation as experts, active team members, influential participants in customer interface, promoters of company strategy as experts, through effective communication in key communicative events in English. The teacher should ensure the learner is aware of the company's communication network with external stakeholders (with suppliers, customers, collaborators) and internal communication partners (organisational units and their representatives) to instigate thinking about the role of communication.
Communication challenge (Global, institutional and organisational knowledge; participant knowledge; social action knowledge)	This activity builds awareness of effective personal contribution in the company's communication environment. The listing of language/communication situations (from Chapter 2, Section 2.3) can be used to draw a general picture of research-based communication needs of engineers, amongst whom the participants can see themselves. Part C of the profile shows some work contexts and organisations with which the learner will be working. Learners are encouraged to tell stories of when and where they were faced with a particular work situation, and what happened (*social action point*).
Language aims (textual knowledge)	• Learning key terms for engineers' communication situations • Learning to listen to others' views and to comment on them
Procedure	In short, the activity consists of a discussion on communication needs followed by needs analysis completion at home or in class. Warning: the needs analysis questionnaire should be given out after the discussion or learners may start filling it in rather than taking part in the discussion. The teacher starts by asking questions such as the following: • How many of you will be using English in your daily work? Weekly? Monthly? • What situations will engineers need English in? • How many of you have experienced a work meeting? Describe what happened. Who talked the most? How were decisions taken? The teacher can use the board to brainstorm communication needs under 'situations' (manuals, websites, meetings, email, telephoning), 'partners' (suppliers, buyers, distributors), 'channels' (face-to-face, web tools, email) and create a mind map.

Learners are encouraged to tell stories of events, which will give the teacher ideas for workplace simulations as well as different company websites they can visit to find out more information. The teacher will add learners' information to the mind map. A copy (e.g. a photo) of the final mind map is taken to be used on the course website.

Teacher input	The teacher • introduces the subject (see the professional challenge and communication challenge content above) • leads the discussion and draws a mind map (or linear list) • gathers the information provided by learners on the needs analysis sheets in one file for course design purposes.
Learner output	Story sharing, discussion participation and sheet-filling for course design purposes.
Learning outcomes	Learners • get to know each other by hearing each other's communication experiences • gain a holistic understanding of the business context and variety of communications • identify personal challenges within communication • increase their interest in mastering those items identified • feel empowered by being able to influence the selection of learning items.
Evaluation	Needs analysis sheets are used by the teacher for deciding on the items to be included.
Language level required	B1 or above
Preparation and materials	Copies of the *Needs analysis questionnaire* below for everyone; possibly also the list of language/communication situations from Chapter 2 (Section 2.3) and/or a copy of Part C of the profile from Chapter 3 (Section 3.2)
Duration	Introduction: 15 minutes Discussion in class: 30–40 minutes
Remarks	A common teacher failure is to include too many elements in the course to be learned. It is better to focus on only a few communication situations and practise them in detail, with plentiful feedback (both by peers and teacher) and comments. Learners should then be able to apply the principles they have learned in these situations to others.
Suggestions for follow-up work	While listening to the discussion the teacher will be able to identify silent members, talkative members and those who express their views with one or two words. Therefore, it may be useful to follow up by introducing some ideas on how to

- interrupt a speaker
- express views
- ask rhetorical questions
- ask for more detailed information
- comment on what others have said and make additional points.

The distribution of the following type of needs analysis questionnaire will already be familiar to experienced ESP teachers. However, the information in the profile gives the teacher a benchmark against which the information collected from the learners can be assessed. For example, if the learner group consists of pre-service professionals, it may be interesting to compare which areas they expect to be confident in against what the profile shows professionals already working in the industry regard as the most demanding situations (Part E). And if (as often happens in our experience) the results of the questionnaire show that the majority of the learner group want further development of their spoken English, then the profile again provides guidance for the most relevant contexts of spoken interaction. These contexts will be exemplified in simulation activities on the course.

NEEDS ANALYSIS QUESTIONNAIRE

A   Personal information

Name: .... Course: ....
First language: .... Student ID: .... Email: ....

B   Knowledge of foreign languages

Complete the table below with information about the foreign languages you know.

Foreign language	Can you speak this language? (*Please write Y (Yes) or N (No)*)	How long have you been learning this language?	What is your level in this language? (*Please use the language level scale in the box below*)
English			
Language 2			
Language 3			

Language level scale

Pre-intermediate (A2): I know some vocabulary and I can understand some words and phrases in conversation and lectures. I do not use this language much, because it takes time.

Intermediate (B1): I understand some texts on familiar topics and parts of clear conversations and lectures; I can deal with many ordinary daily situations with help.

Upper intermediate (B2): I understand texts, conversations and lectures; given time I can manage daily situations without help, and can be an active participant in interaction for limited periods of time.

Advanced (C1): I understand general and professional texts; I understand native speakers' normal conversation and lectures; I can express my views well in conversation and have no difficulty being active.

Proficient (C2): I understand complex professional writing; I understand native speakers' fast speech, including regular accents and a variety of lectures. I take initiative in conversation and can express my ideas fluently in professional conversation.

C　Knowledge of English

What are some of your strengths and weaknesses in this language? Look at the information below and then tick (✓) the option that you believe is true for you.

	I am strong in this area	I am OK but need work in this area	I need to improve in this area
Engineering terminology			
Speaking			
Understanding spoken English			
Understanding texts			
Writing (reports, etc.)			
Grammar and accuracy when speaking or writing			
Other:			

D　English for your career in engineering

1　Look at the list of **communication situations** for mechanical engineers. How confident do you feel about communicating in English in each of these situations? Complete the table by putting a tick (✓) in the column that is true for you.

Communication situation	I believe that ...		
	I will need a lot of practice in this situation.	I can manage quite well in this situation but some practice would be useful.	I am confident in this type of situation and do not need further practice in it.
Giving a presentation about your company to customers or clients			
Giving a product presentation to customers or clients			
Describing processes / how something works (or will work)			
Participating or conducting meetings and negotiations with customers or clients			

Having a discussion with colleagues about different aspects of engineering (e.g. different fields, products, corporate operations)			
Telephoning (making enquiries, reporting fault analysis, giving feedback, making appointments, etc.)			
Socialising in business situations: small talk at trade fairs, before the beginning of meetings/interviews/negotiations			
Making written enquiries			
Producing quotations			
Making a written claim			
Reading and understanding articles, websites, marketing texts, etc. for professional purposes			
Writing reports and memos			
Writing service instructions			
Completing a job application form and/or writing a CV			
Other, which...			

2 Are there any other situations in which you believe you will need English in your future career? Make notes in the space below.

3 Which THREE areas would you like to improve most urgently? Make a note of them below.

1 ....

2 ....

3 ....

E Your expectations for the course

1 What are your personal expectations for the course? Make notes in the space below.

....
....
....
....

2 Planning your time for the course is very important. Realistically, how much time do you have to do study outside of the classroom? Tick (✓) the box which is true for you.

☐ I will only be able to study in class   ☐ 2–4 hours per week
☐ 0–2 hours per week   ☐ >4 hours per week

Thank you for your time.

Activity 4.1.2 Professional communication portfolio

A course built on the profile can easily also become a written performance, as learners should ideally work during the whole course in the same team of four. This being so, all the oral and written work could be done in the same team. Some tasks are individual, for example job applications, but all the work would be organised into the same portfolio. There are good reasons for doing this: learners learn about collaboration and teamwork. The quality of papers improves. Learners learn to sequence work into a table of contents according to some logical order (e.g. chronological, theme-based, genre-based, etc.). Moreover, they learn more about peer work evaluation and the importance of promptness at work. The teacher also gets all of the learners' productions in one go. Since learners do some work in the team and some individually, the checking work is also minimised.

Learning activity description	Written communication portfolio
Professional challenge	Engineers will be working on projects as project managers and team members. The portfolio team approach typically resembles one single project of learning communication. The project needs a project manager and a well-functioning team. The goal of the team – to improve teamwork skills as well as written communication – must be clarified at the start of the course. It is wise to discuss the characteristics of effective communication and constructive team member roles. It is also wise to provide a summary sheet of what needs to go into the portfolio. This can only be done AFTER needs analysis (Activity 4.1.1) has been conducted and the teacher knows which activities the participants need most for their portfolio.
Communication challenge (Global, institutional and organisational knowledge; participant knowledge; social action knowledge)	Many learners in their formal studies will need to produce a major paper or production, and they will need to learn how such papers are typically organised. As each portfolio must have a cover page and a table of contents, the team needs to spend time thinking about the most appropriate organisational principles for their work: chronological, genre-based, team member-based, teacher-provided logic. This activity increases the understanding of logical sequencing. Creating the portfolio in the same team throughout the course has proven to be a good idea: if someone is absent, the rest will take over, and there is always someone to take care of portfolio teamwork.
Language aims (textual knowledge)	• Applying knowledge gained in all the activities to written, professional documents • Producing written papers in an appropriate style • Producing some documents that will be usable later on (CV, abstract)

Procedure	• After needs analysis, the teacher and the group collaborate to decide on portfolio contents. • In collaboration the class agrees on a portfolio delivery date. • The class will need time in their teams to get organised and agree on management and responsibilities. • In connection with each activity, the teacher reminds teams about what they need to complete for their portfolios: teams themselves must be responsible for staying on schedule.
Teacher input	In connection with each activity the teacher should • remind learners about what needs to be put into the portfolio • provide learners with class time for working in teams.
Learner output	• A performance portfolio • Teamwork skills tested over a longer period • Plenty of written practice • Focus on discourse issues and style • 'Real' tasks
Learning outcomes	The learner • learns to adopt a systematic way of thinking of language and communication as a project • is able to progress over time when he or she is clear about what is expected of different documents • builds confidence in being able to operate as a contributing member in a group • learns to evaluate good, average and less good documents in English • takes pride in exceeding the learner's own expectations • gets satisfaction from good results.
Evaluation	Peer evaluation can be used for the portfolios. One week after the portfolio delivery date, the portfolios can be given to a different team: they check which elements are included and which are missing (team A evaluates B, C evaluates D, etc.). They look at the documents and try to find excellent, good and average examples, and explain why. The class selects some of the best documents (starting with tables of contents) for others to look at. At the end the teacher evaluates the portfolios, but the students' pre-evaluation sits as the first page of the portfolio. Team members give each other a grade, one for portfolio work, another for the work in oral reporting tasks. The emphasis in evaluation is on three equally important points: 1. Contents 2. Discourse 3. Language

The *Feedback* sheet below can be issued at the end of the course and provides another overall perspective on the activity. Students give their feedback on the whole course after completion of the written communication portfolio.

Note: The teacher should give a lot of feedback to all learners, but especially to those making progress from a lower level. They need it most.

Language level required	B1–C2
Preparation	A slide (overhead transparency) of the *Portfolio summary* sheet; a copy of the *Assessment criteria* sheet for grading; a copy of the *Feedback* sheet
Duration	Briefing students at the start of the course: one hour Reminders: a few minutes now and then Peer evaluation at the end: 90 minutes

---

PORTFOLIO SUMMARY

Team name:
Team members:

Teacher:

Course title:
Course dates: *From (DD/MM/YY) .... to (DD/MM/YY) ....*

Assignment:		To be completed by:		
Number	*Description*	*each member*	*the group*	*date*
Document 1	Engineering studies: report on the degree programme, studies conducted so far and courses remaining to be completed (Activity 4.3.1 Engineering studies)		✓	
Document 2	Application letter and standard CV or a tailored CV (Activity 4.3.3 Job interviews)	✓		
Document 3	A two-page summary of industries, companies and operations (Activity 4.3.2 Industrial fields, companies and operations)		✓	
Document 4	Illustration of a process supplemented with a descriptive text (Activity 4.6.3 Interaction about a process)	✓		

Document 5	Two business letters (Activity 4.5.1 Responding to a call from the machining workshop or 4.5.2 Telephone and email (related to one-to-one routine situations))		✓	
Document 6	Minutes of meeting (for formal meetings) or a negotiations memo (Activity 4.6.1 Meetings and negotiations in business)		✓	
Document 7	By team choice	✓		

ASSESSMENT CRITERIA

ORAL	WRITTEN
1. **Full understanding** (and courage to ask if not)	1. **Facts** are **correct**
2. **Prompt reactions and courage to speak & active role** (e.g. you say something, even if you don't know the exact answer; you take the initiative; you ask others)	2. **Appropriate discourse** (e.g. you use professional language/format for letters, memos, transparencies, summaries and email; you differentiate between formal and informal style)
3. **Fluency** (your interaction in a group flows as a result of the constructive mindset of participants – comments, questions and reactions are frequent; the outcome is reached; you are not afraid of imperfections)	3. **Good language** (you use professional terms; you use spell-checkers to polish up errors; you avoid mistakes that confuse meaning; your language is clear enough to understand)
4. **Professional discourse** (e.g. normal practices of business/engineering, appropriate language for a letter/ presentation/meeting, etc.)	4. **Completeness/Authenticity** (your documents/productions must be complete and authentic, so they could be used for work as well as in studies; not half-complete and not invented products or texts)
5. **Accuracy** (clear enough language including pronunciation and grammar)	5. **Tidy professional products** (your layout and format should be suitable for the document; you give out no handwritten slips)

FEEDBACK

1. General evaluation

		5	4	3	2	1	
My impression of the course in general	very good						weak
Usefulness for my future career	very important						not really
Supportive atmosphere	very much						not at all
Work load	too much						too little
Contents of the course	well-selected subjects						not well-selected
Teacher	very skilful						weak
Does my grade match my skills?	very well						not so well
Does my grade match my personal input?	very well						not so well
Comments:							

2. Use of the CEF Professional Profile for Mechanical Engineering

		5	4	3	2	1	
We used the profile	too much						not enough
The profile helped me to know what mechanical engineers need English for	very well						not so well
The activity descriptions were helpful	very much so						not really
The practised simulations were easy to follow	very						not very easy
Comments:							
How else would you have used the profile?							

4.2 **Strengthening professional communication identity**

Pre-service learners face three challenges at the start of their career: (i) to come to grips with the engineering field which involves maths and physics and professional studies, which is in itself a tall order for a secondary school graduate; (ii) to master the broader world surrounding engineering, which takes the learner to global competitive business environments and brings them into contact with national and EU regulations, which is also challenging and which is not always explicitly dealt with in an engineering degree programme despite its importance; and (iii) to conduct some or all of this in a multilingual and multicultural environment, becoming an effective communicator in very diverse situations. We now focus on the third of these challenges: strengthening the engineer's identity as a capable communicator in a multilingual setting.

Activity 4.2.1 Becoming an effective communicator

Learning activity description	Becoming an effective communicator
Professional challenge	Groups of professionals are often identified with stereotypical communication expectations, whether they be engineers, medical doctors, lawyers, therapists or marketing consultants. In the education of professionals, the focus tends to be on how to communicate within the profession rather than across professions. Increasingly, however, engineers communicate in projects linking dispersed multicultural teams with multidisciplinary expertise around the globe. Outsourcing and offshoring arrangements in companies strengthen this development and result in more work being done collaboratively. This is why international companies have a major challenge in creating working cultures that promote and foster knowledge-sharing. That is where engineers as well as other professionals need to be able to communicate effectively in multi-user, multi-contributor platforms. Technical tools exist, but it has been identified in research that cross-border, cross-company and cross-disciplinary collaboration can fail at the human level, especially in situations of mergers and acquisitions, where hard feelings may have been caused in the process. Under such circumstances the willingness to collaborate and learn depends both on the individual participant and on team dynamics and management. Effective communicators can facilitate the processes of collaboration.

Communication challenge (Global, institutional and organisational knowledge; participant knowledge; social action knowledge)

The communication challenges of the above environments relate to a number of issues. Firstly, the individual may be involved in *organisational, interpersonal and group communication*. Different modes of communication are expected depending on the category of communication. More awareness is needed of the expectations of these different modes (e.g. written or oral communication). Secondly, communication is painfully susceptible to various kinds of *interferences and barriers* between people, ages, languages, cultures and technologies. Becoming aware of some of the interferences may increase the effectiveness of communication. Thirdly, an individual can develop his or her capacity as an effective communicator by becoming aware of active *contributor roles* as well as passive, less beneficial roles in teams. Positive roles include such tasks as record-keeping, chairing or facilitation. Fourthly, effective communicators follow strategies known by the acronym CLASS:

1. Collaborate on equal terms across professions (C)
2. Listen in five ways (L)
3. Ask questions to understand (A)
4. Seek to change (S)
5. Summarise and check (S)

Learners are given the texts relating to these issues for reporting in class.

Language aims (textual knowledge)

This activity focuses on the content of effective communication rather than language, though the learner may in addition learn vocabulary on business stakeholders, language barriers, group contributor roles, active listening techniques, etc.

Procedure

- The teacher introduces the importance of effective communication, using the professional challenge and communication challenge content above.
- The class should be divided into six teams of four: A, B, C, D, E and F. Each learner should preferably have a copy of each of the team texts below, relating to aspects of effective communication.
- Teams report as the teacher summarises the contents onto a mind map.

Teacher input

The teacher
- introduces the subject of effective communication
- distributes the texts to students
- leads the discussion while drawing a mind map.

Learner output	• Reading a text • Eliciting key points • Reporting the contents to class
Learning outcomes	The learner • gains an understanding of what the engineer can do in order to become a more effective communicator • learns to recognise and improve listening and questioning techniques • gains an enhanced awareness of what is involved in effective communication.
Evaluation	None
Language level required	B1–C2
Preparation and materials	A copy of each of the team texts below for each student. (Learners will learn from the text as well as from listening to presentations from their colleagues.)
Duration	90 minutes

Team A. Act by type of communication

Working in a company or other organisation, the engineer is surrounded by a web of people working towards different goals. In *organisational communication* the professional works with internal as well as external stakeholders. Internal stakeholders may include other members of the team or department, such as engineers, chemists, physicists, accountants or IT specialists, in a word, representatives of other professions. Internal communication can occur upward or downward in the organisation. *Downward communication* concerns information exchange from managers to subordinates, *upward communication* concerns information from positions lower down in the organisation to those above. The communication can also flow *laterally*, between departments and individuals on the same organisational level. Mediated information may be viewed as *formal* when messages are sent along the official lines of authority and responsibility; in other cases we speak of *informal communication*. There is a constant flow of communication in companies between employees through *informal paths* in the hallways, coffee rooms and meeting areas, including virtual spaces. Informal talks at a lunch table may sometimes be the fastest communication path for some useful information.

   External communication is conducted by the company with the outside world, both in and out of the company environment. As a *service provider* or *product manufacturer*, a firm acquires materials from companies, thus communicating with *suppliers* in the field. To communicate their position to *suppliers*, *present clients* and *potential buyers*, companies produce literature for different purposes, from annual reports to *shareholders* to brochures, videos, DVDs, sales literature, and internet pages to clients and suppliers. Shareholders are a key interest group for keeping an eye on the company prospects quarter after quarter year. Since more and more work is now outsourced to *subcontractors* or *partners* in other low-cost countries, collaboration across locations is increasing. Technical tools such as collaboration software and social media tools are also being used for this external communication purpose.

The *media* need good quality information to be persuaded to include items about the company in news or articles. For instance, when new products are launched on the market, a media conference must be arranged to inform the media of the occasion. A *press release* sent as an invitation to the media conference is part of external communication to the public. External communication also includes company communication at trade fairs, conferences, celebrations, seminars, symposia and PR events.

Besides organisational communication the engineer is involved in a number of *interpersonal communications* with his or her colleagues within the unit, with other departments, with clients and partners. Some of this communication takes place in *one-to-one communication* and some in *group communication*. Group communication has been identified as the most challenging type of communication for a professional, as a number of issues make it more difficult. These may include the complexity of the situation, the speaker's shortcomings in expertise or experience, demanding attitudes of the counterpart, the increased unpredictability with multiple participants, cultural differences, stress and the length of time needed for the achievement of satisfactory outcomes (Huhta 1999: 107).

A lot of both internal and external communication may take place through web platforms, social media software, shareware and email. Still, face-to-face communication remains an important human encounter. And even with distances this form of communication can play a major role as sound and picture quality in video and teleconferencing media have radically improved and made such online communication more closely resemble physically proximate interpersonal encounters.

For formal public announcements it is important for the company to involve the best possible experts to create and edit the communications: substance experts, media experts, technical writers and communication managers. Engineering professionals need to involve communication experts in composing and editing formal messages targeting the public and external stakeholders. This is also true of internet communication when it is openly accessible to the public. With internal and interpersonal messages, finely crafted communication is less important.

Team B. Recognise barriers to understanding

If all communication conveyed exactly what was intended by the sender of a message, we would be living in an ideal world, released from misconceptions. Communication, however, is based on *language*, which is a matter of negotiation and interpretation of the meaning of words, concepts and behaviour linked to expressing content. These agreements are implicit, not written anywhere (except for their approximations in dictionaries), and thus understandings of their meanings vary from language to language, culture to culture, and human to human. Some dictionaries portray *denotations*, main meanings of words, but their *connotations,* side meanings remain concealed. Similarly, when words are combined into compounds or phrases, or when they are used in context, their meanings may sometimes be quite different from those found in dictionaries.

A number of interferences cause distortions of the intended message at *the sender end.* Not only may the sender have formulated the message in confusing *language.* The speaker may have prepared the talk to another engineer with a mass of *technical jargon* and details. The audience may, however, be different: an engineer as well as other professionals may need to get through to a mix of technical as well as management and central administration people. *Education, age, cultural background, experience* and *status* all need to be taken into account when planning a message. The message may simply be *wrongly packaged* for this audience. The speaker's *accent or intonation* may be off-putting. A message may be *poorly printed* or presented *in handwriting* that is difficult to read. An expected email is sent by text message to a phone which the user is currently not using. The choice of the right *information channel* is also significant. As for other channels of information, emails may be dangerous. A hasty, angry email is irrevocable. Therefore experts propose that uncomfortable news should first be introduced face to face or by telephone and only later written as messages.

Even if everything goes right at the sender end, *the recipient end* may be failing. The listener may simply not be listening; he or she may be *preoccupied* with other matters for the time being. Sometimes people may just be *uncomfortable* and not listen because they are tired, hungry or are not feeling so well, and thus a well-planned message may not sink in as intended. Some confusion may be caused by *emotions*: the recipient may have distinct attitudes towards the listener which hinder the message from getting through. These feelings may be caused by the presenter's *age, culture, clothing* or similar, and the message gets contaminated. The listener may come to feel that the *motives of the sender* are suspect, and hence either fails to listen or interprets the message in a different way to that intended.

The environment where communication takes place may be *noisy* or uncomfortably located, and there may be *interruptions* by colleagues or telephone calls. The *distance* between speakers may be off-putting, or *microphones* and *loudspeakers* may be inadequately placed. There are also very subtle distractions, which often relate to cultural or interpersonal differences. Communicators may have different *communication styles*: one, for instance, may prefer a *direct approach*, going straight to the point; another may proceed indirectly, firstly providing the reasons behind the suggested solution. Many cultures wish to *establish trust* first by *socialising* in informal groups before proceeding to discussions on significant issues.

Who is to blame if communication is not successful and the message does not get conveyed in the intended manner? Experts say that the sender is in charge.

To avoid barriers to understanding, the sender can do all in his or her power to plan the message specifically for the target audience in order to make it fully understandable. The sender is in charge of organising an environment where everyone can hear well and is placed comfortably, of creating an atmosphere where people trust each other and are willing to hear what is being said.

Team C. Adopt a constructive role in group communication

Groups are formed to reach goals using shared expertise. Group members can complement each other's strengths and counter each other's weaknesses in order to bring forth the best of learning and innovation. Whatever its composition, a given group must strike a balance as to status and expertise in important areas. An effective group shares a common goal to which members of the group are committed. The size of the group may vary. The benefit of smaller groups is that members can communicate easily with each other. Larger groups may combine several kinds of expertise, but conversely, they also inhibit communication, since the interaction opportunities become more limited.

Companies use the term *team* for groups formed to fulfil strategically important tasks. Sometimes the terms group and team are used interchangeably. Teams have typically a clear identity and a well-defined goal, including a time frame within which the project needs to be completed. Teams can function for either long- or short-term projects. Work teams are often given authority to act on their own conclusions. The work of successful teams can be characterised by the four Cs: *Commitment, Cooperation, Communication* and *Contribution*. Members are clearly committed to the mission, values and the goals of the team as they have a clear sense of mutual gain through cooperation. Information flows well between the members of the team, and within the whole organisation. All members contribute to the outcome of the work, using their different skills, capacities and fields of expertise.

Let us now think of roles that members in a team may have. They are in no way exclusive: a person may play several roles during a single communication situation, and may also play different roles in different teams

A *leader* takes the directive approach in a meeting by ensuring all members recognise the agreed goals, work towards them and contribute to the outcome of the team. Whatever the status relationships are in the group, leadership is essential for the group to operate successfully. Leadership may be rotated among the members either formally or informally. *Facilitators* listen a lot, comment on points brought forth in the discussion, ask questions, summarise other members' views and suggest compromises to push the work forward. *Harmonisers* keep the tensions low by using humour, suggesting that the team takes a break, offering ways of finding win-win solutions. *Record-keepers* write down notes, plan memos, draft tables or graphs, type changes to prior documents, create slides for the next session. This *secretarial* role is often no longer the task of an external secretary, but a role that every engineer takes in turn. It is important to notice that the role of a record-keeper possesses a lot of power in the group because it involves deciding what information to document and how to document it – and even more importantly, what to exclude from the documentation. Another role that engineers frequently fulfil is that of the *reporter*, where they search, research or prepare information to be presented to the whole group.

Sometimes when the work is hectic, an engineer may end up being an isolated member: he or she is present but fails to participate. Some other members may have a more permanent flaw of constantly criticising and complaining rather than trying to find solutions to problems. This role of a *detractor* is often harmful for the group, because creative ideas may be blocked by the fear of this 'devil's advocate' approach – always looking for reasons why changes cannot be made. Constructive criticism, by contrast, is a welcome spice to good group communication as it is oriented towards solutions rather than finding faults in others' suggestions. Another less constructive role that a group member can take is that of a *digresser*. A digresser deviates from the purpose of the group by finding interesting paths and new directions to move towards during the process, and invests time in secondary activity. A *socialiser* is a harmoniser role taken to the extreme: the member concentrates on pleasant action, enjoyment and fun, forgetting the actual focus of the group. Companies can hardly afford other more negative roles such as those of *airhead*s, who seldom come to the group prepared. But still some *free riders* may be lazy, allowing others to do their work for them. Unfortunately, even some good leaders can, inadvertently, develop into *dominators,* who like to listen to their own voice, propose all new ideas and comment on all the views expressed in a meeting, rather than listen and invite everyone to contribute. A dominator works on a mode of advocacy: pushing his or her own ideas through. If this is the case, the benefits of team-building are jeopardised and valuable expertise lost. A dominator – whether in a leader or some other role – may inhibit creative ideas, discard valuable types of expertise and spoil the atmosphere of mutual trust and co-creation.

As an effective communicator, it is worthwhile considering your professional and personal strengths and weaknesses in relation to group communication and decide strategically when to concentrate on a specific role.

Needs Analysis for Language Course Design © Cambridge University Press 2013 **PHOTOCOPIABLE**

Team D. Collaborate on equal terms

Like all human beings, professionals whether they be mathematicians, nuclear scientists, therapists or engineers, dislike being underestimated. A good starting point, therefore, is to assume that all professionals are experts, and they have a right to ask for clarification whenever they find a gap in your explanation. Moreover, if the person who wants results is responsible, then you as a sender will make sure that your message is clear and persuasive, and will produce results at the end. As a receiver, you will make sure that you listen carefully and provide feedback to the speaker, by nodding, commenting and asking questions. The point is that mutual feedback is essential for understanding. This often involves assertive questions, repetition and redundancy of speech, especially in contexts where non-native speakers of the language are present.

There is a danger in assuming that all professionals are familiar with related fields and technical terms. This is not always the case. It is amazing how different the central concepts of mechanical engineering are from civil engineering, or mechatronics from software engineering, not to mention economics, law or creative arts. Furthermore, a person can become a president of a company without any technical background at all. Therefore, it is important to have respect for the individual, without assuming that he or she is familiar with your concepts. Every new concept needs to be defined before you can say anything about it. This rule of thumb is useful for avoiding the so-called technical jargon: never talk about a technical solution to a mixed audience before you have *defined* it, *described* it and reported its practical use in the environment. Only then do you have a right to *evaluate* its benefits and problems.

Define
Describe
Evaluate

An example:

The FSB cooling system is a system required for the protection of a flash smelting furnace. The system protects the highly thermal loaded parts of the refractory lining as well as other structures and equipment from overheating. The cooling system must be in operation all the time when the flash smelting furnace is in operation or in a holding state. (define)

Smelting Technology has two kinds of cooling systems. The first one is a conventional one, which is called the 'open cooling system' and the second one is a more developed system called the 'closed cooling system'. The open system is used mostly for the plant which has a long experience of smelting. The closed system is used mostly for green field plants. The open cooling system is controlled manually by operators in the field. The closed cooling system is operated automatically and then all measurements are conducted into the Process Control System (PCS). (describe)

Many plants are very satisfied with the system because you can visually control it, and if boiling or overheating occurs in the process, the system forms steam, which is easily detectable. (evaluate)

When speaking to a mixed audience, general information such as the above about the technology is necessary.

Consider also offering a genuine choice to your audience, asking, for example, which of the solutions the listener is interested in. If you have planned a sequence of information about one thing and the listener is interested in something different, this, of course, means that you have to be more flexible in your preparation. Would you use technical terms in a similar way when speaking to another engineer as when you have a mixed audience? No, you would not. With an automation engineer you can freely use all the technical automation engineering terms required, expecting a similar level of familiarity with technical concepts. With the purchasing manager, you would concentrate on the needs he or she has expressed and the necessary technical terms for precisely that purpose. You would also provide this client with the option to be sent technical information which would be delivered to the technical persons using the equipment in his or her organisation.

Team E. Listen and ask

Communication is a two-way street of input and output. Your role as the engineer is a mixture of listening, hearing, commenting on what you hear, speaking and making yourself heard. Our common experience shows us that we have a number of *strategies for listening*.

A good listener gives feedback to the speaker to indicate what he or she has understood. This can take place by commenting, nodding or other physical gestures, by asking questions or summarising. Effective listeners are constant learners because they continuously gain knowledge and skills via others' experience and insights. People place trust in good listeners.

When you are watching TV and someone is trying to talk to you, you may resort to *casual listening*: you may respond with a smile or nod or a comment or two, but your mind is on the TV, that is, elsewhere. Casual listening is typical between people who know each other very well. Stories, experiences and recapitulation of past events may lend themselves to casual listening. The listener may throw in comments or questions, but since people in a casual situation usually know each other well, silences, grumpiness, joking and any free behaviour can also be expected. Casual listening does not show much respect for the speaker's message.

Another strategy of listening used between people who know each other well is so-called *empathetic listening*. While listening, the listener demonstrates understanding of the speaker and sharing of the speaker's feelings. What happens in practice is that the listener comments sympathetically, suggests solutions or courses of action or remedies or tells similar stories from their own experience to show they understand how the speaker feels. In business empathetic listening is important when dealing, for instance, with an unhappy customer. In that case it is vital to acknowledge the problem and show understanding, apologise and suggest a solution.

All professionals use *selective listening* strategies in the workplace. With excessive information flows, selective listening is a necessity. A person's concentration can span over an hour or two at the most, frequently only 15–20 minutes. The listener can simply tune out and start planning his or her own day, the mind drifting away from the overload. Similarly, a student may listen to the core content of the lecture and let his or her mind drift away when less important procedural information is given. A selective listening strategy is a clever tool for professionals.

The fourth strategy for listening is *active listening*. Active listening is used when the listener really wants to internalise what is being communicated. The listener comments, asks questions, asserts by using rhetorical questions and provides compliments to the speaker. The concentration on the message is such that the listener is able to summarise what the speaker is saying. There are cultural differences in active listening. For example, Finns and the Japanese may communicate active listening by a concentrated silence, whereas the silence in Anglo-American communication practice would be interpreted as lack of interest in the message.

The fifth type of listening can be called *critical listening*, which involves listening at a deep level, comprehension, analysis of the message, comparison to current knowledge and an evaluation. This type of listening requires good logical thinking skills and time for assimilation. This may be difficult if the listener is forced to comment directly after the message has been delivered. Critical thinking takes time, and equivocal responses may be more appropriate where immediate comments are required.

Listening – in all of its forms – is an important interpersonal skill. Good listeners can switch from one type of listening to another, understanding when it is appropriate to listen actively, when empathetically, and when it is necessary to listen critically. Good listening opens doors for ideas and encourages creativity. Good listeners are able to separate fact from fiction and cope with false persuasion. They can also avoid being exploited by others.

Asking questions is part of listening in that it is another way of seeking to understand the situation. In Anglo-American communication practice, questions are often introduced to link them with the current discussion (*You mentioned ... Why is it that ...?*). In other cultures, too, many questions may be interpreted as a cross-examination rather than an attempt to understand the viewpoints of the parties involved.

Open questions like 'How do you feel about that?' or 'How would your co-workers feel about that?' produce answers that allow respondents to say whatever they feel like. These kinds of questions often help improve the atmosphere, as all parties have the opportunity to express their views. One of the drawbacks of such types of questions is that the answers may become too general and lose direction, making it difficult to work through a problem. For that purpose we need questions that use the precise question words: *who, where, what, why, how* and *when?*

Team F. Summarise and check

Summarising in a communication is part of what is called the 'metatext'. Metatext means simply text about text, to help the listener or reader to follow the logic of your thinking. Metatexting, including summarising, helps the recipient to keep on track with the communicator's logic, whatever it may be.

An example of metatexting in presentations might help to see what it is and how it works. In a presentation you could use metatexts in the following ways:

• to introduce a presentation	Today I'm going to talk to you about Cubing, a method of collecting previous knowledge of a subject, and practise some higher order thinking skills to organise the content into a text.
• to show your plan	I have structured my talk around the following outline. First, ...
• to show where the presentation is at within the outline	So much for the definition of Cubing. Let's now move on to our second point, which are the labels of the cube, all in all six of them.
• to make an intermediate summary	So, basically, what I'm saying is this: ....
• to recap to an earlier point	Let's go back a moment to what we were discussing earlier.
• to show you want to keep on giving more details of a theme	I'd like to expand that a little, before we move on.
• to summarise what has been said so far	So, just to give you the main points here, ...
• to demonstrate how the end of your presentation links with the start: the objective	Let me conclude by repeating what I said at the beginning of this presentation.

There are a number of logical structures around which a talk or a text can be organised.

A presentation can follow *the 4Ps Structure*. In that case, the *position* is first described: where, when and how a problem occurs. This is followed by the definition of the *problem*. Various *possibilities* are then reported for solving the problem, weighing the possibilities against each other. At the end the presenter evaluates the possibilities and makes a *proposal* for the best one. This kind of structure would be suitable for topics related to fault analysis, market research or persuasion to take on a new system as an introduction to a recommendation.

A second common option of organising subject matter into a logical whole is to sequence it as a *chronological structure*. This is suitable when describing the history or developments of some activity, technology or solutions. The point of a chronological presentation is to systematise the occurrence of an event and spot favourable or unfavourable stages in the development.

A common structure is to describe two systems and compare their different aspects. This *comparative structure* results in an interesting outcome, where the listener may take his or her choice depending on the variables he or she prioritises. In this kind of logic it is common to first establish the criteria against which the comparison is being made.

The fourth common logical structure of articles and research papers is the *research structure*, also used in project reports. This structure starts with the Introduction, existing knowledge in the format of Literature review or description of the current system, moving on to Method and material, Results and Analysis, Discussion and Conclusions. The core logic is surrounded by shortcuts of Preface, Abstract and Table of contents, Abbreviations or Acronyms and Appendices. Basically, the purpose is to provide the results of the project, to evaluate their significance and to provide enough information for the reader to be able to evaluate the soundness of the research.

These structures and their combinations may constitute your own presentation. The key point is how your communication becomes a *neat package*, with a clear destination. The neat package has a logical order from beginning to end, starting with the objective and culminating in the *key message*.

Activity 4.2.2 Mechanical engineer's communication profile

Learning activity description	Mechanical engineer's communication profile
Professional challenge	This activity is especially helpful for pre-service learners in getting familiar with the communication life of a mechanical engineer. It focuses on future positions or occupations that the participant may envisage and potential companies the learner might be employed by, including extended knowledge about typical communication situations that mechanical engineers experience.
Communication challenge (Global, institutional and organisational knowledge; participant knowledge; social action knowledge)	Reading the profile the learner will familiarise him- or herself with those key organisations and institutions that a mechanical engineer's work relates to in the roles of suppliers, customers, collaborators and standardisation bodies in the global business setting. It is useful to stress not only the importance of technical expertise, but also how engineers are capable of communicating their valuable expertise and know-how to stakeholders from a variety of backgrounds (technical, business, law, chemistry, etc.) and with different cultural experiences (national, corporate, professional).
Language aims (textual knowledge)	• Mediating cryptic, list-like information to storytelling, requiring imagination in re-creating missing elements • Learning to ask questions for points too hazily or cryptically formulated • Sharing information with others and linking profile information to participant's own experience • Learning to discuss and interact
Procedure	Learners are given a brief description of what a CEF Professional Profile is before receiving a copy each (see Chapter 3, Section 3.2, *Sample profile: mechanical engineers*). The following questions are then written on the board. Learners skim the whole document and answer the questions. • What kind of information does the Professional Profile provide? • How may the information in the profile be useful to an engineer / an engineering student? How was the information in the profile collected? • How does the profile information match with the learner's experience?

After discussion of the answers, learners are then told that they are going to read one (or possibly more if the group is small) section of the profile in more detail and report their findings back to the class. Each learner is then given one (or more) of the slips below, each of which sets the learners some questions. Learners answer the questions and then report their answers orally, first to a partner and then to the whole class. Finally, learners are asked to write up a short summary of the section(s) of the profile they investigated. The summaries are then checked by the teacher and distributed to the group as a single document.

Teacher input	The teacher

- gives a 15-minute introduction to the subject (see the professional challenge and communication challenge content above)
- instructs the class to (1) skim through the whole profile and (2) read their own part well, ready for reporting in class, either at home or in class (takes 45 minutes). No visuals are asked of learners.
- asks learners to share with the whole class.

Learner output	

- Skimming a longish text
- Reading and reporting on a short text
- Discussing a mechanical engineer's career profile
- Understanding the kinds of professional communication needed

Learning outcomes	The learner

- gains an improved understanding of the target profession
- understands mediation as a different discourse from reporting precisely the text of a profile
- learns more vocabulary of the field of mechanical engineering.

Evaluation	Teacher and peer feedback is given, especially for extended examples of communication situations.
Language level required	B1 or above
Preparation and materials	One copy of the profile (e.g. *Sample profile: mechanical engineers*) for each learner; enough copies of the guided questions for each group of three–four members (see *Mechanical engineer's communication programme* worksheet below)

Duration	Introduction: 15 minutes Skimming and reading: 1 hour (in class or home) Oral reporting and discussion: 60 minutes
Remarks	The CEF Professional Profile is mainly designed for course design purposes, but this trialled activity has shown that it can also be utilised for learners. Note that quite a few other profiles are also available as appendices in this book or at the CEF Professional Profiles Project website http://www.proflang.org. If you end up using a profile that does not fully match your student group, you could focus on how the country-specific profile differs from practice in your country.
Suggestions for follow-up work	Examples of communication situations deviating from the profile are worth listening to. Given by in-service participants (or any other learner who may have experience), they can be directly utilised as simulations in later activities.

Mechanical engineer's communication profile

Your group reads the assigned part of the profile (A–F), and reports the information orally to the whole class.

- Start by introducing the focus of your task. For example:

    Our task is to give an overview of the contexts where the mechanical engineer works and of the collaborators with whom he or she needs to communicate. This is given in Part C of the profile, which we have read.

- Use metatext between parts.

    Antti will start...Thank you, Antti. I will now hand over to Rick for...

- End clearly and decisively. For example:

    This is all we planned to say about the contexts. Are there some questions you want to ask?

Group A. Chairing the activity
This group's task is to chair the whole activity.

First introduce the activity (Aim: get an overview of the communicative demands made on a mechanical engineer; use information in Part A). Then hand over to each group for their report. After each report lead a short discussion (5 minutes). You could ask questions such as:

Did you get a clear picture of (the routine situations)? Was there anything that was hard to understand? Can we look at it together?
Did you know this before, or was some of this information new to you? Which part? Can we now say that we have a pretty good idea of what could be considered demanding situations?

After discussion invite the next group to present.

Group B. Section B
What positions are mechanical engineers found working in?
What kinds of companies are mentioned? In what fields do they operate?

Group C. Section C
In what situations do mechanical engineers need to communicate at work?
In what situations do mechanical engineers need to communicate during their studies?

Group D. Section D
Explain types of routine situations for a mechanical engineer. Which of the most frequent routine communication situations of a mechanical engineer do you think would be most difficult for you? Why? Which situation would be least difficult for you? Why? Role play one of the situations.

Group E. Section E
Explain one demanding situation for a mechanical engineer. What makes this one demanding? Can you think of any other reasons why professional mechanical engineers found these situations demanding?

Group F. Section F
Which activities in the snapshots require the specific skills or technical professional knowledge of a mechanical engineer?
Which activities in the snapshot are common to other kinds of business?
How does your own day compare with a day in the life of a mechanical engineer?

Group G. Whole profile guiding question
What is metatext and how is it used?

4.3 Contributing to knowledge of the professional field

Activity 4.3.1 Engineering studies

The benefit of *this* activity is that learners become confident in expressing matters concerning their university and their studies in English through having to look at three different universities. This generates discussion on how the studies at different universities compare. The curriculum description helps them to spell out course titles and explain the contents of courses they personally have taken. Learners give good feedback about this activity, as they are talking about their own interest area and projects and courses they have already experienced.

Learning activity description	Learning to communicate about engineering studies
Professional challenge	Many engineers' first employment starts with a CV and interview (some through personal connections – the grapevine – which highlights the importance of social ties). They may be novices, but they must be able to communicate clearly and fluently about their educational background and specifically those interest areas where applicants are expected to perform well. This activity focuses on the vocabulary of job applications; a later activity covers CV writing and participation in a job interview.
Communication challenge	Employing companies come in all sizes and have different communication preferences. By looking at a company's job advertisements, it is possible to identify what style the company favours: modern and dynamic, traditional and corporate or something different again. A clever applicant recognises style preferences and tailors the message to suit the purpose – including the speaking, writing, dress code and body language that are associated with those styles.
Language aims	• Being able to report and explain the learner's educational background effectively, convincingly and fluently (since a recruiter wants this information in a convincing package) • Being able to use the terminology of engineering education without hesitation
Procedure	Topic introduction: aims of professional and communication challenge. The teacher takes up some terms for engineering education to see how familiar students are with them. *What is it going to say on your business card once you graduate?* *What degree/qualifications do you expect to have?* Then the teacher gives out the group task from the *Engineering studies* worksheet for next time. The weekly schedule task (see the Group E task) should be saved for the weakest group, since it gives plenty of practice on weekdays, clock times and prepositions.

Teacher input	The teacher
	• shows two job advertisements, one a traditional one, the other a dynamic, thematic one
	• recommends that the learners adapt the style of the advertisement and communicate accordingly
	• asks one learner to tell a story of his or her educational background, from elementary to the current position, in order to encourage the learner to use the terminology of education necessary for describing this background
	• writes the following on the board:
	  o country-specific terms for primary, secondary and tertiary education
	  o instead of blank verbs such as *I **was** in high school*, informative verbs such as *complete, finish*
	  o instead of *I went to university*, clearer expressions such as *I applied, I was accepted, I completed/took a degree in ...*
	  o subjects studied and subject categories (core requirement studies, professional studies, etc.)
	  o names used of Master's/Bachelor's degree, vocational qualifications, traineeships, etc.
	• shows one syllabus (e.g. of the teacher's own university) and asks learners to explain its parts
	• gives the learners the task for preparation (see *Engineering studies* worksheet below). The tasks should be divided among teams of three or four learners (teams A, B, C, D, E, F). Teams should report on the team topics as given below.
	They will need to be given any missing terminology.

Learner output	• Searching results for universities and degree programmes on the Internet • Oral group reporting (no visuals) • Practising commenting, asking questions and discussion
Learning outcomes	The learner • improves oral reporting and discussion skills • consolidates his or her engineering education terminology: curriculum, syllabus, Bachelor's degree, core requirement studies/professional studies, names of specialist subjects, concise descriptions, learner's own university, traineeship, Bachelor's or Master's thesis or dissertation, special projects, etc. • demonstrates how to communicate convincingly about an interesting project.

Evaluation	Peer evaluation can be used for group reporting; as the activity is part of class work, it is not graded separately.
Language level required	Level B1–B2 (work experience not needed); mainly pre-service learners
Preparation and materials	Learners study the contents of their own degree programme, subjects and schedule, plus the websites of two other universities. If the university has an exchange programme with another institution, this is a good opportunity to promote the link, since some learners have become interested in student exchange through this activity. Copies of the *Engineering studies* worksheet Learners work in teams of three–four nominated at the start of the course (A, B, C, D, E, F). This makes all work run smoothly even if there are absences. The teacher can copy a description of the mechanical engineering syllabus from one university to show direction.
Duration	Introduction: 15 minutes Learner preparation: 30–45 minutes Time for reporting and discussion: 90 minutes
Suggestions for follow-up work	Vocabulary work or translation is a useful follow-up activity. The teacher asks the learners to recount their educational background, including times and names of schools, e.g.

> *I started elementary school at the age of ___. Elementary school in my country generally goes from age __ to age __. At the age of 11, I entered …*

This may seem to be an easy task, but several trial rounds of this activity have demonstrated that it is not the case. Translations are used instead of student reporting because the learner's own text ends up avoiding more precise and informative verbs (*took an entrance examination, attended, was accepted, completed*), using a repetitive series of general words instead (e.g. *first I went to ..., then I went to, then I went to*). The translation option is not available if student native languages are too varied. Verbs and names of schools, degrees, entrance examinations and acceptance are not easy even for level B2 learners, especially as there may not be exact equivalents between different countries.

ENGINEERING STUDIES

This activity helps you to describe, discuss and compare engineering education in different places and at the same time become more fluent in talking about your own education and its contents to your employer and your collaborators.

Engineering education language includes the knowledge of a number of items, e.g. those referring to

- levels of education (secondary, tertiary; vocational school, college education, etc.)
- degrees, degree programmes and specialisations (e.g. BSc, BEng; degree programme in Mechanical Engineering, specialisation in Machine Automation)
- syllabus, curriculum and course descriptions (prerequisites, extent, evaluation, grading, learning outcome)
- categories of subjects (core requirement, professional studies, specialisation studies)
- names of subjects and descriptions of course content.

Each group finds information on one of the six topics given below (A–F). This is reported to the other members of the class as a group presentation of 8–12 minutes. Some ideas: search for Bradley University, USA, Umeå University, Sweden, Metropolia University, Finland. No visuals are needed; you may show the webpages of the relevant university.

NB. No reading from the original information is allowed. All the information must be presented orally in non-technical language. Make an effort to 'sell' the benefits of your university or programme.

Learners report orally the contents of

A. University A (size, degree programmes, number of students, academic programme, benefits)
B. University B (size, degree programmes, number of students, academic programme, benefits)
C. Students' own university (size, degree programmes, number of students, academic programme, benefits)
D. Curriculum of the student's own degree programme (focus on how the elements are important for a future engineer)
E. Weekly schedule of Group E members (explain to the class your weekly programme from Monday to Friday; if the group has many different ones, choose one and then let others compare to the given one)
F. One course, project or traineeship and its contents described in a convincing manner to an employer (focus on how this builds up the student's skills for the employer)

Needs Analysis for Language Course Design © Cambridge University Press 2013 **PHOTOCOPIABLE**

Activity 4.3.2 Industrial fields, companies and operations

Mechanical engineering and specifically machine automation students may end up working for a variety of companies linked with the production, processing and packaging of goods in various fields. Therefore industry-specific terminology, linked with practice of oral skills, can be a motivating activity for this target group. The *Occupational information* of Part B helps the language instructor to look for relevant webpages and make suggestions. The *Contextual information* given in Part C of the profile gives further information on the institutional and social action perspectives of the engineer's *language* contexts. The following activity is designed to help learners to formulate communication about the company environment and its operation. The need for this activity type is related to the *text- and discourse-types* column in Part C of the Mechanical Engineer's profile: *Discussion about industry (fields, products, corporate operations).*

Learning activity description	Industrial fields, companies and operations
Professional challenge	A mechanical engineer's work may take place in numerous organisations, as shown in Part B of the profile. The employing company may be specialised in one field or several fields. For language and communication purposes, it is therefore vital to recognise key fields, be able to talk about them and follow current developments in the field by scanning news on websites and trade papers.
Communication challenge	Mechanical engineers communicate not only about engineering issues and their own company, but more broadly about other suppliers, competitor companies, other agents in the field, and trends in the industry and economy. Thus knowledge – and its formulation in a second language – is worth taking up in class. This makes it necessary to read current news and business trends in the field.
Language aims	• Searching field-specific and country-specific information and terminology on the Internet (including main fields of industry, names of major product categories, economic indicators of corporate annual reports, terminology for economic trends) • Learning to refrain from copy–paste knowledge, avoid plagiarism, and package the knowledge to slides, and thus mediate knowledge in another format • Learning the discourse of the bullet-point style of slides, and unlearning copying of sentences and paragraphs from existing texts

Procedure	Learners are divided into five working parties of three or four at the beginning of the activity. Each group is then given one of the tasks outlined in the *Industrial fields, companies and operations* worksheet below.

After completing their search, each group then prepares and delivers a presentation to the class in which they explain their findings. All groups make use of visual aids (such as slideshow presentation software). Those learners whose research tasks included searching out statistical information may wish to distribute copies of this information.

Teacher input

The teacher
- introduces the importance of industry knowledge by focusing on the reasons for being able to discuss current events in business and industrial trends in the field using the professional challenge and communication challenge content outlined at the beginning of this activity
- shows the genre of 1) slides and 2) text and discusses the differences between discourses: slides have a distinct discourse (condensed, bullet-pointed, elliptical, visual) from textual or internet site material (sentence-based, built in paragraphs, causal links, hyperlinked, rich with examples, references). The teacher then demonstrates how a coherent text becomes a slide
- discusses plagiarism and shows how to document a reference in a slide
- divides participants into groups of four and delegates tasks using the worksheet below
- listens to reports, and guides the discussion.

Learner output

- Internet information search
- Selection of relevant information and conversion to a slideshow format
- Functioning as an active, contributing group member
- Participation in a group presentation
- Learning and consolidation of new terminology
- (giving peer feedback)

Learning outcomes

The learner
- gains a better knowledge of industrial fields, product categories and companies, including associated terminology
- improves searching skills and knowledge of nationally important sites for economic and business information
- gains practical experience in group work
- improves presentation skills.

Evaluation	An extended version of this activity is to ask learners to peer evaluate the quality of the presentations according to a set of criteria agreed on by the group (e.g. interest value, preparation, contents, use of illustrations, etc.).
	The teacher needs to make sure that positivity prevails in the comments. This can be done by making two positive points before any single critical point because learners learn best by encouragement. However, learners should not be left with the impression that everything went perfectly, if this was not in fact the case. The teacher could say, for example:
	Can we help Ville to identify improvement points for the next time he presents? When Ville does this, how can he improve?
Language level required	B2–C1; pre-service and in-service learners
Preparation and materials	Copies of the set of research tasks (see *Industrial fields, companies and operations* worksheet below); computers and/or access to the Internet; access to printers and photocopiers (for learner use) or projector facilities and slideshow presentation software.
	A group should be nominated in advance to ask the presenters a few questions. The worksheet should be copied to all.
Duration	Pre-class preparation: 2–3 hours (learners) Class time: 60–90 minutes
Remarks	This activity can be used for other fields of engineering as well as public sector organisations in the fields of social services and healthcare, law, banking, insurance, etc.
Suggestions for follow-up work	This activity is very terminology intensive. Such a wide repertoire of terminology is not acquired just by listening to group presentations. Therefore some exercises introducing field-relevant terminology may be appropriate.

A few ideas:

- Groups are nominated to listen carefully and pick up 5–10 words that are new to learners that came up during the presentation. The words should be written down so that they can be discussed the following week.
- Many of the words relating to this topic may present pronunciation difficulties. It will help to write their phonetic script on the board and practise (e.g. sound problems: *manufacturing, produces, subsidiary, executive, technology, engineering,* etc.; word stress problems: *personnel, employees, materials, established,* etc.).
- One group could draw a mind map of all the presentations on one transparency. Learners are then asked to fill in the mind map structure with key content from the group presentations, adding elements to it. (Assignment text: Fill in the different parts of the mind map with key points from the presentation.) All learners should look at the information and then different groups (not those who presented the actual information) could come and report on the content they have just heard orally in front of class. This gives more terminology consolidation and further presentation practice. A skeleton of a mind map is given in the *Summary of industrial fields* worksheet below.

Another extended version of this activity more suitable to groups of advanced (C1+) learners is to ask the whole group to make notes during the presentation and use these to write up an Industry report summarising the key points, exemplified in the worksheet tasks below.

INDUSTRIAL FIELDS, COMPANIES AND OPERATIONS

Your group task is to communicate well about your topic to the rest of the class. In order to do this you need to

- discuss your topic within your team and share the work
- conduct internet searches on the topic
- create 5–6 slides to incorporate the essential information
- decide how to divide the parts of the presentation so that all participate
- make sure you do not copy directly from internet materials
- make sure you use bullet-point items and not full sentences or paragraphs in slides
- present your findings in class for about 15 minutes.

The group tasks are the following:

Group A. Why invest in your home country?

In your group, prepare a report outlining some reasons why foreign investors should do business in your home country. Search the websites of the Ministry of Trade and Industry, Chambers of Commerce, and other organisations in your country for information for foreign investors. Try to see this information as a potential investor might and consider advantages and disadvantages.

Group B. Main fields of industry

In your group, prepare a report on the main fields of industry in your home country. Search the Internet for national statistics and factual reviews of industry in your home country.

Group C. Major groups of products

In your group, prepare a report on the major groups of products manufactured in your home country. Search the Internet for information and statistics on the main categories for commodities.

Group D. Major international companies

In your group, prepare a report on the major international companies operating in your home country. Search business journals such as *Business Week* or *The Economist* for information and statistics on major international companies that play a significant role in your home country.

Group E. A company in your area

In your group, prepare a report on a company active in your area (not necessarily from your home country). Search the Internet for information on the company, including its origins, organisation, finances, locations, major products and markets.

After completing this search, your group should prepare and deliver a presentation to the class in which you report on your findings. Those learners whose research tasks included searching out statistical information may wish to distribute copies of this information and/or make use of visual aids (such as slideshow presentation software).

Summary of industrial fields

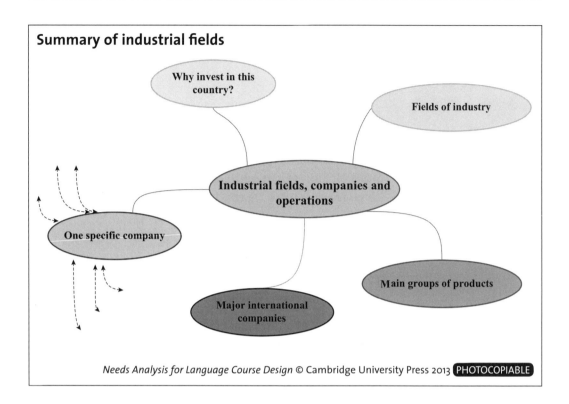

Activity 4.3.3 Job interviews

Learning activity description	Learning to prepare for a job interview
Professional challenge	Recruitment of the best engineers has become a major undertaking in business. More and more of the job market and its advertising has been moved onto the Internet; fewer recruitment announcements are published in print. Applications are primarily advertised and accepted online. Those invited to interviews are often expected to bring their testimonials with them.
	With the shrinking job market, the selecting personnel face increasing numbers of applications to choose from. The applicant must find a way to make his or her application stand out from the pile of other ones.
Communication challenge	The challenge for the engineer is how to be able to communicate about his or her skills and competencies in a brief, positive, attractive and yet truthful and authentic manner that will increase his or her chances of being invited to an interview.
	One significant challenge is how to speak about one's own personal characteristics in a comfortable manner. Teaching experience tells us that engineers have trouble thinking about their strengths and weaknesses, not only in a foreign language but in any language at all. Therefore this activity focuses on learning to be at ease when talking about oneself as a person.
Language aims	• Preparing to communicate about one's competencies, capabilities, skills and character in a natural way • Rehearsing answers to typical job interview questions
Procedure	• The teacher asks learners to bring a job advertisement to class. They may use the Internet, newspapers or trade papers. They are asked to think about themselves as they will be three years after graduation when they are looking through job advertisements (they must then 'invent' the missing part of their history – this improves the quality of their responses). • The teacher gives an introductory lecture on why the first impression both in writing and face to face is significant and on the personal qualities required of a good engineer, using the slide *Personal qualities of a good engineer* provided below. Learners may wish to add further qualities to the list.

- The learners are asked to write down six strengths and four weaknesses and to exemplify them in a convincing manner to the employer. '*Why should the employer hire you and not someone else / your classmate?*' '*How can you demonstrate / have you demonstrated that you are good at x (e.g. design software)?*'
- Learners are then divided into groups (A–F) and a group interview is arranged so that team A interviews team B members, team C team D members and team E team F members. This can then be reversed, so the interviewers have a turn at being interviewed. The questions from the *Interview questions* sheet are used to help groups prepare for the interview.
- Team members who are not interviewing use the *Interviewee observation form* to evaluate the sample job interviews that are conducted subsequently.

Teacher input

The teacher
- asks learners to bring in a job advertisement
- leads a discussion on the desired competencies and capabilities of a good engineer as evidenced in advertisements
- asks participants to list their strengths for their future employer
- circulates around the class and helps learners personally to find their best stories to back up why they can be called 'inventive', 'systematic', 'determined', 'open-minded', 'persistent', 'ambitious'
- shares some of the good examples in class
- divides participants into teams (A–F)
- asks them to rehearse asking and answering job interview questions.

Learner output

- A personal list of strengths and weaknesses (not shown to any other person, but helped by the teacher) with good examples of what events provide convincing evidence that they are realistic
- Some good answers to interview questions
- More confidence in talking about oneself

Learning outcomes

The learner
- achieves a well-considered evaluation of personal competencies, capabilities, skills, characteristics, motivation and communication
- (consequently) is able to devise some plans for improving areas where weaknesses are identified.

Evaluation	Part of continuous assessment OR
	After the evaluation form has been explained, learners take turns to go over to the other group to be interviewed. When all learners have had an opportunity to be interviewed, the observers use their notes to give feedback and discussion on the experience.
Language level required	B1 or above, mainly pre-service learners
Preparation and materials	A slide of the list *Personal qualities of a good engineer*; copies of the *Interview questions* worksheet for all students; a copy of the *Interviewee observation form* for observers
Duration	Introduction and listing of personal competencies and qualities: 45 minutes
	Group interview rehearsal and shared answers: 45 minutes (possibly longer if the teams are large and/or every learner needs the opportunity to be both interviewer and interviewee)
Remarks	The activity requires discretion and confidentiality in talking about personal issues that the learner may not have expressed even in his or her native language. The teacher should reassure learners at the start that the lists of personal issues will not be shared in class: understandably some learners may feel anxious about discussing personal qualities, being interviewed and observed by their peers in the class.
	Learners should be reminded that they were asked to envision themselves as having graduated three years ago. This partly fictional alternative persona helps learners to be more imaginative and may lead to a more courageous and less inhibited involvement in the activity. The teacher should convince learners that it is safer for them to rehearse blushing in class than blushing in a job interview.
	Variation Group rather than individual interviews can be proposed. In this case, three or four learners can be interviewed at once by the panel and observers can be assigned one interviewee each to make notes on.
Suggestions for follow-up work	This activity can easily be followed up by asking learners to produce either: Option A: a thematic application tailored to their job application (1–2 pages) or Option B: a traditional application letter (1 page) with a chronological CV (1 page)

PERSONAL QUALITIES OF A GOOD ENGINEER

ambitious

high level of commitment

dynamic (interested in continuous change)

flexible

able to work under pressure

humble (conscious of continuous change)

a life-long learner

international

open-minded

professional expert

resourceful

self-confident

good communication skills

willing to move around

the x factor for the company

INTERVIEW QUESTIONS

Use the questions below to help groups prepare for the interview.

A   *Introduce yourself to the candidate then ask the following four questions:*

- Why did you apply for this job?
- How did you prepare for this interview?
- How do you see your career developing in the next five years?
- You have had very short periods of employment, according to your CV. Why is that?

B   *Choose two or three of the points below to ask the candidate:*

Please tell us about a time when you ...
- worked under pressure
- worked effectively with others
- organised a major project
- motivated and led others
- solved a difficult problem
- accepted constructive criticism.

C   *Choose two of the points below to ask the candidate:*

- What are your weaknesses as they relate to this job?
- Please tell us about a time when you had difficulty in persuading others to accept an idea of yours.
- What leadership qualities do you think you have?

D   *Ask the learners to think of a typical workplace problem and ask the interviewee how they would deal with it, for example:*

We'd like you to imagine that you are working for us. Your department has trouble coping with your printed material because of the printing department's failure to deliver your copies in time. This has been a growing problem for three months. The printing department manager and his deputy are doing their best to cope with the problem. How would you go about trying to find a solution to the problem? (Huhta [2000] 2002b: 231)

E   Why do you think we should hire you?

In pairs, encourage learners to think about how they might answer each question on the list. Each group then selects two or three members to be the interviewers. The rest of the group are observers and are given a copy of the *Interviewee observation form*.

Needs Analysis for Language Course Design © Cambridge University Press 2013 **PHOTOCOPIABLE**

INTERVIEWEE OBSERVATION FORM

Candidate information	Notes
Name	
Education and work experience	
Personal qualities and competencies	
Motivation and enthusiasm	
Confidence in communication	

4.4 **Raising awareness of professional genres**

A few words need to be said about why we consider it useful to introduce the concept of professional genres to mechanical engineers in their language course.

Genre can be understood in the sense of 'a more or less standardized communicative event with a goal or set of goals mutually understood by the participants in that event and occurring within a functional rather than a personal social setting' (Swales 1981: 10–11). The 'standardization' of the event implies some regulation by the professional community (Robinson 1991: 26). A wide range of research has been conducted to identify the nature of professional genres.[1] Besides an analysis of the text, genre analysis may also focus on levels beyond texts. For example, Swales (1990: 24–7) has analysed discourse communities that produce the genres and discovered socioculturally essential defining characteristics.

Genre analysis has proven its value to the practice of language teaching. There is an ongoing discussion about whether the linguistic features identified as genre research outlines are fully realised in practice in any profession (Bhatia [1993] 1998: 18). Without taking a stance on this discussion (Huhta 2010: 54–6), we recognise that genre research has helped second language teaching significantly. Genre analysis has proven very useful for second language learners based on our experience in delivering these courses. If a learner is able to identify and recognise genres as existing 'templates' for a communication, even a weaker learner can get the overall functions of the communication in place and achieve a coherent text despite shortcomings in the technical command of linguistic resources, whether spoken or written. This is why this activity is useful for second language learners.

We recommend that the teacher introduces a few example genres at the beginning of this activity. Here are two of them: instructions and a telephone call. Bring an instruction booklet with you and ask a couple of learners to analyse its discourse. They will find some of the following:

Technical *instructions* are typically short version 'manuals' for non-technical users whereas manuals are mainly intended for technical users. Writing of manuals and technical instructions may be done by technical experts and specialist technical writers working in collaboration, or they may be written by one person who combines both technical and communication expertise. Instructions aim to give a brief understanding of how to use – and how not to use – the equipment. In overview, instruction booklets normally have a clear

---

[1]   See, for example, analyses of sales promotion letters and job application letters (Bhatia [1993] 1998: 118), self-published web résumés (Killoran 2006), weblogs (Miller & Shepherd 2004), collaborative genres (Yates et al. 1997), meetings (Ponzini 2002), academic writing (Dudley-Evans 1994; Ventola et al. 2002), interdiscursivity in academic writing (Candlin & Plum 1999; Bhatia 2000; Bhatia & Candlin 2001; Candlin 2006), social interactions in academic writing (Hyland 2000), business correspondence (Louhiala-Salminen 1999; Yli-Jokipii 2001; Bhatia 2002; Kankaanranta 2005; Louhiala-Salminen & Kankaanranta 2005).

structure for selective reading, with a number of clear illustrations – pictures, numbering, colours, graphs, arrows, font size, bold type, etc. – suited for the target group. Many instruction booklets also include an abstracted guide at the beginning for fast reading.

The *text functions* typically include an overall description of the piece of equipment and an outline of its uses and purpose. This typically includes a description of the elements and structure of the equipment, including an overview of the functions of the equipment and the procedures for operating it. Every instruction booklet also includes points about safety, service and maintenance. Warnings are frequent. The *style* of instructions is typically very neutral. *Forms of politeness* are quite few, with perhaps some imperative comments such as 'Please remove before inserting …'. As for *language features*, it is typical that instructions are written in imperative form (*open, remove, insert, do not touch …*) with instructive text (*you attach, you press …*) and the passive voice (*the indicator light is turned on*). References to sequence are frequent (*first, then, after, before …*). Sentences tend to be short, unambiguous and easily readable. The conditional is used for facilitating use or avoiding undesired activity (*If you do this then something will happen …*).

After this introduction the learners are ready for this activity.

Activity 4.4.1 Creating templates for professional genres

Learning activity description	Creating templates for professional genres
Professional challenge	Engineers' most frequent communication situations are:

88% socialising
87% telephoning
82% travelling
77% writing for work
76% client contacts
70% professional reading
62% meetings and negotiations (Huhta 1999)

Getting familiar with the genres of the most frequent communication events helps the engineer to establish standard formats for routine communications and save his or her creative energy for dealing with changing, complicating elements of communication, as discussed in Chapter 2.

Communication challenge

This activity looks at genres from an overview perspective of sequence of events, to establish templates for communication events, for example meetings, presentations, application letters, complaints, project proposals or report abstracts.

This activity raises awareness of genres used in mechanical engineering companies and their discourse community expectations. The social action around the genres is discussed for each communication event.

It is sometimes easy to misjudge how to communicate in a certain situation. For example, an enthusiastic expert *giving a presentation* on his or her specialist area may easily get carried away with the content area and pack the presentation with masses of detail, consequently losing audience interest. Or a *planning meeting* may end up without any results if no one takes responsibility for structuring what to do and where to meet. These are examples where participants are not aware of professional communication genres and discourse expectations for the communication event. In these two examples, an expert communicator knows that presentations are meant to be tailored for the audience, and thus the level of detail must be radically trimmed for a mixed audience. Planning meetings, in turn, typically end in decisions being made on measures to be taken.

Language aims

- Learning to look at a text from an overview perspective of communication
- Recognising the discourse of a number of professional genres
- Becoming aware of overall general expectations of key communication events

Procedure

The teacher introduces the subject of professional genres: what they are and why it is useful to analyse them. The professional challenge and communication challenge content from the start of this activity is used for this stage.

First, the teacher shows the class the telephone call text below and analyses it together with them (see *Example text: telephone call* and *Discourse analysis of this text* below). Then each group gets their text and is given 20–25 minutes to analyse it. Groups are asked to report.

Results are summarised by drawing the genres in a mind map on the board. The teacher tells the learners which genres they will study in more detail later on during the course; the mind map is drawn on the board as the groups report on the genres.

In the centre: professional genres. Second level: the six genres you chose. Third level: participants, sequence of events, style, forms of politeness, features of language, other. This is a good way of summarising the whole activity.

We recommend that many of these texts can later on be studied in more detail in the course.

Teacher input

The teacher
- selects six different genres – some that the learners will be studying later on in the course, i.e. from their coursebook, if appropriate, and perhaps some additional ones. Dialogues of the following genres will be needed, one for each group. For example:

  A   meeting
  B   presentation
  C   process description
  D   negotiation
  E   application letter
  F   email
  G   instructions
  H   project proposal

- shows the text of the telephone call and analyses it together with the class
- distributes six different genres to learners and gives them 20–25 minutes to analyse the text
- draws a mind map on the board about the six genres and their template.

Learner output
- Analysis of one genre
- Listening to and commenting on others' analyses

Learning outcomes

The learner
- gains an awareness of genre features above sentence level
- learns to recognise common elements
- hopefully increases confidence in knowing how to deal with a genre despite minor language flaws.

Evaluation	None
Language level required	B1–C1; both in-service and pre-service learners
Preparation and materials	Copies of five examples of the six selected genres, a different one for each group (examples of genres from a coursebook or other available sources can be used). For lower-level classes, the texts should be given out in advance for reading at home; slides of the *Example telephone call* and *Discourse analysis of this text;* one copy of the *Analysis of a communication situation* template for every team.
Duration	Introduction: 5 minutes Analysis time: 30 minutes Reporting and discussion: 60 minutes
Remarks	Genres rely on discourse practices based on Anglo-American business standards that are fairly well recognised and accepted in international business. Communication problems may occur if one or more communication partners do not conform to the practices or standards of discourse for the event. Cultural differences also have a major impact on what happens in actual practice.
	Weaker learners derive a great benefit from this activity. They learn to get the overall items right and the outcome of a situation will be much better in practice.
	Even if the teacher does not find a perfect text, a good discussion is created by describing what the chosen sample of genre is and how that differs from the common 'norm' (something that is difficult to establish with confidence in any discourse community). The point of this activity is not to establish a 'norm' but to raise awareness of alternative norms, styles and approaches and to make learners work out for themselves how to act in those situations.

Some humorous examples that deviate from the standard format are a good idea: for example using a presentation that adopts an impolite stance towards the audience can generate a good discussion on audience expectations. Another useful 'awkward' text is an abrupt email that simply says: 'Our factory is on strike. Your order will be delayed.' This will lead on to a helpful discussion on the use of direct and indirect communication strategies when delivering a bad news message. For example, Anglo-American business practices sometimes prefer the use of indirect approaches where the actual fact of a strike and a delay is accompanied by an explanation of the cause of the strike, steps taken by the company to try and prevent such an event, and apologies for its occurrence.

Suggestions for follow-up work

A far-sighted teacher chooses those six communications he or she will use later on in the course for other activities. This will give weaker learners more time for learning first the holistic events, the discussion on the communication and its language and finally for rehearsing them in simulations. We have used fairly long and complex texts of meetings, negotiations, presentations, bad news, application letters and project proposals.

EXAMPLE TEXT: TELEPHONE CALL

RS: Salmi. (Riku Salmi)

JH: Hello, Riku. This is Jim Haines speaking.

RS: Hi, Jim. Good to hear from you. How're things?

JH: Fine at this end. I think you'll like this. The planned project is on.

RS: Finally? That's exactly what I was hoping to hear.

JH: The question is: are you still interested in making the offer for the marine engines we have discussed?

RS: That goes without saying. Of course we are.

JH: So how long would it take you to get the quotation on the way? We seem to be in a bit of a hurry.

RS: Are we talking about the same specifications we discussed last week?

JH: Oh yes. Nothing has changed on that front.

RS: In that case I can get it going within the next 24 hours.

JH: Good. Can you email it and snail mail a copy?

RS: Yes, we can do that.

JH: I look forward to receiving your quotation tomorrow afternoon then.

RS: Sure thing. Let me check I have all the details: yes, I have your card — right here, with address and everything.

JH: OK.

RS: Thank you for the good news. I'll be in touch.

JH: Goodbye for now.

RS: Bye.

DISCOURSE ANALYSIS OF THIS TEXT	
Type of situation	Telephone call
Participants	Representative of the supplier Representative of the buyer
Sequence of events (Text functions)	Greetings Introductions Social language Introduction of the problem Treatment of the problem (alternate strategies) Summary of the measures decided upon Pre-closing act(s) Closing of the call
Style of situation	Informal business register
Forms of politeness	Social contact Reference to previous contacts Offering favours Referring to next meeting/contact/improvement Easy-going suggestions instead of demands
Features of language	Set telephone phrases Short sentences Clear requests Plenty of confirmation
Other factors	Brief and clear sentences

ANALYSIS OF A COMMUNICATION SITUATION

Work with your own team. You will receive a text from your teacher of a genre typical of business communication. First skim through the text and avoid looking at details. Focus on the main events happening in the communication. Write down the typical features of the text in the grid below. Be prepared to report your findings to the class.

Genre	Typical features of international business communication in the text
Type of situation	
Participants	
Sequence of events (text functions)	
Style of situation	

Forms of politeness	
Features of language	
Other observations	

4.5 Consolidating one-to-one routine communication exchanges

In this category we will deal with the situations presented in Part D of the profile. We will present activities that derive from the situations described. Since the foreign language course in our case is to prepare learners for actual workplace communication in their field, they have to be closely modelled on situations that might happen in the workplace. Creating scenarios is a way to achieve this for more complex situations. Di Pietro (1987: 41) defines a scenario as 'a strategic interplay of roles functioning to fulfil personal agendas within a shared context'. By a strategic interplay, we mean that several human beings interact, sharing the same context, i.e. situation, while pursuing different motives for the conversation. Participants in scenarios take over roles in the context and try to achieve their conversational aims (Di Pietro calls this 'personal agenda' (1987: 47)), bearing in mind the conventions of the interaction situation. The outcome of the communication situation is usually open. The following example for two participants has been taken from Di Pietro (1987: 47f.):

1   You have been assigned to write an important report. It is due in the boss's office tomorrow. However, if you could have an additional day, it would be a much better report. Prepare to discuss the matter with your boss.

2   A meeting with an important client has been pushed up from tomorrow to this afternoon. As a result, the report being written by your assistant is needed today rather than tomorrow, as originally planned. How will you encourage your assistant to speed up the writing of the report without endangering its quality?

When we take a good look at the situations and the snapshot in Parts D, E and F of the CEF Professional Profile, we can see that the situations and therefore a large number of potential scenarios are already there. What remains to do is to assign roles to the participants and make sure they know about the conversational aims they want to achieve. The discourse-type and the medium for the communication situation (e.g. email, telephone call) has to be determined and instructions for learners need to be formulated. In some cases, language support needs to be given.

The first situation in the Mechanical Engineering profile takes place in the office. The project manager gets a call from a machining workshop. The project manager and her designer (the mechanical engineer) had previously designed equipment for a web-dryer and done the drawings for it. The caller, the client from the machining workshop, wants to speak to the project manager responsible for the drawings in order to get some additional information on the drawing. Therefore he sends a message with the information he has available on the product. The project manager forwards the information to the designer, the engineer, who has to get back to the client on the phone to provide the requested information.

The situation is fairly clear and there are several learning tasks that could result from the scenario. We start with the layout of the fax that is forwarded to the engineer as this is a text-type that the engineer has to be familiar with regarding contents and layout. The simulated phone call between the engineer and the customer from the machining workshop follows. The outcome of the conversation is clear in the two cases presented below: the exact information needs to be provided so that the customer can continue manufacturing. Therefore the phone call that learners will be asked to simulate in pairs will be fairly stereotypical, but in a positive sense. After all, the most frequent situations are to be used for learning tasks here.

Activity 4.5.1 Responding to a call from the machining workshop

Learning activity description	Phone call from a client from the machining workshop with follow-up email to be written
Professional challenge	Routine communication exchanges such as this are in no way insignificant work, despite what the word 'routine' might imply. A significant number of companies include customer-orientation, or customer focus as part of their primary vision. Therefore, the technical person closest to customer interface is a key agent to produce good customer experience. Firms measure customer satisfaction and customer experience in their regular customer surveys. Customer experience has also been recognised as having a correlation with company profitability and performance. Thus the engineer in this customer interface is contributing significantly to the key metrics of company performance. This makes it important to ensure that 'routine exchanges' are satisfactory, and preferably excellent, for the customer.
Communication challenge	The communication challenges of an encounter such as this are as follows:

- Contacts like this are frequent and locating the right order, the right company and the right person in one's own company is vital: therefore backgrounding in the encounter is important. It is important to know who in one's company has the best knowledge.
- Customer experience is important; therefore, it is important to recall any previous contact, ask about past service, compliment on good procedure, confirm that everything is running smoothly, make the client feel served.
- It is important that the company keeps its promises despite any time and resource constraints.

Language aims	

- Reacting to a request from one's supervisor
- Conducting a business telephone call as exemplified in the discourse analysis of Activity 4.4.1 (greetings, small talk, introduction, etc.)
- Becoming aware of the communication requirements (politeness, etc.) in a supplier–customer relationship

Procedure	Learners are told that they are going to role play a real situation based on a description given by a professional engineer. They are given the following information: *A client of the engineer's firm is a machining workshop based in Sweden. The client has some queries for a project manager at the firm.*

Learners are then given a copy of the client's email (*Sample business email* below). After clarifying the context and the situation, learners are assigned A or B. A is Sami, the engineer responsible for the drawings and B is Tomi, the Swedish client. Learners are given the relevant role card (see below) and then asked to role play the phone conversation. Feedback and reflection on the activity and communication situation follows.

The teacher introduces the situational context of this professional communication. The professional challenge and communication challenge content from the start of this activity is used for this. For less advanced learners, a revision of the text-type 'business emails' might be appropriate.

The teacher provides learners with the email, and then the context is clarified. Leading questions might be:

- Why has the client contacted the engineering firm?
- What action does the client want the project manager to take?
- What preparation will the engineer need to do before replying to the client?
- If you were the engineer, how would you contact the client (i.e. fax, email, phone) and why?

The teacher divides the learner group into pairs and provides them with role cards (below). If possible, learners use real telephones or (if not) they sit back to back so that they cannot see each other, as in a real telephone conversation. Learners then exchange partners and roles, so that each learner has an opportunity to play the role of the engineer.

During feedback, learners are asked to reflect upon what they felt the critical success factors were for the communication situation. A comparison can then be made between the suggestions of the learners and those suggested by the professional engineer in the profile:

- clarity of the question
- sufficient background details correct

Teacher input	The teacher
	• introduces the situational context of this case
	• shows the sample business email and makes sure all understand why it is sent
	• divides the class into pairs and provides them with role cards (below)
	• asks them to simulate the telephone call, all at the same time
	• asks learners to exchange roles
	• asks one or two of the pairs to repeat the case again, with the others listening, and then gets the class to discuss the solutions.
Learner output	• Discussion of sample business email based on a frequent communication situation
	• Role play of telephone conversation
Learning outcomes	The learner
	• learns to react spontaneously during a telephone conversation
	• practises commenting on the success factors of a frequent professional communication situation
	• builds confidence in dealing with telephone calls.
Evaluation	Teacher feedback and peer assessment on role-played situations; might also be done in small groups evaluating each other's performance.
Language level required	B1–B2; in-service and pre-service learners
Preparation and materials	Copies of the *Sample business email* and a role card for every learner
Duration	Introduction time: 5 minutes Analysis of email: 15 minutes Role play and reflection: 25 minutes
Remarks	More advanced learners could be asked to write the email message themselves first, starting from key words to help them.
Suggestions for follow-up work	The situation can be extended into a more complex situation, e.g. by having another email from the client stating a problem related to the details given. The problem must then be fixed on the telephone.

SAMPLE BUSINESS EMAIL

To   : info@suomi-solutions.fi
Sent   : Monday, 28 April
Subject   : Web-dryer WD-505

Dear Sir or Madam

We placed an order with your company for drawings for our new equipment (product number VL-13) for web-dryer model WD-505. When we started manufacturing this week we noticed that there seems to be a problem with measurements in the drawing. Please contact me asap to check some details of the drawing. I have enclosed the customer details below.

Yours faithfully

Tomi Wadell

Client: FPM Paper
Product number: VL-13
Year/week: 2006/20
Project number: 328
Revision number: 02
Designed by: SAA-EM
Checked by: SAA-EM
Approved by: CEM-SA
Program: CATIA

Filed in: S/webdryers/EM
         FPM Paper
                Specialists in pulp processing machines
                Gjuterigatan 5
                SE-55111 Jönköping
                Tel. +46 36 10 10 10
                Tomi.Wadell@fpm-paper.se

Role card A: Sami

You are Sami, the designer from Suomi Solutions Ltd. You have made the drawing for equipment for web-dryers used for drying paper. Your project manager has given you a fax with the request to contact the customer.

Check the request carefully and apologise for any mistake you might have made (see some measurements from the drawing below). Offer to be of assistance any time.

Rotating disk measurements:

inside disk diameter: 1256 mm
outside disk diameter: 2453 mm
rotating disk diameter: 293 mm

Role card B: Tomi

You are Tomi, the project manager of the Swedish company FPM Paper. Your company has been commissioned to build a web-dryer and you have just started work on it. However, you have found a problem in the drawing. The diameter given for the rotating disk seems to be much too small – it is 29.3 mm only. There must be a flaw in the drawing.

Before you make any serious mistakes in the workshop by wasting material and time (you are a bit behind already), you decide to call the engineering company that did the drawings for you, Suomi Solutions in Finland. You do not know who is responsible for the problem, so you have sent the information with details of the drawing as a fax message.

Prepare to be called by the person in charge and phrase your request politely. You need the information urgently for production to run on time.

Activity 4.5.2 Telephone and email

Learning activity description

Several brief telephone calls to look for green light suppliers, in order to be able to draw up a quotation

Professional challenge

Sami Salmi, the design engineer, needs to send a number of emails to investigate sources and search for a supplier of green lights for the processing system. The standard red light is part of the original system delivered to the US customer. The telephone calls go to potential suppliers and the email to the customer.

Here, as in Activity 4.5.1, customer experience is important. Though the customer has clearly given incomplete information, forgetting to mention that US law requires a green indicator light rather than the red one used in the current system, the style of the emails needs to be considerate and kind. It is a not infrequent problem that a customer placing an order does not necessarily think of all the details needed that might impact on the drawing-up of a quotation.

Communication challenge

- To become aware of the complexity of quotation drawing, which requires that all specifications are clear in respect of the components needed, their subcontractor delivery times and prices. This impacts on the pricing of the quotation.
- To become aware of the communication requirements in a supplier–customer relationship in written communication

Language aims

- Learning about the email genre: style, greetings, closings, backgrounding, security requirements on data put in emails
- Learning about the telephone genre, as in Activity 4.5.1

Procedure

Learners telephone several prospective clients in order to find out which of them could supply the green lights they need for the US customer. Sami has used the services of the following companies before, so it is likely that he would start with these:

FLG Electronics, Brad Wernecke
Metravib, Liu Hong
Texelco Ltd., Dominick van Heugen

When they find one, the learner writes the quotation to the poultry-processing plant, with delivery, price and installation information.

A poultry-processing plant in the USA urgently needs a modification to their processing line. By US law, signal lights on automated lines indicating GO must be in green, whereas the processing line installed at the plant currently has a red signal. The US firm therefore needs to be sent a quote from an engineer for changing the colour of the signal lights. The quote is needed urgently and is to be sent by email.

Learners are presented with the following basic details of the case (which may be written on the board or distributed as copies):

Client:	*Maple Leaf Pharm*
Client address:	*1801 W. Taylor St, Chicago, IL 60612*
	+1 312-413-7704
Client contact:	*Jack Cloud (jack.cloud@maple-leaf.com)*
Requires:	*Push-button signal indicator (green)*
Product no.:	*7856855*
Estimated cost:	*$124.95 (P & P included (express mail))*
Engineering firm:	*TZ Engineering, Satamakatu 53,FIN-67900 Kokkola, Tel. +358 6 8242 400, Fax +358 6 8242 460, E-mail: info@tz-engineering.com*

Learners are given a copy of the *Quotation template* (see below) which they have to complete, using the information they have been given. They will have to formulate brief emails asking for the measurements of the button and the type of machine it will be used for.

Teacher input

The teacher
- introduces the situational context of this professional communication, using the professional challenge and communication challenge content from above and procedural information
- if necessary, revises the features of a quotation, providing the list of details to the learners
- directs attention to the missing measurements and the lack of information on the type of machine for which Mr Cloud is ordering, the push-button signal indicator
- asks pairs to simulate the telephone interaction, either back to back or using telephones.

Learner output	• Making a telephone call • Writing an email for quotations • Completing a quotation form
Learning outcomes	The learner • gains confidence in making telephone calls, including good backgrounding information • practises writing emails • practises drawing up quotations.
Evaluation	Teacher feedback and evaluation of telephone and email communication
Language level required	B1–B2; for both in-service and pre-service learners
Preparation and materials	Copies of the details (if applicable) and of the *Quotation template* below for each learner
Duration	Introduction time: 5 minutes Telephoning time: 20 minutes Email and quotation-drawing time: 20 minutes
Remarks	To simulate more details of the business case, the teacher could provide the learners with a sample of the company's catalogue and price list – here it could become obvious that there are several types of push-button signal indicators available, depending on their use.

QUOTATION TEMPLATE

Quotation No. 6832/10	
NAME OF COMPANY:	ADDRESS:
TELEPHONE NUMBER: ( )	QUOTED BY:
EMAIL ADDRESS:	WEBSITE:

Item #	Description of item	Quantity	Unit price	TOTAL
			TOTAL BID PRICE:	

DELIVERY TERMS:

PAYMENT TERMS:

INSTALLATION:

For further information, please contact me at:

Telephone: Cell Phone:

_____
Signature

Activity 4.5.3 Keeping appointments

Learning activity description	Written negotiation activity requiring an agreement on a date and a time for an installation process
Professional challenge	In this situation, a slaughterhouse requires an engineer to oversee the installation of an automated processing line. Dates and times for supervising the installation need to be arranged and confirmed. For this client, installation must take place overnight only.
Communication challenge	Appointment confirmation is often done either by email or by telephone confirmation, in this case email. Email writing challenges the writer to give enough background information about the case and events that have occurred before the contact. A second challenge is to manage to communicate friendliness and politeness, even though email is a tool for quick messages. The third challenge is to use a style that is informal enough not to make them formal letters. The teacher may remind students on features of email communication before the task. Repetition is a key to good email writing. If one mentions a point of time, this needs to be repeated and confirmed to make it 'an agreement'.
Language aims	• Learning about the email genre, politeness in email, salutations, pre-closings, closings • Using language for confirmation
Procedure	Learners are told that they are going to reply to an email from a client based abroad. They will need to make arrangements for a visit to the client to supervise the installation of some machinery. Learners are then divided into pairs and given a copy of the client's email (see *Appointment confirmation email* below). In pairs, learners are also each given a page from one of the diaries of the two professionals (see *Diary page: Hans, Diary Page: Mirja* below). In pairs, they role play the telephone call and find a suitable date and time for the installation process on-site.
Teacher input	The teacher • introduces the situational context of this professional communication, using the professional challenge and communication challenge content from above • if necessary, reviews the phrases for fixing appointments • provides the learners with the information sheet for availabilities and asks them to conduct the interaction back to back or using a telephone • provides feedback and language terms for the activity.

Learner output	• Role-played telephone conversations • Follow-up email
Learning outcomes	The learner • gains confidence in making telephone calls, including developing negotiating skills • gets practice in writing routine emails (if applicable).
Evaluation	Teacher feedback and evaluation of follow-up email (if applicable)
Language level required	B1–B2
Preparation and materials	The teacher and learners should be familiar with Situation 6 in the Mechanical Engineering profile (Section 3.2, p. 70); copies of the *Appointment confirmation email* and *Diary pages: Hans/ Mirja*, one set per pair
Duration	Introduction: 5 minutes Telephoning time: 10 minutes Writing time: 10 minutes (if applicable)
Remarks	Learners can be asked to write a confirmation of the installation date to the client as a follow-up activity.

APPOINTMENT CONFIRMATION EMAIL

From: Hans van de Groot <vandegroot@meatprocessing-groot.be>
To: Mirja Kantelinen <kantelinen@suomi-engineering.fi>
Reference: Installations for slaughterhouse in Ghent

Dear Ms Kantelinen,

Thank you for your communication and your offer to come to supervise the installation at our plant in Ghent. After confirming with our production manager, we would be able to stop the night shift for the time of the installation. However, we cannot possibly stop production in the two remaining shifts, i.e. from 6 am to 10 pm. So the installation would have to be done during the night shift in week 25. As you said in your previous mail, it would take approximately one shift with two mechanics on-site. We would like you to confirm the date of your visit, so that we can make arrangements.

Best regards,

Hans van de Groot

Diary page: Hans

Wk 25
Mon - giant KFC order due 6 pm
Tue
Wed
Thu - no mechanics available
Fri - no mechanics available

Diary page: Mirja

Wk 25
Mon
Tue
Wed - public holiday
Thu - holiday
Fri

4.6 **Making use of complex simulations to mirror authentic workplace communication**

Simulations in this category are inspired by Parts C (context information) and E (demanding situations) in the profile. Each of the tasks in this section is related to the same demanding communication situation reported on in Part E of the Mechanical Engineer's profile. It is worth observing that the difficulty experienced in a situation is not always caused by language only. The reason for difficulty may be the fact that there is a lot at stake. The speaker may be short of expertise. The counterpart may not understand the speaker or his or her logic, or vice versa. It may be that the counterpart has such demanding attitudes that the speaker has difficulty in coping with him or her. Moreover, problems are tackled in very different ways in different cultures. The situation may occur unexpectedly, for example someone may have to step in to do a full morning's work as an interpreter without having time for any preparation. Speakers without much experience may find having to cope with certain situations in a foreign language stressful. Sometimes talks may last so long that a speaker may find it difficult to maintain his or her concentration in a foreign language context (Huhta 1999: 107).

The needs analysis shows that the broad background to this situation is a very common one. Representatives of a foreign client have shown interest in an engineering firm's product and have travelled to the engineer's home country to be given a full presentation of the product and to negotiate terms.

Activity 4.6.1 Meetings and negotiations in business

Meetings and negotiations play a significant part in most workplaces and this is true for those of mechanical engineers as demonstrated in Part C of the profile (*Dealing with expert and client contacts in meetings and negotiations, including unexpected face-to-face interactions* under *Communication situations* and the *interaction situations* of *meetings* and *negotiations* under *Text- and discourse-types*) and in Part E (*Situation 2: Negotiating with public authorities*).

The proposed activity combines many learning interests: learning about meetings and negotiations and interaction in general, about relevant record-keeping and reporting practices and active participation. The activity is time-consuming: it use 8 hours of class time, which can be further increased by asking students to produce slides for use during the reporting stage, minutes of meeting, memos and materials and to communicate about the results of the case. However, judging from the comments of students who have completed this project, the activity is well worth doing. This simulation has been tried out in several classes over many years, and works well.

Learning activity description	Meetings and negotiations in business
Professional challenge	Business is conducted in collaboration with various groups of people, on informal or formal terms, but mainly informal. The progress of these encounters much depends on how well the subject matter is prepared and the extent to which the selected group of people are aware of the aims and are capable of moving forward. Meeting and negotiation skills are seen as management skills, and they are vital for any professional's progress.
Communication challenge	The effectiveness of informal meetings depends on how well they have been prepared for. Therefore, those in charge should make informal meetings resemble the structure of formal meetings, with an agenda (minimally a shopping list on scrap paper), a nominated record-keeper (someone to jot down points) and a memo (email to inform everyone about the points agreed on). If a chair has not been nominated, the leader in charge will make certain that all of this happens and that progress is being made.

Language aims

- Identifying different types of meetings
- Giving constructive criticism to peers
- Using meeting and negotiation language
- (Gaining confidence from seeing themselves present on video)

Allowing only two hours for teacher input may not seem much time, but experience has shown that increasing teacher input to four hours does not add to the learning: the learning takes place during the simulations and the discussion and during the evaluation discussions after the simulations.

Teacher input

The teacher

- divides the class into teams of four persons again, so if there are 24 students, for example, there are six teams: A, B, C, D, E and F. The first three teams (A, B, C) simulate a meeting (which is the easier genre), the remaining three a negotiation.
- allows two hours of lectures on meetings and negotiations and includes examples (e.g. showing a video clip of a meeting) especially if the group is heterogeneous and has a mixed skills level
- gives participants two to three weeks to prepare
- arranges a series of 30-minute simulations, followed by peer evaluation (see worksheets below). If possible, the simulations should be videotaped.

For the discussion, see 'Evaluation' details below.

Procedure

The teacher prepares the two introductory lectures and starts by asking the following questions:

How many of you have attended a work / an association / any meeting? Who was present? How long? Why was it convened? What was decided? What was your role?

The teacher then draws a mind map on the board about meetings based on what they say.

Lecture 1 (1 hour) to include the following: what are meetings? (typically in-house, informal, order predictable); language of meetings (introduction of the terminology of formal meetings). Learners could perhaps listen to or watch a meeting taking place.

Lecture 2 (1 hour) to include the following: what are negotiations? (typically two parties with different interests, informal/ formal, order unpredictable); negotiations language (setting the atmosphere, suggesting conditions, proposing, making concessions, compromising, agreeing).

Learners are provided with good ideas on how to choose and prepare the simulation. Part E of the profile provides two options. Other suggestions for meetings:

- Weekly in-house departmental meeting (if you have a learner with experience of such a meeting who can describe how it runs)
- Introductory meeting with a buyer and a potential seller (of a web service, for example a device or system)
- Planning meeting between a product manufacturer and client

Some suggestions for negotiations:

- One of the situations described in Part E of the profile
- A simulation where a sales department has sold a system to China with a shorter delivery time than normal (12 weeks). The negotiation on meeting this order is conducted between the sales department and the production department (more employees, contacting summer trainees, discussing with employees on extra work, perks)

Learners are advised to look at models in books or on the Internet, or to simulate a situation they themselves have experienced at work. Those who have no work experience will need special help or perhaps even written dialogues of meetings found in coursebooks. They are allowed to use precisely the same set-up, but need to expand it to a 30-minute meeting.

We have experimented with a number of closely described cases, but this way of giving a loose idea seems to work better as it allows learners to choose a situation they are comfortable with and are willing to do. Giving out existing cases does not allow for variations in learners' level and interest. If one or two groups fail to find one, then the teacher could give them an existing case.

Learner output

- Preparation of a 30-minute simulation in a team of four learners

NB: Everyone needs to be an active participant in the simulation.

Learning outcomes

The learner
- gains confidence in being able to cope in a demanding situation
- practises interacting in a meeting/negotiation situation
- improves facilitation skills
- gains an awareness of the importance of positive feedback and feedback giving in general
- learns about different types of meetings and their applicability to different purposes
- learns about the characteristics and practices of meetings and negotiations
- carries out professional communication in a meeting and negotiation
- practises drawing up professional reports, memos and minutes related to a meeting (this is optional).

Evaluation

To structure the evaluation discussion, it is wise to use a peer evaluation tool. The peer evaluation sheets are given to learners. At the beginning of each simulation, learners should be nominated to focus on observing different parts of the simulation: some should be nominated to comment on points 1–3 in the peer evaluation sheet, others to comment on 4–5, and the rest to give personal feedback to each individual.

It is useful to introduce a rule of peer evaluation: before a commentator may say anything critical, he or she must find two or three positive points first. This is essential to support everyone's positive identity building.

Learners should not use the third person, e.g. *He did not look at the person he was talking to.* The feedback tends to become more diplomatic if feedback-givers speak directly to the person they are evaluating: e.g. *You could have looked more at the person you were talking to.*

Language level required	B1–C1; for both pre-service and in-service learners
Preparation and materials	B2-level learners do not necessarily need models for meetings and negotiations. Less experienced ones need good examples of meetings and negotiations, either as texts or on video, so the teacher should look for them in coursebooks.

- A slide of the *Summary of meetings and negotiations* (see below)
- For weaker students, an example dialogue of a meeting and a negotiation from any coursebook
- Copies of the *Peer evaluation sheets*, one for meetings and one for negotiations, for each student in the group
- Name cards

Duration	

- Teacher input: one hour on meetings, one hour on negotiations
- Two weeks for students to prepare
- Three hours for meeting cases (30 minutes meeting for teams A, B, C, followed by evaluation and discussion); three hours for negotiations cases (30 minutes negotiation for teams D, E, F, followed by evaluation and discussion)
- 20–30 minutes for simulation + 15 minutes to evaluate and discuss times 6 teams = 6 x 45 minutes
- In total eight hours of class time, with one lesson lasting 90 minutes.

This time is well worth spending. If the simulations are video-taped, two more hours will be needed. Only a very short piece of each simulation should be shown; learners can look at the complete videos during self-study time or at home.

If the simulations are being used as an oral examination, learners should be told that the meeting must be of at least 20 minutes in length or it will not generate enough input by each participant. To make it of this length, a meeting can include presentations of background organisations, product information and other typical introductory content. Learners must explain their roles at the beginning of the simulation (organisation, titles, name cards for the table, field of business, etc.).

Remarks   Learners should limit their choice of the type of meeting to a professional one in a workplace community which provides suitable roles (e.g. supplier/client/auditor/principal/employer/employee) rather than one, e.g. a meeting to plan a trip to take in their free time, which may result in informal student chit-chat.

It may be surprising to devote such a lot of course time to this activity. However, given all the elements of learning it offers, it is worth it, especially as this activity allows the learner to choose the simulation precisely from his or her own experience and interest area, which promotes the specificity of English for professional purposes as well.

If it is not possible to devote this amount of time to the activity, then it is a good idea to include presentations in this simulation as well. Two groups should give the presentation. However, this makes the task significantly easier for learners, as the difficult part of communication is having to interact in an unpredictable situation. For this reason, it is worthwhile finding time for the whole activity.

Although it is rare for this activity to fail, it is possible that weaker learners may be unable to do it. In such circumstances it is useful to set up a simulation where the group of four are at a helpdesk and have to respond to callers. For example, if the learners are studying software engineering, two learners could call the helpdesk for advice and the other two play the role of the IT people who have to either solve the problem there and then or forward the problem to an expert, who does some more research and solves the client's problem. It is thereby also possible for such learners to learn about interaction within their limits.

Suggestions for follow-up work   Watching video recordings gives a good opportunity to have a lesson on body language in business.

Learners can also be asked to send in agendas and memos or preparation documents to the teacher.

SUMMARY OF MEETINGS AND NEGOTIATIONS

	Meetings	Negotiations
Nature	formal/informal; brainstorming; briefing; discussion; can also include phases of negotiation	resolve deviating or conflicting interests; can also include phases of meeting
Purpose	pooling ideas; planning; sharing information; evaluation; monitoring process; making decisions; scheduling work	testing ground; learning the counterpart's stance; communicating own views; reaching progress
Typical documentation	agenda; oral reports presented as introduction (slides) to discussion; written reports prepared for introduction; minutes of meeting kept during the meeting; minutes of meeting (formal) or memo (informal) sent after meeting; release or memo sent to a distribution list	invitation (no agenda); planning documents; documentation on negotiation targets; memo sent to stakeholders
Roles	chairperson secretary experts (in charge of reports)	two or more parties, represented by one or more persons
Terminology	formal meetings: set phrases used related to changes in the agenda, election of officials, making of proposals, seconding of motions, proposing of voting, announcing voting informal meetings: variety of style	dependent on degree of familiarity and company/field culture

PEER EVALUATION FORM: MEETINGS

Meeting by: _____

Evaluated by: _____

1. Contents Were the contents real and authentic? Did all members have a thorough understanding of their role? Were the issues dealt with thoroughly enough? Did the meeting stay coherent? What was the purpose of this meeting? Were decisions made? What was decided? What was not decided? Was progress made?	
2. Planning, timing Did all members contribute actively and productively? Had the preparation been done carefully? How long was the meeting?	
3. Culture Which cultural aspects came up in the meeting? Were there any problems caused by similarities/differences of culture – national culture, work culture, professional culture? How were they resolved?	
4. Documents Were an agenda, minutes and/or reports produced? Were they adequately used? If not, why not? Were they professional/adequate in this case?	

5. Chair A Role – realistic, constructive? Planning? Logical? Jumping from item to item? Democratic/Dominant leadership? Did he or she involve everyone efficiently? Facilitation*? Summarising? What follow-up measures were decided?	
6. Secretary B Role – realistic? Did he or she do all a secretary should do? Planning? Taking accurate notes? Facilitation?	
7. Participant C Role, views – realistic? Active/passive participation? Way of presenting? Facilitation?	
8. Participant D Role, views – realistic? Active/passive participation? Way of presenting? Facilitation?	
Comments:	

* Commenting or agreeing on others' views, continuing from another person's statement, summarising, complimenting, suggesting compromises, looking for solutions, keeping tension low, being constructive.

PEER EVALUATION FORM: NEGOTIATIONS

Negotiations by:

_____

Evaluated by:

_____

1. Contents Were the negotiations real and authentic? Were the roles of each member clear to all? Was the setting and purpose clear? What were the negotiations issues? In which points was agreement found? Were follow-up measures decided upon? What were they?	
2. Planning, timing Did all members contribute actively and productively? Was the contribution democratic or did one person dominate? Did all have a clear role? Who kept records? Did the parties have a strategy?	
3. Culture Which cultural aspects came up in the negotiation? Did they have an impact on what happened? If so, how were these resolved?	
4. Atmosphere How was the atmosphere established? How was trust established? By small talk? Did everyone contribute to establishing a good atmosphere? Were any impolite or disrespectful expressions used? How did they influence the meeting?	

5. Party X / Person A Role – area of specialisation? Realistic, constructive? Planning? Participation active/passive? Logical sequencing and linking? Facilitation*?	
6. Party X / Person B Role – area of specialisation? Realistic, constructive? Planning? Participation active/passive? Logical sequencing and linking? Facilitation?	
7. Party Y / Person C Role – area of specialisation? Realistic, constructive? Planning? Participation active/passive? Views expressed? Logical sequencing and linking? Facilitation?	
8. Party Y / Person D Role – area of specialisation? Realistic, constructive? Planning? Participation active/passive? Views expressed? Logical sequencing and linking? Facilitation?	
Comments:	

* Commenting or agreeing on others' views, continuing from another person's statement, summarising, complimenting, suggesting compromises, looking for solutions, keeping tension low, being constructive.

Activity 4.6.2 Comparing cultures

Activity 4.6.2 can be used stand alone or as a preparatory activity for Activities 4.6.4 and 4.6.5, as they all reference a specific business situation. Sequencing activities will result in a complete business case. In this particular situation, a South Korean company has shown interest in purchasing a palletising robot system from a mechanical engineering firm in Finland. A delegation from South Korea arrives and is given a tour of the premises. On the same occasion, the sales engineer presents the potential product /project to the delegation and answers any questions its members might have. After the deal has been struck, arrangements need to be made as to the payment, and then the robot needs to be installed on-site in South Korea. Any problems that might occur must be solved by the engineer, who is responsible for the project.

This situation requires a comprehensive range of skills that an engineer will require for English use and provides a rich source of activities for the ESP course. The whole scenario can be turned into a real task that is simulated from beginning to end, or isolated features of the situation can be simulated, depending on the learners' needs.

Learning activity description	Reflecting on cultural similarities and differences; considering different business cultures
Professional challenge	Cultural awareness development stands as one of the key development areas of training surveys conducted by Human Resources (HR) departments in international companies. At the same time, it is a demanding area for development that may be approached in different ways. There is a strand of the dos and taboos approach, applied in many practical business books, focusing on one country at a time. The German Landeskunde tradition suggests a deeper dive into the culture, through knowledge of history, geography and customs. The anthropological approaches of Hall, Hofstede, Trompenaars and many others suggest the use of common variables prevalent in all cultures whereby any culture can be looked at: time, context, power distance, semantic systems, non-verbal language. A language programme for professional purposes always needs to focus on the issue of culture in one way or another, irrespective of which approach the teacher chooses. This activity offers one suggestion.
Communication challenge	This activity raises awareness of cultures and potentially gives the learner tools to think about cultural aspects (individuals and collectives, speed, noise, silence, distance, language) and our understandings of culture (guesses, stereotyping, facts, feelings, prejudices, assimilation). In business a wise communicator takes the other parties into account, considers adapting to the client's culture and respects the client's way of doing business.
Language aims	• Practice in formulating assumptions and giving reasons for them • Putting cultural knowledge into words

Procedure	Learners are told they are going to think about culture in the workplace. In class, learners are asked to suggest whether or not they believe in a national character and to suggest typical traits for their home country (i.e. Finnish learners describe what they think are typical Finnish characteristics). They are then asked to say how true (or not) they think these traits are.
	The teacher tells the class that business culture(s) in South Korea have been exemplarily chosen for the activity. Learners are then given copies of the worksheet *Culture comparison: South Korea* (see below). The teacher takes the learners through the activities in the order presented on the worksheet. A Hofstede-based analysis for several countries can be found at www.cyborlink.com.
Teacher input	The teacher • introduces the situational context of this professional communication, using the information from the Professional and Communication challenges above • gives a brief explanation of the activity before conducting debriefing in plenary.
Learner output	• Reflection on the concept of culture(s), starting from learners' own cultural frame of reference • Discussion of assumptions based on learners' cultural knowledge of differences and similarities in business cultures
Learning outcomes	The learner • develops an awareness of different business cultures in general • gets to know details of Korean business culture(s) • builds discussion skills
Evaluation	Teacher feedback on discussion skills
Language level required	B2, for both in-service and pre-service learners
Preparation and materials	The teacher and learners should be familiar with Situation 1 in Part E of the Mechanical Engineering profile (p. 70); copies of the *Culture comparison: South Korea* worksheet for each learner (see below)
Duration	30–40 minutes
Suggestions for follow-up work	This activity can be a preparatory activity for Activities 4.6.4 and 4.6.5. Sequencing activities will result in a complete business case.

CULTURE COMPARISON: SOUTH KOREA

Work in pairs. Look at the following statements (1–8) and decide if they are generally True (T) or False (F) for the business culture in your society.

1   When someone gives you their business card, it is normal to read it slowly and carefully as a sign of respect for the person. It would be rude to only look at it quickly as you put it away.

2   It is more appropriate for women to wear skirts rather than trousers for both business and social events.

3   Business relationships have to be built up first, so you should not expect a significant result when you meet a new business partner for the first time.

4   It is acceptable for a senior executive to be a few minutes late for a meeting or appointment.

5   Nowadays, it is more normal for employees to consider their own personal needs and interests before loyalty to the company they work for.

6   If you can control your emotions and remain calm in difficult or stressful work situations (i.e. you do not complain in a loud voice, you do not show that you are angry or upset, etc.), you will gain respect and status with your colleagues and other business partners.

7   Making a sound by sucking in your teeth is a way of showing other people that you think there is a serious problem or saying you don't agree.

8   Asking for a cigarette break in the middle of a long meeting or presentation is not acceptable.

Activity 4.6.3 Interaction about a process

Part of a mechanical engineer's role is to describe how a particular system works and to deal face to face with client queries and feedback. This can be a challenging experience for engineers as they may not be able to predict what questions and concerns the client may have. These aspects of an engineer's working life are commented on in Part C (*Context information*) and Part E (*The most demanding situations*).

The following activity gives learners an opportunity to think about the nature of the situation, to prepare for it and finally to rehearse it. In making predictions about the requirements and demands of this communication situation, learners are also introduced to the concept of active listening. For a non-native speaker, active listening practice in English is not self-evident. This activity is also useful for reminding learners that most communication situations involve dialogue rather than monologue and that they should be prepared to deal with participation from the 'listener'.

The input session needs to focus on two themes: how to present a process in an interesting manner, and how to function as an active listener. The learners are given the task of interacting in a situation between a process expert and a client, i.e. a face-to-face encounter. The aim of the communication is to get to know each other and familiarise the client with the relevant process. Monologue presentations (which are too easy) are strictly forbidden: the students are allowed to speak *only* for a sentence or two before the client is given a chance to comment, ask or compliment.

Learning activity description	Communicating about a process interactively
Professional challenge	This activity helps the engineer interact in a common situation of information exchange around a process. Typically the process presenter is in an expert position to promote the process and the counterpart persons are to be convinced of the qualities of the process.
Communication challenge	This activity was designed specifically to fight a cultural imbalance between expected communication modes. In this case, when a Finnish engineer communicates about a process, he or she normally prefers the monologue mode that allows the speaker to present the process all in one go, perhaps answering a few questions at the end. The Anglo-American tradition favours interaction, where each party contributes and the listener has a chance to influence the amount and type of information about the system. A focal area of this activity is therefore to make participants interact and use active listening techniques of commenting, complimenting, rhetorical questions and informative questions and, at the same time, keep the interest level high.

In a situation like this, the expert often represents the supplier or manufacturer side and the listener often the customer or purchaser side. A logical process description includes initial small talk, overall view of the system, initial stages of process, sequenced stages, stopping for details by client interest, final conclusion and answering questions. It is good to illustrate this process with some examples. Active listening concerns frequent commenting, compliments, rhetorical questions and informative questions.

Language aims

- Using active listening tools consistently:
  Commenting (*Yes, I see, that's right, Why not …*)
  Complimenting (*What a huge area! Looks like a park to me.*)
  Rhetorical questions (*Really, all these years? Are you serious?*)

- Sequencing a process presentation logically, including:
  initial talk
  overview
  steps in order
  wrap-up
  smooth transitions from one phase of the conversation to the other
  inviting questions

Procedure

Before starting the activity, learners need to search for an illustration of an interesting process or system in their field to bring in. The learner needs a slide (or at least be able to do a drawing on the board) to show the process, such as paper production, packaging line, software production (Waterfall or Scrum method), testing procedure, installation procedure or any related technical process.

The teacher introduces the subject early on in class and reminds learners to bring a slide of a process or system to class. The teacher gives a lecture (45–90 minutes) to demonstrate how a process is presented in a structured manner, how active listening can be a significant part of this interaction, how cultures may expect different kinds of presentation and how to do active listening.

The class is also introduced to the scale (see the *Interaction assessment scale* below) which will be used by the class to rate (on a scale of 1–5) how successful the learner's performance was, in terms of delivering either a monologue (1) or a full dialogue (5) and mark them on the scale accordingly.

Learners then prepare a dialogue of 10 minutes in pairs for the next lesson, where one learner is an expert (e.g. a product engineer) and the other is a visitor (client) who knows nothing about the product and is interested in learning more.

In the next lesson the class listens and gives feedback to the expert as to how well he or she was able to communicate interactively and listen and respond to the visitor's interest. They also give feedback on how well the visitor participated in the interaction. This class feedback is done using the *Active listening log* (see below).

The teacher draws the scale on the board, for the class to measure the extent to which the interaction was either monologue or dialogue.

Teacher input

The teacher
- asks learners to find a slide about a process a week or two in advance
- gives a lesson on interaction and the importance of listening to each other (talking about a process; active listening). For weaker learners, show an example.
- asks learners to prepare a 10-minute interaction between a process expert and an interested visitor
- (a week later) conducts 10-minute pair simulations in front of the class
- uses evaluation tools at the end to create a discussion (*Active listening log* and *Interaction assessment scale* on the board).

Learner output

- Bringing in a slide illustrating a process or a system
- Practising the dialogue in a pair
- Demonstrating the interaction in class (10 minutes)
- Marking active listening utterances in a table and reporting on the number of these made during the interaction
- Giving peer feedback and identifying monologue/dialogue quality in classroom discussion

Learning outcomes

The learner
- gains an understanding of cultural differences concerning turn-taking
- increases his or her ability to be fully involved in interaction using active listening techniques, the best outcome being that the process presenter and listener roles become blurred
- practises communicating about the process clearly, logically and professionally.

Evaluation

Peer evaluation is an essential part of this activity. In a group of 20, two members (who have just finished their dialogue) are asked to keep records of how many comments, compliments, rhetorical questions and informative questions were used, using the active listening log below. Two other members are asked to assess whether the listener on the one hand and the presenter on the other hand promoted good interaction, using a scale of 1 (monologue mode) to 5 (dialogue mode).

This is not something that the teacher necessarily needs to make a note of, but is used rather as a clear learning process for all in the room. After a dialogue the teacher asks first for the records of the active listening functions used (e.g. Kari made three comments, only one compliment, used no rhetorical questions but asked seven informative questions). Then the two other learners are asked to assess the pair's performance, positioning them on the scale on the board as described above.

You will find that after several pairs of learners have performed their dialogues, the quality of all the following interactions will keep improving. This is called progressive learning.

Language level required

B1 or above; suitable for both pre-service and in-service learners. In-service learners appreciate this activity very much, as they get to use their workplace expertise in a natural setting.

Preparation and materials

Learners have to find a process in their field (from packaging lines to automated production) to discuss with an interested visitor in the company (the teacher additionally needs two/three slides of processes in case some learners forget to bring any); a copy of the *Active listening log* for recording the statistics for active listening (this can be one list that circulates).

Duration

• Approximately 45 minutes' teacher input about the activity before presentation week, depending on group size and depth of analysis
• 2 x 90 minutes' class time for a group of 24 students

Remarks	This activity is especially good for classrooms where learners come from different disciplines and where the expert knows a lot and the listener only a little about the process or system.
	Learners give very useful feedback for this activity by ticking the *Active listening log* (see below). Some learners have commented that this was the first time they were able to understand the meaning of interaction in practice.

At the evaluation stage, the teacher asks the student whether the communication was more of a monologue or dialogue. The teacher marks the estimate of both the active listener's and the process expert's style of communication either as closer to the dialogue mode or the monologue mode. Sometimes the expert does not allow any chance for interaction, but continues with a monologue.

The pair interactions start improving as learners recognise how the process expert has a responsibility for allowing time for the active listener to react and comment, and participate in the communication as a contributor.

This activity becomes interesting if the teacher asks two students to give feedback to the pair, one to the process presenter, the other to the active listener. The following table is used for keeping track of how interactive the situation becomes.

ACTIVE LISTENING LOG

Learner	Number of comments (*Ah, I see, That's right, Sure ...*)	Number of compliments (*How clever! I bet you know the details.*)	Rhetorical questions (*Really? 10 000, did you say? You mean first?*)	Informative questions (*What is your capacity, exactly?*)	Other

Needs Analysis for Language Course Design © Cambridge University Press 2013 **PHOTOCOPIABLE**

170   Needs Analysis for Language Course Design

INTERACTION ASSESSMENT SCALE

Draw the scale below on the board. Ask the learners to mark on the scale to what extent they identified the observed interaction of each pair as monologue or dialogue. Mark the process description above the arrow and the active listening below the arrow. Pairs to be labelled A, B, C, etc.

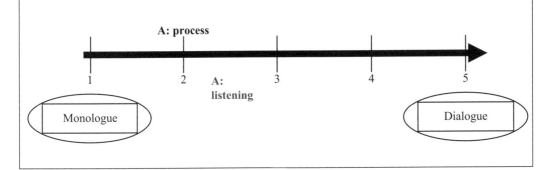

Activity 4.6.4 On-site troubleshooting

This activity represents an instance of the everyday necessity of solving problems of current clients, as described in Part C of the profile. It involves acknowledging a problem and negotiating a solution to the client's problem – in this case a problem with deadlines for an installation.

Learning activity description	Acknowledging a problem and negotiating a solution in terms of installation deadlines for a client
Professional challenge	Customer experience (CE) is produced as a result of successful encounter in situations such as in this activity where practical scheduling questions are dealt with. If CE is satisfactory or, better still, exceeding expectations, this customer will return to the same supplier again and again, establishing a sustained relationship of customer loyalty. This makes a simple question such as this scheduling event not only routine but important for company profitability, as loyal customers can be the key 'cash cow' of a company, bringing in a flow of revenue each year.

Communication challenge

This situation involves an unexpected complication in the installation, namely miscalculation of space, or a planning problem, or miscommunication of the space requirement to the customer.

In such 'bad news' situations, it is essential that the problem be solved without causing any hard feelings. It is a natural human tendency to resort to blame, but finding the scapegoat does not really solve the problem.

In good communication the following steps often work:

- Report the problem, acknowledge it and apologise (even if you are not sure whether the fault is yours or that of your company).
- Suggest options for solutions.
- Implement the solution as promptly as possible and report meticulously the progress/delay of the implementation to those in charge and discuss remuneration at a later stage.

Language aims

- Acknowledging a problem, communicating it and offering a solution
- Negotiating a solution with a communication partner

Procedure

Learners are presented with the following workplace situation:

An engineering firm has a won a contract to install a palletisation system for a client based in South Korea. The installation will take five working days. Meeting the agreed deadline for installation is very important to the client. However, on the Monday of the week in which installation begins, the project engineer quickly discovers that the client has not allocated the 3 x 4 metre space necessary for the control unit of the robot. A suitable space can be cleared from the production hall, but the engineer learns that this cannot be done for another three days (in other words, until Friday) because another machine is taking up the space needed. The project engineer has arranged to meet the production manager of the client's firm to find a workable solution that will not involve extending the originally agreed deadline and that will not generate too much extra cost.

After the situation has been described, learners are asked to work in pairs to come up with a solution that will be satisfactory to both the engineer and the client. Learners are then asked to change partners to form new pairs. Learner A takes the role of the engineer and learner B the role of the production manager and they role play the situation. When this first role play has finished, each learner A finds a new partner B and roles are reversed, so that every learner has had an opportunity to play both roles. The activity concludes with discussion and feedback and a summary of the best solutions.

Some possible solutions are:

- Once the space is clear on Friday, mechanics work double shifts, thus catching up on time.
- Extra workers must clear out the hall, thus generating extra cost.
- Everybody gets on as before and hopes for the best.

Teacher input

The teacher

- introduces the situational context of this professional communication, using the professional challenge and communication challenge content from above
- advises learners to conduct the role plays, all pairs at the same time
- monitors role-playing pairs and takes up language points for the debriefing phase if desired
- conducts the debriefing session with learners presenting their best solutions
- conducts in-class discussion of best solutions in terms of practicability, impact on customer relationship, etc.

Learner output

Negotiation practice with partners, taking on the role both of the engineer and of the client

Learning outcomes

The learner

- gains confidence in conducting more complex negotiations
- practises goal-oriented communication.

Evaluation

Teacher feedback of role-played negotiations, teacher and peer feedback of best solution presented.

Language level required

B2–C1; pre-service and in-service learners

Preparation and materials

None

Remarks

This activity can be stand-alone or done as a follow-up activity to Activity 4.6.2.

Activity 4.6.5 Driving a hard bargain

Learning activity description	Giving a persuasive presentation about a potential robotics line
Professional challenge	Negotiations belong to the daily activities of project engineers who need to present their company in a positive light, emphasising in particular that the company will be able to deliver solutions to individual problems the buyer might have. This case is about palletising solutions that are needed by companies who wish to improve their packaging lines. The ultimate goal lies in speeding up the manufacturing operation. In this activity, the product consists of motor blocks which come off the production line in crates.
Communication challenge (Global, institutional and organisational knowledge; participant knowledge; social action knowledge)	In the following activity, a detail from Situation 1 from Part E of the profile (p. 70. *The most demanding situations*) provides the main focus. A Finnish engineering firm was required to pitch to a Korean client. In addition to presenting the details of the robotics line, the sales engineer respondent was required to negotiate terms for the project, including dealing with custom specifications, the cost and the schedule for manufacture and installation. The activity below requires learners to focus on business negotiation within the context of mechanical engineering.

As for the negotiation, some of the vital issues to consider include:

- establishing a good atmosphere (small talk, good shared feeling)
- establishing common ground (same information, same documents, same level of knowledge about the case)
- practising good listening (asking questions, summarising heard views)
- sales talk (consolidating company credibility, product benefits and performance)
- suggesting solutions
- ceding ground where necessary, but securing profitable sales (price, payment schedule, realistic delivery time, realistic installation scheme, practical maintenance programme).

Language aims
(textual knowledge)

- Developing the discourse for negotiations (if you analysed a negotiation in Activity 4.6.1, it is easier to assist in language matters for negotiations)
- Negotiating an outcome (linguistic functions such as establishing a starting point (e.g. a sent email), requesting details, agreeing to a compromise, proposing solutions, compromising, suggesting concessions, declining concessions, as well as more general functions of commenting, asking questions and summarising)

Procedure

The general situation is outlined to the learners, based on the following elements from the profile summary (see also p. 70):

Communication situation: giving a persuasive presentation about a potential robotics line to a foreign client in English
Location: office
Persons: project engineer, group of potential buyers from South Korea
Details: In this case the engineer was selling a project; this sometimes involved sorting out problems such as scheduling and detailing of contents.

Learners are asked to predict what they think might be the most challenging aspects of the communication situation described here. The profile can be drawn on as a source of suggested answers to this question:

Challenge factors: new experience, attitudes of the listeners, presenting in a foreign language

Learners are told that they are going to role play a negotiation based on this situation. The class is divided into groups of four (with optional groups of five if the number of learners doesn't divide neatly into four) and assigned a role, A–D (and optional E). Learners are given some preparation time. All learners with the same role are asked to get together before the role cards are distributed. Learners are asked to read through the situation to make sure they understand their role and then discuss what they might say during the role play. Learners then form groups of four or five members, each with different roles. Each group then role plays the situation. The teacher monitors and then conducts feedback with the whole group.

Teacher input	The teacher • introduces the situational context of this professional communication • uses the information of professional and communication challenge above • explains the content of the role cards as well as the aim of the activity thoroughly.
Learner output	Role-played negotiations (in small-group setting)
Learning outcomes	The learner • gains confidence in conducting more complex negotiations • practises goal-oriented communication.
Evaluation	Teacher feedback on role-played communication situation (whole-group activity); debriefing
Language level required	B2–C1
Duration	Explanation of context and activity: 10 minutes Rehearsal: 30 minutes Role play: 10 minutes Feedback and debriefing: 15 minutes
Preparation and materials	The teacher and learners should be familiar with Situation 1 in Part E of the profile (p. 70); enough copies of each of the *Role cards* A–D (see below) for each group of four; at least one copy of role card E if a group of five is necessary.
Remarks	Note that these role cards have been designed specifically for the learners for whom the Mechanical Engineer profile was developed, and therefore include references to concepts which would be unknown (e.g. *palletising solutions, a robotics line for motor blocks which come in crates, stacking*) and tasks which would be impossible (e.g. *You must try to give as much detailed information about the schedule and design of the robotics line as you can, and answer any technical questions the Korean delegates may have*) for learners who do not have specialist domain knowledge. In this sense, this activity may challenge the learners' professional as well as linguistic competence. It will therefore be necessary for anyone using this activity with engineers in a different specialisation to either adapt the details or be prepared to incorporate an additional stage in which the learners familiarise themselves with this area of machine automation and the specific vocabulary associated with it.

This activity also presents the opportunity to explore aspects of intercultural communication more thoroughly. Learners playing the role of the South Korean delegates in the original Finnish context for which this activity was designed were also challenged to think about differences in contrasting communication styles (e.g. Mr Lee's aversion to open disagreement or refusal). See Activity 4.6.2: *Comparing cultures*.

Suggestions for follow-up work   The activity may be used as a stand-alone or it can be the main focus of a task involving Activities 4.6.2 and 4.6.4, both focusing on Situation 1 from Part E of the profile.

Role card A: Ari Malinen, Finnish sales director of SIMC Corporation

Character profile

You are **Ari Malinen**, the CEO of SIMC. Your company is the market leader in Finland for palletising solutions, and you do a lot of business with companies from South-East Asia. The Korean customer is important for you as the business relationship with other customers in South-East Asia depends on that client. You have asked **Mirja Mäkinen**, your sales engineer, to provide the technical details; you are in charge of financial matters. The Korean customer, represented by **Mr (Min-Sik) Lee**, is interested in a robotics line for motor blocks which come in crates.

Key information for the negotiation:

- A standardised line costs about €230,000 with some leeway for reduction (around 5%). Your annual commission will be greatly affected if you exceed this limit of 5%.
- Customised solutions do not have any rebate options.
- In previous dealings with customers from South Korea, you have noticed that the standard term of delivery is ex works and the payment is usually done via letter of credit with 20% downpayment and two further instalments of 40% (after delivery and after completion).
- You may offer other kinds of concession such as after-sales service, warranty issues, etc.
- Success with this customer will help you consolidate access to the South Korean market.

Role-play task

You must try to accommodate the customer as much as you can, but do not forget that 5% is your limit as far as reductions are concerned or a prolonged payment time.

Role card B: Mirja Mäkinen, sales engineer at SIMC Corporation

Character profile

You are **Mirja Mäkinen**, a sales engineer for SIMC Corporation. Your company is the market leader in Finland for robotic palletising solutions, and you do a lot of business with companies from South-East Asia. A South Korean delegation, led by **Mr (Min-Sik) Lee**, is interested in buying a palletising robot for crates. Your company sales director, **Ari Malinen**, has asked you to be present as you are most familiar with the requirements of the product.

Key information for the negotiation:

- The standardised robotic solution takes four weeks to manufacture and two or three weeks to install.
- The standardised robotic lines are capable of stacking only one type and size of load.
- Any customisation requires new engineering drawings to be made and this would extend the manufacturing time.

Role-play task

You must try to give as much detailed information about the schedule and design of the robotics line as you can, and answer any technical questions the Korean delegates may have.

Role card C: Mr (Min-Sik) Lee, Korean, senior executive

Character profile

You are **Mr (Min-Sik) Lee**, a Korean delegate and senior executive. You need a palletiser for crates (really for motor blocks which come in crates), as a turnkey project. You have travelled to Finland to meet with **Ari Malinen, sales director** of SIMC Corporation, whose company is the market leader in Finland for robotic palletising solutions. As the most senior member, you will lead the negotiation on behalf of your delegation.

Key information for the negotiation:

- You are used to a business culture in which it is unacceptable to say 'No' directly. Any disagreement you have in the negotiation with the SIMC Corporation team must be expressed indirectly.
- Your budget is limited to €200,000.
- The palletisation solution must be installed and ready to go in six weeks – you are expecting a huge order which you will only be able to fulfil if the solution is in place.
- A letter of credit is acceptable.
- Your assistants, Mr Kim and Mr Jung, are in charge of the details.

Role-play task

You must not exceed your budget and must have the machinery installed within the time limit.

Role card D: Mr (Dong Wook) Kim, Korean, junior executive

Character profile

You are **Mr (Dong Wook) Kim**, a junior executive, reporting to **Mr (Min-Sik) Lee**. You are responsible for processing the details of the order once the deal has been struck. Therefore you are interested in the details of the payment and the schedule.

Key information for the negotiation:

- The budget is limited to €200,000.
- The palletisation solution must be installed and ready to go in six weeks from completion – you are expecting a huge order which you will only be able to fulfil if the solution is in place.
- A letter of credit is acceptable.
- The terms of delivery and the exact terms of payment are your responsibility and so are of particular importance to you.

Role-play task

Make sure you understand all the details; if necessary ask a lot of questions.

Needs Analysis for Language Course Design © Cambridge University Press 2013 **PHOTOCOPIABLE**

Role card E: Mr (Hyung Joon) Jung, Korean, junior executive

Character profile

You are **Mr (Hyung Joon) Jung**, a junior executive, reporting to **Mr (Min-Sik) Lee**. You are responsible for processing the details of the order once the deal has been struck. Therefore you are interested in the details of the payment and the schedule.

Key information for the negotiation:

- The budget is limited to €200,000.
- The palletisation solution must be installed and ready to go in six weeks – you are expecting a huge order which you will only be able to fulfil if the solution is in place.
- A letter of credit is acceptable.
- The terms of delivery and the exact terms of payment are your responsibility and so are of particular importance to you.

Role-play task

Make sure you understand all the details; if necessary ask a lot of questions.

Needs Analysis for Language Course Design © Cambridge University Press 2013 **PHOTOCOPIABLE**

4.7 **Conclusion**

In this chapter we have illustrated that a variety of activities can be created using the contextual information of a CEF Professional Profile. The tasks and activities presented above are based on one sample profile, the higher education profile for Mechanical Engineering. With the help of the information provided in the other sample profiles in the appendix, it is easily feasible to create similar tasks and activities for the other professional fields. Customised profiles for your particular professional background can also be created; methods for creating your own CEF Professional Profile will be discussed in the following chapter.

5 Creating your own CEF Professional Profile

Chapter overview

In this final chapter, we will give guidelines for creating your own Professional Profile. We will give guidance on how readers can carry out their own needs analysis for their particular fields, using a template of our Professional Profile as the starting point.

The Professional Profiles created as a result of a series of projects (reproduced in Appendix C) cannot of course cover all the fields and all the professions for which language courses might need to be designed. The nature of these profiles also means that they are at times rather specific and so may not fit every professional context. Therefore a need for a profile particular to the reader's purposes might arise.

Against this background, we would like to highlight once again the importance of needs analysis prior to course design in ESP. To plan and teach tailor-made courses, the teacher (or the organisation that the teacher works for) has to make sure that he or she has a detailed background knowledge of the professional activities in question. Therefore, creating a new Professional Profile might make the teacher's job of designing the course syllabus much easier. A situation may arise in which a teacher has to teach an ESP course in a subject area with which he or she is unfamiliar. A Professional Profile provides an answer to the question of what has to be taught.

Creating a profile does require the investment of a certain amount of time and effort, but the results are worthwhile. New profiles can be re-used within an institution and updated or modified for specific variations in a particular context. In the case of an individual teacher (such as freelance language trainer of working professionals), the profile can be used for several courses over time and, with regular updates, can also function as course material.

In this chapter, we will:

- outline the procedure for creating a profile
- give hints on different, manageable data-collection procedures for a new profile
- provide a template profile with guiding questions and key words to fill in
- briefly summarise how to apply a newly created profile to the design of an ESP course.

A copy of a profile template is given in Appendix A and sample questions as well as advice and hints on collecting data for each of the six parts of the profile are summarised in Appendix B.

Creating a Professional Profile involves five basic steps:

1 considering the depth and coverage of your profile
2 defining the target group
3 collecting data
4 processing the data for the profile
5 applying the profile

We will discuss each of these steps further in Sections 5.1–5.4.

5.1 Considering the depth and coverage of your profile

The basic template for creating a Professional Profile should be treated as a flexible set of guidelines rather than a strict set of rules. The template has been designed for use in a wide range of language and communication training contexts, and variations in personal, institutional, regional, national and professional needs will all have an influence on how a particular profile is created. Some course designers may be creating a profile for an institution where the students are required to use a particular coursebook or else where the students have to follow an established curriculum. Others may find themselves responsible for creating a completely new course in a company which is sponsoring language training for the very first time. A flexible approach also makes it possible for the profile to be revised and updated over time, thus ensuring its contemporary relevance to the professional group the document serves.

As a first step, we recommend that the course designer review the examples of the profiles in this book (Chapter 3 and Appendix C). The profiles are somewhat different as they vary in their depth and coverage of the specialist field. The Mechanical Engineering profile (Chapter 3) was the first to be produced and as a result is more comprehensive in scope than the others. For example, the researcher of this profile (Huhta) has clearly marked the elements in the profile that will constitute the core content of the course, whereas other researchers have not done so. Some of the profiles place greater emphasis on certain parts of the profile than do others. Górska-Poręcka's professional profile, created for Master's students at the University of Warsaw (Appendix C, pp. 229ff.), extensively explores the communication situations in Parts D and E. This level of detail was a response to the results of the needs analysis, involving interviews with legal professionals from five different law firms. A review of the profiles shows how the researchers made practical decisions about the depth and coverage of the needs analysis conducted for the profile.

The scope of the profile can of course be extended if two or more researchers agree to collaborate, as in the case of Hämäläinen and Järvinen's profile for registered nurses (Appendix C, pp. 219ff.). Not only can the quantity and diversity of the data collected be increased, but the different views and opinions of researchers and informants may also improve the quality of the profile as well as different forms of interaction between them.

To summarise, we suggest:

- reviewing existing profiles (Chapter 3, Appendix C or see also http://www.proflang.org)
- considering the restraints and resources (in terms of number of researchers, time, budget, institutional requirements, etc.).

5.2 Defining the target group

The next step is to define the target group for the needs analysis which will inform the profile. The course designer's final decision may be complicated by several factors. Budget reductions or falling student numbers may force a university language department to merge students with different needs into one group (for example, putting biology and engineering students into the same language programme). Conversely, a programme of expansion or an increase in enrolment may prompt an institution to diversify and specialise (for example, by splitting a business English course into distinct language programmes in finance, management and marketing).

Creating a profile can be a time-consuming endeavour, so we advise starting with a broad target group. The profile's flexibility means that the original document can be amended or extended to accommodate more specific needs or institutional changes, such as those we have already mentioned. A broader definition of the target group can be approached in four ways. The course designer can look at an occupational group (e.g. engineer, lawyer) or a sphere of professional activity which may be relevant to one or more professional domains (e.g. design engineering, EU law). The other two ways are perhaps less common but equally useful in ESP course design. These are to define the group by function or by organisational unit. A target group defined by 'function' may include those who fulfil specific tasks, such as auditing or research and development, whereas those grouped by 'organisational unit' may include those working within a specific department of an organisation, such as in a university admissions office or a company's human resources department.

The course designer's final choice will be influenced by the specific circumstances. A teacher who has been asked to prepare an English course for airport staff from different departments (e.g. baggage handlers, immigration, security) may find it more useful to focus on a function such as customer services. This could be a useful focus for communication training across the different occupational roles of the students in the group. A teacher preparing a course for undergraduate medical students may, on the other hand, be more likely to focus on doctors as a broadly defined occupational group.

Once the target group has been defined, the course designer needs to think about who the key informants for communication in the professional field will be. The choice of informants will depend on circumstances; it can take time to arrange interviews with professionals working in the field, for example; if the proposed course is running for the first time, there will be no precedent to work from. So while not everyone in the list below may always be available, key informants for the profile may typically be drawn from the following groups:

- Companies and other organisations in the target professional domain
- Teachers who have taught the programme in previous years
- Subject area specialists such as university lecturers, professors and researchers
- Professionals in the field attending adult education courses part-time at the course designer's language centre or school
- Graduate students from previous years now in work.

The ideal situation is to gain access to professionals currently working in the field. However, it can be understandably difficult to secure an interview, and time is likely to be limited to one or two hours at the most (especially if the respondents are helping the researcher in their own time). Former students now in work may be more inclined to give their time, especially if they know the researcher or his or her institution.

To make the most of the time you have with a professional, it is important to go to the interview prepared. Talking to colleagues with experience in this field of ESP and subject area specialists (some of whom may have worked in the profession before becoming a lecturer) can help to narrow the focus of your questions and means the professional doesn't have to waste valuable time explaining basic background points to the researcher.

5.3 Collecting data

As we noted earlier, the profile can be created by an individual or a team. Although more data can be collected by a team of researchers, we would like to recall what we said in Chapter 1: it is not the quantity of data that matters but rather the quality. To arrive at a thick description of complex communication situations in the workplace, the amount of information gathered (quantitative data) is less important than having data which is reliable and takes into account different contextual factors.

There are different procedures for gathering data for a new profile, some of which will be more suitable to a course designer's situation than others. In the suggestions below, we will assume a single researcher creating a profile for mechanical engineering undergraduate students and working alone. However, it should be easy to adapt the procedures below to suit other circumstances.

A useful step in the data-collection process is for the course designer to do a thorough search of the Internet for online sources of information. Naturally, the quality of information about the target profession will vary considerably, and where the purpose of gathering such information is to explain the basics of a specialist subject to a non-specialist audience, it is worth remembering that while an online encyclopedia (such as Wikipedia) may be useful in giving the researcher an overview of the background to the professional domain, it may not be suitable as the basis of a course syllabus or as a resource for course materials. For the profile, the researcher needs information on the industry, on the kinds of roles and positions occupied by the professional group and what kinds of communication situations professionals most commonly encounter. For this information, searches such as the following may help:

mechanical engineering industry
mechanical engineers careers
mechanical engineering companies
mechanical engineering universities curriculum
mechanical engineering universities syllabus

An industry search can provide useful links to professional associations (such as the Institution of Mechanical Engineers, IMechE) which often include information about professional training and development courses, thus giving the course designer an indication of what professionals do or need to do in the workplace. Careers sites provide detailed background information on the profession and may include profiles of student or working engineers aimed at encouraging newcomers to the profession – exactly the kind of information that can be found in the Snapshot (Part F of the profile). Searching for companies provides the researcher with a list of possible contacts in their area. Listings of companies may also include useful background information on typical activities in the profession, such as we find in the following example from an engineering website:

Specialisation

The installation and removal of electrical and mechanical plant and equipment.

Description

Within the construction, mechanical and electrical services sectors, Machine Movers are the first choice for companies who need fast, reliable professionals for transportation, offloading, rigging, crane hire and installation. Machine Movers can offer a variety of services, including: craneage and hoisting, full method statements and risk assessments, transportation, road closures and traffic management, liaison with police and local authorities, on-site assembly of mechanical and electrical plant, and building services for site installation. We specialise in problem-solving the unexpected and in dealing with challenging projects, installing difficult objects in the most unlikely places.

A detailed syllabus document may give a good idea of what knowledge is needed for coping in the professional workplace. A less detailed course description outlining the general aims of the programme may be less useful for the profile. Searches in all these areas should help the course designer to locate relevant organisations, functions and activities in the field quickly.

Internet searches may also bring up advertisements for jobs in the target profession. Detailed job specifications are useful for describing the requirements, roles and responsibilities for positions in the field, as in the example for an operations manager below:

The Role
* Implementation of prototype control systems into vehicles
* Development of Simulink models and support of algorithm development
* Define requirements and specifications for Mechatronic components: sensors, actuators, connectors, wiring and electronic controllers, and define appropriate test requirements and specifications
* Code generation using Rapid Prototype platforms
* Validate and test of models using MIL
* Project management, including tracking of timing and open issues
* Electronic hardware and software development
* Development of new product concepts
* Support IPR activities
* Act as technical mentor to engineering teams
* Interface with customers and suppliers in order to meet agreed objectives
* Education and Experience
* Minimum Degree in Mechatronics, Electronic, Electrical, Control Systems or Computer Science Engineering
* Significant professional experience preferred
* Expertise in MATLAB/Simulink/Stateflow modelling
* Experience with Rapid Prototyping systems, such as MotoHawk or dSPACE, including code generation utilizing Real Time Workshop
* Experience and understanding of sensors (displacement, pressure, temperature, acceleration) and actuators (valves, air compressors, electric motors)
* Ability to create component specifications and wiring schematics
* Skilled in electrical troubleshooting of prototype systems
* Advanced knowledge of electronic hardware

Knowledge of details like this can be very useful in providing examples of what the needs analyst can ask in any interviews conducted with professionals. In addition to the Internet, job centres and careers advisory services can be good sources of information about the target profession. Data gathered on the industry, jobs and courses for the profession can later feed into Parts A and B of the profile.

Interviews represent another source of data that, in our view, is one of the most important for ensuring that the information in the profile is authentic and up to date. With this type of data collection, it is vital that different types of stakeholders are considered in order to obtain triangulated data (see Chapter 1). Fellow teachers, training supervisors in companies, former students working in the job, university lecturers and experts at the local chambers of commerce, the **Guild of Master Craftsmen** or other professional organisations could be contacted and asked.

A list of potential questions has already been presented in Table 1.2 in Chapter 1 (p. 29). Of course that list can be shortened, added to or altered depending on local needs.

The Professional Profiles themselves can be used with learners in courses or in situations preceding courses, for example while establishing their needs. In fact, asking learners to describe their professional activities and provide details of routine and difficult situations, either before or during courses, is a task to which learners usually respond very well. Here it is important to remember that learners with experience on the job can be considered experts in the subject matter and therefore as perfectly trustworthy and relevant sources of information. When regarded in this way, learners will readily comply with requests to contribute to your profile, thus facilitating a good working atmosphere on the course.

If you can be confident that respondents will return them, questionnaires might represent an additional source of data for new Professional Profiles. Open-ended questions will yield more qualitative data and will be more likely to give insights into the professional background of the respondent. Whenever results of the questionnaire are not clear or raise further questions, a possibility for follow-up interviews would be ideal. This option would provide a further data source. At the same time, it would ensure **communicative validation** of the data provided by the respondent. Communicative validation means that the researcher has ensured that he or she has understood correctly what the respondent meant, and this is another step towards obtaining the thick description we advocated for needs analysis in Chapter 1. Experience with questionnaires, however, reveals that profile information can best be collected by interviews rather than questionnaires. Time and interest may be problems, but a more serious difficulty is that the questions set by linguists are not always well understood by professionals. For example, a question such as 'Which are the most common communication situations for you at work?' may not work at all in a questionnaire. The answer will probably elicit a very general response, such as 'ordinary situations' or one specific example. If the analyst wants to collate a more comprehensive list of genres for the profession he or she is investigating, personal interviews with professionals in the particular field are recommended. This is a direct way of clarifying responses provided by a questionnaire and as such the results of such interviews offer valuable information for the profile.

The data-collection procedures we have outlined here apply equally to all contexts of needs analysis for course design, whether an analyst is working alone or in a small team, or if the context includes a larger organisation and/or if there are enough resources for the researcher to carry out a very detailed analysis. However, when, for example, more interviews can be conducted with a variety of respondents, the chances of obtaining a thick description are higher. In turn the potential of the outcome, the Professional Profile, is likely to be higher in terms of the comprehensiveness of the data.

To summarise, we suggest the following steps for collecting data:

- Obtaining input from teachers with experience in the target profession and adding this to the first draft of Parts A–C of the profile
- Searching the Internet for useful background information on the target profession and using the findings to inform interview questions with professionals

- Making contact with former students now working in the profession and revising the profile content accordingly and/or arranging interviews with professionals (as discussed in Section 5.2)
- Interviewing multiple professionals and deciding which parts of the profile you will concentrate on for each interviewee (the questions in Appendix B provide a basic template)
- Asking your informants to review your interview notes and check them for accuracy (alternatively, you can record the interview and complete the profile later). For research purposes, audio (or video) recording is necessary, but for practical purposes having the interviewer's notes checked by the informant may save time and still serve the practical purpose.

5.4 Processing the data for the profile

Once the data has been collected, it then needs to be processed and the document revised. In this section, we work through the questions which each part of the Professional Profile template has been set up to answer.

The purpose of Part A of the Professional Profile is to provide general background information on the target profession. *Field* is a broad category and is useful for the comparison of the professional communication needs of related professions. A doctor, nurse and social worker may share certain communication situations with each other, but their needs for the same event may be quite different. *Education/Programme* and *Specialisation(s)* are used to describe the academic or vocational qualification the students are working towards as part of their career progression. It is not intended to refer to the details of the language course the profile has been created for.

Degree/Qualifications concern the education the relevant professions require. Often the needs analysis is done for an educational institution for some formal qualifications. Is a university degree necessary? What type of degree is it? Are there multiple pathways to the jobs in the field? What specifications are possible in the field? The section should include the answers to these types of questions. *Language* refers to the foreign language(s) the students need (English, German, etc.) and may also include the level of proficiency learners are expected to have at the beginning of the course.

The information contained in the last three sections of Part A makes the data-collection process comprehensible, traceable and thus transparent to any user of the profile. *Drawn up by* and *Date / City and Country / Organisation* are especially useful in situations where the profile is going to be used by teachers other than the designer of the profile. Knowing the authors of the profile can make it easier to adapt or revise the original for a different context or as circumstances change. Information on the date should include both the date on which the profile was first created but also the dates of any subsequent revisions. Anyone using the profile will then be able to see at a glance how up to date the content is likely to be and whether or not the profile is in need of updating. The other details tell us something about the cultural context in which the profile was created. This may prove very important if a teacher wants to use the profile to design a course for students in a country other than the one the original information was drawn from. So a profile from southern Europe will probably look slightly different from one from eastern Europe. Even within a country, there might be differences between rural and urban areas that could be reflected in the content of the profile. Besides, all communication information is contextual, and therefore it is important to know where the information originated.

The final section of Part A is *Methods used for collecting the information (methods, persons, dates)*. Dates for interviews and other data-collection methods are again useful for showing the contemporary relevance of the information. This section also gives an indication of the types of sources that have been used to create the profile and should be used to answer questions such as: Do we have information from several stakeholders so that triangulation takes place? Are the persons interviewed professionals who actually work in the field and have the latest background information? Are they teachers or lecturers who have educational processes and their teaching objectives in mind? Are they, perhaps, representatives of more general needs, such as administrators in educational institutions or supervisors in companies with their specific viewpoints? Their respective views might reflect different needs – and they might yield considerably varied data. Ideally, there is a variety of different sources to be found in the data in order to achieve the triangulation of sources we advocated in Chapter 1.

Parts B and C are similar in that they both provide a detailed overview of the target profession. Part B contains occupational information about professional aspects of the field and so is not concerned with foreign language communication (as described in Part C). Its function, therefore, is different from that of Part C in that it provides general background information for those less familiar with the professional activities of the job, namely the course designer or teacher.

The first section of Part B (*Typical examples of professions/occupations/jobs*) concerns the types of positions or functions someone in the job holds and the overall fields of activity in which the professional is involved. It answers the questions: What positions do the professionals generally hold? Are they rather in middle management in business, or would they be found in the more technical positions? Are they involved in production, design or sales?

The next section highlights *Typical organisations, companies, communities to be employed in*. These might vary from companies to public authorities via institutions like unions or other job-related services. When speaking of companies, it might be important to note the size of the company as the context of an SME (small and medium-sized enterprise) will be very different from that of a multinational. Questions focusing on the type of organisation or community would have to be asked here, so professional respondents should be asked to describe the size, nature and aims of the organisation they work for in order to achieve varied and comprehensive data.

Typical job descriptions provides an overview of the target professional's field of activity, including the central activities of his or her everyday working life, not only those conducted in a foreign language. This is necessary for a holistic understanding of the communication setting. Note that core activities of respondents from the same target profession may vary.

In the case of mechanical engineers, the core activity of one might be designing systems, whereas for another it might be programming software or selling or purchasing items for others. The questions to ask here could include: What exactly is your line of work? What are, generally speaking, the core activities you perform in your job? What would be considered the most typical tasks in the profession, not only in one specialised area? Only a rough description is necessary as more detailed information on professional activities routinely carried out using the foreign language is provided in Part C of the profile.

Although a more detailed description of the use of the foreign language (or languages) is given in Part C, the final section of Part B is *To what extent foreign languages are needed*. This section addresses questions such as: What languages are usually needed? Could a professional get by without a foreign language? If not, what skills – reading, writing, speaking, listening, mediation (i.e. translation and interpretation) – are generally required to be able to accomplish the necessary tasks in the workplace? What groups of people does the professional use the foreign language with?

Part C of the profile focuses on the foreign language component and should include the most important results of the foreign language needs analysis. It is also the part in which the CEFR is matched with the relevant aspects of the foreign language needs analysis, so filling in the information for the target profession of your profile will yield a comprehensive needs analysis (see Section 2.5 in Chapter 2 for more information). This part of the profile can be divided into *work contexts* and *study contexts* (though this need not always be necessary and was not included in early versions of the Professional Profile template). *Work contexts* highlight the tasks that are carried out in the foreign language in the workplace itself, in other words in the communication situation in the professional context. The *study context* centres on communicative tasks in the foreign language classroom. There might be some overlap when, for example, a situation from the work context is simulated in the classroom. Other activities in the classroom, however, go beyond the professional communication situation, for example when an activity presents companies or examples of texts from the field to fellow learners in the classroom.

The first column indicates the setting for the communication (*Location*). This can vary from the professional's office, a client's premises or workshops to trade fairs or restaurants in which a business meeting takes place. The variety of locations usually reflects the variety of the professional's communication tasks. Typical questions to be answered here are: What are the most important locations for the professional? Would the majority of activities take place in his or her office or elsewhere? Where does he or she meet customers, clients, suppliers, etc.? Are informal events linked to particular places? For example, do brief chats often take place in hotel lobbies or in lifts? Do important meetings and negotiations generally take place on the customer's premises, in public buildings (e.g. at a court of law) or elsewhere? Establishing the locations for the study context will probably be easier, particularly if the profile is created by a teacher already familiar with the study environment. Note that the classroom may not be the only location of the study context. Students working towards a professional qualification (e.g. engineers, lawyers, nurses) may be sent on industrial placements as a course requirement of their studies, and so other locations will play a role as well. The latter are likely to be the same as or similar to work context locations.

Locations are linked to the *persons* involved. Again, it is important to note that *persons* does not mean only individuals, although these of course play a role in face-to-face communication. Other interlocutors such as *communities, companies* and *institutions* have to be taken into account as well. This second column addresses the following questions: What individuals does the professional have business with in his or her everyday working life? And on another level, what organisation or institution does the individual belong to? This determines the nature of the *communication situation* (and the language used). If a professional is on friendly terms with a supplier or a client, then the tone of the conversation is more likely to be informal. However, if the professional has to communicate with an important customer or a representative of a public authority he or she does not know, then the language used will be much more formal and polite. So the nature of the interlocutor is directly linked to the communication situation. This should be borne in mind when drawing up a profile, particularly when summarising frequent or challenging situations in Parts D and E of the profile.

The professional may also communicate with groups of people, such as delegates from a different country on a visit to his or her company or organisations. On the institutional level, communications could involve chambers of commerce, governmental agencies, standardisation bodies, legal authorities or public health authorities, depending on the target profession and the field. Regional differences within a country would also play a role as there might be different codes of practice in use depending on the local business culture. We can see that the cultural aspects involved in workplace communication are sometimes rather subtle, so they cannot be directly expressed in the profile.

The study contexts of the *Persons, communities, companies, institutions* section need to be seen on an *educational* level and a *private* level. Contexts on the educational level refer to communication that takes place in a school, university or training institution. In addition to the teacher and other students, the learner might also come across guest lecturers, either from the home institution or from outside and even from abroad, or exchange students. If the learner's programme of professional education includes an industrial work placement, then we would also see the relevant aspects of the workplace in the educational context. The private level refers to contexts in which a pre-service learner becomes involved in a professional communication while still a student, for instance when an undergraduate student makes a job application while still at university, when he or she meets prospective colleagues and employers during a job interview. Questions related to this part of the profile include: Who does the learner usually communicate with in the context of the educational institution? Is it only the teacher and fellow learners? Are outside guests (e.g. lecturers or international students) invited to class or do they participate in the course? Has the learner completed a placement? Has he or she communicated with professionals in the field when visiting trade or careers fairs? In the private sphere, does job hunting form a part of a learner's activities in the foreign language? Will the learner have to complete part of a job interview in the foreign language?

Communication situations (the third column) is likely to be the most extensive section of this part of the profile. Firstly, communication situations may be quite diverse and secondly, their descriptions will be related to the two earlier categories of location and persons.

Situations can range from informal conversations with colleagues or customers to product presentations or formal hearings at court. They will possibly comprise face-to-face situations as well as mediated (i.e. telephone or email) communication. Different situations will take place in different settings with different interlocutors.

The most relevant situations should be written into the profile in a systematic way, and there are several ways of going about this. Firstly, communication situations can be organised according to the locations they take place in (in which case information in locations and communication situations are linked). This entails finding out what situations the professional is most likely to encounter in his or her places of work, e.g. office, building site, hospital staffroom and so on.

Another way of organising the results of the needs analysis in this section is by activity. In this case, the linguistic function of the situation is made less generic and more specific to the professional context: welcoming visitors, presenting a solution for an engineering problem, apologising for a late delivery, negotiating dates for installing a machine at the client's premises. Alternatively, the information can be organised by interlocutor type (i.e. by the persons, institutions and organisations). In other words, communication situations are grouped according to the persons involved: colleagues, superiors, patients, defendants and so on. Depending on the profession to be described, all approaches have their advantages. It is up to the individual to make choices, while the overall goal is the systematic and comprehensive organisation of the communication situations in the workplace.

Text- and discourse-types are the last category of Part C. They show what kinds of (written and oral) texts the professional encounters and what the linguistic demands are. For some professionals, for example, manuals are important, although the linguistic focus may not always be the same. For others, understanding the text might take priority, in which case reading would be the key skill. Other professionals, an engineer for example, might need to interpret the functionalities of the machine or device that was described in the manual for a customer. For this text- (or discourse-) type, the professional needs to be able to draw on the manual's content to give a process description. Text- and discourse-types are also linked to situations and persons and form the final element of the situational factors that we would like to highlight with our profiles.

Parts A–C of the profile give the course designer important background information on the target profession, taken from a number of professional informants approached for the needs analysis. Parts D and E, by contrast, describe specific cases related by individual interviewees. The information in these sections should be as detailed as possible and, whenever possible, include examples of actual texts used: these could be emails, drawings, patient observation charts, product brochures and so on. Companies are inclined to be cautious about releasing these kinds of texts, so we recommend that you explain why you need copies of the documents and come to an agreement on how you can use them (for example, by agreeing to delete or mask out key information such as a specific name, date or value). This is worth pursuing with your respondent (or the company he or she works for) as the more detail you have, the better the case studies in the profile will be.

Part D presents the course designer with *The most frequent routine situations* in the working life of a professional. Key questions to be asked here are: Would other professionals in the field encounter similar situations? Is the situation applicable to different industries the professional works in or to different functions performed? However, it is neither desirable nor useful to include every frequent situation which requires the use of the foreign language. The situations you choose from your data should be common, of course, but you should also try to identify situations which are suitable for learning. These would include situations which share one or more features of language and communication with other typical events in the target profession. While detail is important, a certain degree of generalisation will be more practical for the course designer as the content of the situations are more likely to be relevant to a wider range of learners.

During the interview with the professional informant, you will need to get a detailed and comprehensive description of the communication situation. You first need to establish the setting, finding out what the main part of the activity is (*communication situation*), where the situation occurs (*location*) and who is typically involved (*persons*). Information about the context should also include a summary of how the situation came about: What is the background to this situation? How is it related to other work activities? What exactly does the professional do using the foreign language? For completing the *Details* section, a good place to start is to ask the informant to describe the sequence of events in the situation. Then you can ask for further clarification of the details within each stage. An example of some interview questions (for mechanical engineers) might be: 'After greetings what does he say? … So he explains the background of when and where the machine element was designed? And then what?' You should try to get as much information as you can during the interview – it is better to have to edit the information at a later date when compiling the profile than to find you don't have all the details you need. It is important that you are able to grasp the situation fully. This is especially true if the profile is being created for other teachers as they are likely to be non-specialists in the target profession. The details of the situation are then given so that the learner (and the teacher) can use the situation as a basis for further discussion and, in the case of the teacher, for designing course activities. A crucial question to be addressed is: What makes the communication successful? In other words, what are the *critical success factors*? Examples of questions to be addressed here are: Does the situation require only an efficient transfer of information, or is it also important for the interlocutors to establish or maintain a good social relationship?

Part E goes on to consider *The most demanding situations*. As in Part D, specific situations reported by the respondents are described in detail, but the situations here give the course designer an idea of what difficulties can arise in the workplace communication of the target profession. These more complex situations also provide a basis for the analysis of contextual factors of this particular situation. The course designer should therefore be looking for situations which provide good models for learning and analysis, but which are nevertheless challenging in their specific details. The situations in Part E form the basis of more complex tasks and activities to be designed for the foreign language classroom.

As with data collection for Part D, it is necessary to elicit a detailed description of both the situation and its context. Although the situation will be more complex, the questions asked are essentially the same as for Part D. That is, you will need to get information about the context (*location* and *persons*) and identify the *challenge factors* presented by this situation. The last point is again of particular importance as it details the critical success factors of the communication from the point of view of the professional involved. The *Details* section will be more extensive here than it is for Part D, so it is useful to begin with a short summary of the event(s) before giving more in-depth information.

Examples of the kinds of activities that could be written for an ESP course were given in Chapter 4. Course activities and tasks based on situations in Part E tend to be linguistically, as well as professionally, more demanding and so are generally better suited to more advanced learners (B2–C2 on the CEFR scale). For example, demanding situations may be the starting point for a simulation in the classroom that encompasses several communication situations. The profile is useful not only for designing the ESP course but as a classroom resource for learners. This is particularly true in the case of Parts D and E, which can be used as input information for role play and simulation. It is therefore worth considering this when writing up your notes for these two parts of the profile. That is, you should include any information that the learners are likely to need to carry out a successful simulation: names of companies, products, problems, solutions, etc. – in other words, all the details learners might otherwise have to invent.

The information in the last part of the profile, the Snapshot, can also be used as a classroom resource with the learners. However, unlike Parts D and E, the Snapshot is usually not based on the data from a single respondent but is taken from various respondents and then collated into the account of a fictitious character whom we accompany during a typical working day. Ideally, the Snapshot should read as a record of a day spent shadowing a professional in his or her workplace. The Snapshot therefore gives an insight into the target professional's routine activities in a linear sequence. The writing of the Snapshot can be approached in several different ways, so we advise you to look at the examples used in the profiles in this book (in Chapter 3 and Appendix C) before writing your own.

To create a new profile, we have included a template version in Appendix A and Appendix B provides a handy summary of the advice and sample questions discussed in this chapter. We would like to remind those wishing to create their own profile that the template should be seen as a flexible document and that the approach should be adapted to your local context. We would also like to encourage you to do research for this, even if it is 'only' small-scale. The important thing is to get started on this!

5.5 **Applying the profile**

Here we summarise how profiles can be used.

1 *Find or create a profile for the target profession.* Profiles for your target profession (or for a related profession in the same field) may be found in this book or by visiting the website including CEF Professional Profiles (http://www.proflang.org). If you cannot find an exact match, then you should consider adapting an existing profile or creating your own.

2 *Review the profile within the local context.* Once you have found or created a suitable profile, you will then need to consider the specific context of your course. For example:

- Institutional requirements: Are students on the course working to a set curriculum? Will the programme have to reflect or match existing descriptions of course content? Are students required to have a minimum level to enter the course? Does the course include formal assessment of some kind? How many classroom contact hours are there on the course?
- Resources: How many teachers are there? Will the course be taught by one teacher or by a team of teachers? What materials are available? How much time do the teachers have to design courses?
- The learner group: Has a needs analysis for the group already been carried out? What are the age(s) and level(s) of the learners? What professional experience (if any) do the learners have?

3 *Design the course syllabus.* Once the local context has been considered, the course can then be designed:

- Select the core content, that is, identify which communication situations and texts are likely to be most relevant to the needs of workplace communication for the target profession and of any course or institutional requirements.
- Consult the learner group. Before finalising the core content for the course, you should ideally give the learners an opportunity to prioritise their learning for the course. This involves having learners review Part C of the profile (Context information) and asking them to suggest which communication situations and texts they consider to be most important.
- Write a course syllabus document. The plan should aim to include a variety of communication events, subject matter and activities. A varied syllabus is in keeping with a holistic perspective on the language and communication needs of the target profession.

4 *Design learning activities and create materials.* Using your course syllabus, find appropriate case studies of communication situations in Parts D and E and the Snapshot in Part F to design tasks and materials which are suitable to the level of the learners and which accurately reflect the needs of the target profession. Chapter 4 presents examples of activities that have been based on profile information.

Materials for the course should, where relevant, make use of any texts and documents supplied by professional informants during the creation of the profile.

5 *Assess and evaluate learner progress.* Assessment and evaluation will depend to some extent on the local context of the course. However, two basic approaches are suggested below:

- Create exam materials using the profile and other professional source material. Learners' knowledge and understanding of language and communication can be evaluated through the content of the profile. Learners can be asked to summarise a part or parts of the profile, or the information in Parts D, E and F can be used as a framework for assessment through role play. Information in Part B of the profile can suggest sources for exam material. For example, an exam task could be to write a covering letter for an actual job advertisement taken from the Internet. In this example, the learner's knowledge of the language is evaluated in the context of a realistic representation of a communication situation which is relevant to his or her professional needs.

- Peer evaluation and peer feedback. Asking learners to comment on each other's progress can be useful in building up an identity for professional communication. Feedback and evaluation from peers can be powerful tools for making a life-long learner reflect on the language and communication skills needed for professional use. Peer feedback encourages and improves a learner's ability to reflect on and analyse his or her own performance and the performance of others in relevant communication situations.

This helps the learner to understand that the use of the foreign language in the workplace is not a discrete skill but one that is integral to the broader context of Language and Communication for Professional Purposes, the focus of this book. A holistic perspective on language and communication will help the learner to build a greater self-awareness of him- or herself as a professional in the field.

Glossary

action-oriented approach   An approach (adopted by the CEFR) that is based on communicative tasks and actions performed in the foreign language.

authenticity   A term applied to content that is realistic, existing and meets the needs of the learner. Authenticity also relates in what 'chunks' the learning takes place, whether single functions or complete communication events (Huhta 2010). It also involves the use of authentic materials and authentic tasks. Authenticity also relates to self-knowledge and to communication between learners, as well as between the teacher and the learner (van Lier 1996: 125).

CEFR   *Common European Framework of Reference for Languages* (also known as CEF). Published in 2001, this document was created to provide a comprehensive description of language learning, teaching and assessment for all languages. Its scales and descriptors provide a description of language proficiency on six levels in order to make language proficiency (and related tests and certificates) more transparent and comparable throughout Europe.

communicative approach   A now mainstream approach to the teaching and learning of foreign languages. It posits that a foreign language is learned most efficiently when embedded in communicative contexts and it stands in opposition to previous approaches, such as audiolingual language learning.

communicative event   An interaction involving a combination of verbal and non-verbal interaction between participants in a specific setting.

communicative practices   Communication conducted by a discourse community of professionals. Discursive practices (e.g. of doctors, nurses and technologists) may be relatively strongly or weakly demarcated (Fairclough 1995), because there may be various sorts of relationships for different purposes of communication.

communicative validation   Determining whether the researchers have understood correctly what the respondent meant, for example by providing interview notes made by the researcher for the informant or asking for clarification in an interview of a point that was raised in a questionnaire/survey or during a previous interview.

content-based learning	A teaching approach in which a particular content is integrated with language learning aims. The content the lesson is based on need not be academic, so content-based learning has proved a popular approach within LSP.
context reliance	Addressing one's thoughts in an indirect manner, being at the same time confident that the recipient can interpret the meaning based on the context in which it is expressed.
Council of Europe	A regional body, founded in 1949 and consisting of 47 member states throughout Europe. Its aim is to develop democratic principles, based on the European Convention on Human Rights.
discourse	A term that refers to language and communication beyond the sentence level, including strategic, cultural and non-verbal aspects of communication (Council of Europe 2001). Discourses are intertextual in that they manifest a plurality of text sources (Candlin & Maley 1997: 203). When associated with some institutional and social meaning, such discourses are at the same time interdiscursive (Candlin & Maley 1997: 203).
domain	A situational environment in which communication occurs, such as in professional, educational, public or private contexts. Discourse practice differs among social domains (mobile communications, banking, law), each of which has its own discursive practice associated with a particular social domain or institution (Foucault 1982; Candlin 2006).
domain-specific language	Language typical of a situational environment such as mobile communications, banking, law. Each domain has its own discursive practice associated with the context.
ecological validity	This type of validity (Cicourel 2007) relates to what extent the teacher succeeds in organising learning activities that increment the competences required by the workplace in realistic units and contexts in the context of classroom practice.
ELP	The European Language Portfolio is a document, closely linked to the CEFR, that was developed and piloted by the Council of Europe. Generally consisting of three parts (language passport, language biography, dossier), its aim is to support the development of plurilingualism and pluriculturalism as well as learner autonomy in order to enhance lifelong learning. There are more than a hundred different versions available throughout Europe.

ESP	English for Specific Purposes. A branch of English that is learned and taught for particular purposes, such as health, electronics or chemistry.
function	Refers to the purpose of the language used for a particular communicative aim, e.g. apologising, contradicting, declaring etc. An important type of syllabus (functional-notional syllabus) is organised around functions and => notions.
genre	A term that refers to the generic resources of a written or spoken communication event with the same purpose of communication and textual organisation in the same setting, e.g. a CV, a meeting or telephone call. Variation of genres occurs both between professional domains and within professional domains.
Guild of Master Craftsmen	The body of experts representing different types of crafts; similar to the chambers of commerce and industry.
holistic	A word derived from the Greek word *holos* (total) and representing the idea that the whole system or person has to be considered and cannot be reduced to the individual parts.
interlocutor	A person who interacts in an oral communication situation.
language-in-education planning	An area of language learning and teaching that focuses on user-related decisions which need to be made to develop programmes and to teach language for specific purposes.
LCPP	Language and Communication for Professional Purposes. Purposeful human interaction typical of knowledge work of professionals. Professional communication involves both communicating as a professional and communicating to a professional standard (Boswood 1999) applied in various communities of practice (Lave & Wenger 1991). The interaction includes the use of verbal and non-verbal communication. LCPP arises from the interests of professional language and communication usage in a second language and serves the purposes of effective language and communication utilisation in professional settings (Huhta 2010: 26).
LSP	Language for Specific Purposes: includes the term ESP and designates a branch of language teaching and learning that centres around language skills for a particular academic subject or vocation.

mixed methodology	Refers to the combined use of methods from the quantitative and qualitative research paradigms within a single study in different combinations, e.g. quantitative methods with qualitative methods dominating the study design. Mixed methodology has become increasingly popular in foreign language research as mixed methods are believed to produce more significant results in terms of quality and scope.
multimodality	A term referring to degrees of certainty in conveying meanings in discourse (Scollon 2001; Ventola et al. 2002; O'Halloran 2004). e.g. *I will/can/may surely/naturally/certainly sign.*
multisemiocity	A term referring to a mixture of meanings intended by different individuals and a variety of interpretations of their messages in discourse (Scollon 2001; Ventola et al. 2002; O'Halloran 2004).
needs analysis	The formal process of establishing the particular (language or language learning) requirements of a particular target group. In this book, the term is used to establish the foreign language needs of different stakeholders in professional communication in the workplace.
notions	Refers to language used to express abstract concepts such as time, space or quality. In language teaching, notions are usually associated with => functions.
organisation culture	The specific collection of values and norms that are shared by people and groups in an organisation and that control the way they interact with each other and with => stakeholders outside the organisation.
professional community context	Conditions where professionals (e.g. engineers, accountants, business specialists) form networks of professionals (communities) to perform knowledge work in social domains (e.g. mobile communications, banking, law).
professional discourse activity	A communicative task that is essential in working life and that is primarily fulfilled through language and communication, as opposed to an activity that mostly requires other professional knowledge and skills.
professional discourse community	Networks of professionals (e.g. engineers, accountants, business specialists) with common goals for knowledge work in an organisation or a part of an organisation. The discourse community typically uses discursive practice associated with the particular social domain or institution.

professional domain	professional => domains (e.g. mobile communications, banking, law) have discourse practices that differ from each other. EU family law is an example of a professional domain. To what extent professional domains differ depends on the plurality of text sources and the association with institutional linkages as well as social meanings.
qualitative research	Research that has a more exploratory function in that it attempts to gain an in-depth understanding of various, often complex, phenomena, such as human behaviour. Qualitative research is limited in generalisability because it usually refers to a smaller sample (i.e. a limited number) of informants.
quantitative research	Refers to the systematic empirical investigation of phenomena and their relationships, with the help of measurement. Often hypothesis-based, results of the measurement process help to verify or falsify the hypothesis formulated.
rhetorical function	A social sciences term for speech acts such as promising, ordering, greeting, warning, inviting someone and congratulating.
second generation needs analysis	A type of needs analysis which is based on the professional task, and *not* on language or genre as the primary unit of analysis. Empirical data and methods are required for the task to be analysed; therefore, e.g. analyst intuitions are not sufficient.
situational communication	Recognising the range of varieties of language use a person has and choosing the appropriate alternative in a particular situation.
SMEs	Small and medium-sized enterprises.
social agency	Capacity (i.e. knowledge, skills and identity) of human beings to act independently and to make their own choices.
stakeholder	In needs analysis, any society, organisation, group or individual that influences or is interested or involved in, or affected by the needs analysis at hand.
stratified random sampling	A method of sampling for a study. In the attempt to have subjects in a study represent the total of a population in the most accurate way, the subjects are grouped to reflect the proportion of the real population. In other words, in a population with 60% of the people under 25, 60% of the stratified sample will consist of subjects under 25.

tenor	According to systemic functional linguist Halliday (1978, 1985), tenor refers to the participants in a communication situation and their relationship.
text-type	A language unit, either written or oral, with a shared purpose (e.g. to inform, describe or negotiate a solution) with a beginning and an end.
thick description	Type of enquiry that seeks not only to explain human behaviour but to interpret its context as well, making such behaviour meaningful to the outsider. The concept was developed by the American anthropologist Clifford Geertz.
triangulation	Triangulation implies different perspectives on a given object of research or on answering research questions. These perspectives can be derived from applying different methods, using different sources of data and different researchers, etc. The combination of results affords a deeper insight on different levels.
VOLL	Vocationally Oriented Language Learning. A term coined by the Council of Europe for language learning that addresses needs in vocational training and at work. It also goes beyond the vocational domain in that its aim is to enable learners to communicate in a foreign language, in both professional and private situations.

Appendix A
Template of a CEF Professional Profile

CEF PROFESSIONAL PROFILE

A. BACKGROUND INFORMATION

Field	
Education/Programme	
Specialisation(s)	
Degree/Qualification	
Language	
Drawn up by	
Date / City and country / Organisation	
Methods used for collecting the information (methods, persons, dates)	

B. OCCUPATIONAL INFORMATION

Typical examples of professions/ occupations/jobs	
Typical organisations, companies, communities to be employed in	
Typical job descriptions	
To what extent foreign languages are needed	

C. CONTEXT INFORMATION

	LOCATION	PERSONS, COMMUNITIES, COMPANIES, INSTITUTIONS	COMMUNICATION SITUATIONS	TEXT- AND DISCOURSE-TYPES
Work context				
Study context				Texts:

D.   THE MOST FREQUENT ROUTINE SITUATIONS

Situation 1.

Situation:
Place:
Persons present/involved:
What is essential to make the communication successful:

Details:

Situation 2.

Situation:
Place:
Persons present/involved:
What is essential to make the communication successful:

Details:

Situation 3.

Situation:
Place:
Persons present/involved:
What is essential to make the communication successful:

Details:

E.   THE MOST DEMANDING SITUATIONS

Demanding situations mentioned by the interviewees:

Situation 1.

Situation:
Place:
Persons present/involved:
Why the situation was demanding:

Details:

Situation 2.

Situation:
Place:
Persons present/involved:
Why the situation was demanding:

Details:

F.   SNAPSHOT

Narrative of a day in the working life of a professional, based on the data available.

Appendix B
Guiding questions for profiles

It is advisable to fill in the parts of the profile that are already known, such as field, qualifications, occupations or contexts, in advance, to speed up the documentation of valid knowledge. Recording the interview is a good idea, as is asking the interviewee to check whether you documented the findings correctly.

Questions relevant to Part A: Background information

The formal qualifications necessary to take up employment in the respective job: Is a university degree necessary? What type of degree is it? Are there multiple pathways to the job? What specifications are possible in the field?

Do we have information from several stakeholders, so that triangulation takes place? For example, are the persons interviewed professionals who actually work in the field and have the latest background information? Are they teachers or lecturers with the educational processes and their teaching objectives in mind? Are they, perhaps, representatives of more general needs, such as administrators in educational institutions or supervisors in companies with their specific viewpoints?

Questions relevant to Part B: Occupational information

What positions do the professionals generally hold, e.g. are they rather in middle management in business, or would they be found in the more technical positions? Are they involved in production, design or sales? Is there any other function they might be involved in?

What exactly is the professional's line of work? What are, generally speaking, the core activities performed in this job? What would be considered the most typical tasks in the profession, not only in one specialised area?

What languages are usually needed? Could a professional get by without a foreign language? If not, what skills (reading, writing, speaking, listening, mediation) are generally required to be able to accomplish the necessary tasks in the workplace? What groups of people does the professional use the foreign language with?

Questions relevant to Part C: Context information

What are the most important locations for the professional? Would the majority of activities take place in his or her office or elsewhere? Where does he or she meet customers, clients, suppliers, etc.? Are informal events linked to particular places, e.g. brief chats in hotel lobbies or in the lift? Would important meetings or negotiations take place on the customer's premises, in public buildings (e.g. at court for law) or elsewhere?

What individuals does the professional have business with in his or her everyday working life? And, on another level, what organisation or institution does the individual belong to?

Questions related to this part of the profile would then be, e.g.: Who does the learner usually communicate with in the context of the educational institution? Is it only the teacher and fellow learners? Are outside guests, e.g. lecturers or international students, invited to class or do they participate in the course? Have learners completed work placements or do they visit trade fairs during which they communicate with other professionals in the field? On a private level, does job hunting form a part of the learner's activities in the foreign language? Does he or she have to complete part of a job interview in the foreign language?

What situations is the professional most likely to encounter in his or her office, on the building site, at a trade fair, in the prosecutor's office, in the staff room at the hospital, etc.?

Questions relevant to Part D: The most frequent routine situations

The exemplary character of situations is achieved when it can be applied to many different contexts. When gathering the data for this section, make sure that the situation itself is suitable for the profile. Would other professionals in the field encounter similar situations? Is the situation applicable to different industries the professional works in and functions performed?

Other information includes a description of the location (e.g. office or workshop? In the country or abroad?) and of the persons present or involved in the communication situation apart from the professional. In other words, what are the critical success factors? Is it about the efficient transfer of information, is it about building up or maintaining relationships, or does the achievement of a compromise play a crucial role?

Questions relevant to Part E: The most demanding situations

This category illustrates challenging professional communication situations. When gathering data for this section, consider the following questions: What kinds of persons were involved in the communication setting? Where did it take place? What made the situation demanding? Was there a language barrier? Did cultural differences cause any misunderstandings or misinterpretations? What kind of communication was there? Written? Spoken? Face-to-face? Did any of these cause problems? Did any conflict arise? How was it resolved?

Questions relevant to Part F: Snapshot

Tell me about your typical working day. What kinds of communication situations does it involve? Written communication? Oral communication? What communication devices do you use? To what extent do you need foreign languages in your communication?

Appendix C
Sample profiles

The following sample profiles have been selected and adapted from the ones developed in the CEF Professional Profiles Project. They are different as different needs analysts have found different elements more useful than others. For example, the Law profile includes stages of communication situations, whereas the Mechanical Engineering profile does not. The number of sample situations varies. This illustrates how the teacher can modify the profile concept to his or her own needs. The profiles in this chapter have not all been trialled, so the abbreviation 'C' for core areas in Part C might be missing in some profiles for this reason.

The full list of profiles that can be accessed on the team website (http://www.proflang. org) at the time of writing are:

Field	Professional profile(s) available	
	for secondary education	**for higher education (tertiary)**
Business	Assistant in export sales Clerical worker	Business administration and management International business
Healthcare and social services		Registered nurse (RN) Registered public health nurse
Law		LLM Law
Technology	Metalwork and machinery	Information technology Mechanical engineering Structural engineering

Here, we reproduce four profiles (one from each field): Business, Healthcare and social services, Law and Technology.

BUSINESS – ASSISTANT IN EXPORT SALES; CLERICAL WORKER – SECONDARY EDUCATION

CEF PROFESSIONAL PROFILE

A. BACKGROUND INFORMATION

Field	Business
Education/Programme	3-year trainee programme: 3 days in the company, 2 days at the vocational college
Specialisation(s)	Basic qualification, specialisations only possible after completion of the traineeship
Degree/Qualification/Occupation	Assistant in export sales Clerical worker
Language	English
Drawn up by	Karin Vogt, University of Education in Karlsruhe
Date / City and country / Organisation	10 May 2006, Karlsruhe, Germany
Methods used for collecting the information (methods, persons, dates)	**Sources:** text analyses and interviews 13 July 2005 Analysis of job descriptions provided by the job centre information service 15 July 2005 Analysis of curricula (job-related, Standing Conference of Ministers of Education in Germany, state specific curricula) and materials (textbooks on the German market) 10 October 2005 Interview with three export sales assistants in a large automotive company in Karlsruhe, Germany 3 December 2005 Interview with an assistant in export sales working in a small steel company 4 April 2006 Interview with a teacher at a vocational school in northern Germany 20 April 2006 Interview with a teacher at a vocational school in western Germany 21 April 2006 Interview with a teacher and teacher trainer at a vocational school in south-western Germany Previous interview data (with assistants or HR managers)

B.   OCCUPATIONAL INFORMATION

Typical examples of professions/ occupations/jobs	Assistants in export sales typically work in multinational companies or companies that are involved in international trade, e.g. in machine construction, automotive engineering; also in smaller companies that have parent companies or their production plants abroad. Assistants in export sales are generally engaged in the processes of international trade, e.g. enquiring and exchanging information about markets / companies, dealing with customers abroad and writing or responding to tenders. They can be found in different departments of a company, e.g. in sales and marketing, purchasing, distribution, cost accounting or human resources.
Typical organisations, companies, communities to be employed in	Examples include: advertising agencies; steel trade; automobile manufacturers; printing, supply chain management, packaging; textile industry Assistants in export sales are to be found in a huge variety of industries and in companies of varying size.
Typical job descriptions	Assistants in export sales typically buy goods with producers or suppliers and/or re-sell them. They are usually involved in international trade, see to cost-effective storage and cater for a steady flow of goods. They monitor the goods on arrival and check stocks as well as order new goods and plan distribution. Assistants in export sales work in companies in numerous export-oriented industries. Their job description includes: • organising the exchange of goods in international trade • corresponding with suppliers and customers worldwide • writing and responding to offers and enquiries • negotiating terms of payment and/or delivery (on the phone, via email or via video conference) • cost accounting (invoicing, reminders, statistics, profit and loss accounts, balance sheets) • purchasing (planning, coordinating, organising, negotiations, placing orders, complaints, monitoring receipt of goods, etc.) • carrying out sales and marketing duties and responsibilities (writing offers, monitoring orders/cases, planning marketing campaigns, key account management, sales negotiations, dealing with complaints) • dealing with minor legal questions in international trade • dealing with customs, banks and tax authorities (filling in export documents and other forms, making customs payments for incoming consignments, dealing with banks, forwarding agents and insurers) • Human Resources (payroll accounting, training schemes, personnel statistics)

Depending on the size of the company, assistants in export sales can accomplish highly specialised tasks in a particular department or can be entrusted with a huge variety of activities. The job advertisements extracts below complete the picture of the requirements of the job:

Fluent French Export Sales Assistant

Our client is a well-established international company looking to expand their European desk by recruiting a new person within the Export Team.

Main responsibilities:
- Customer service (dealing with a portfolio of French & other European customers)
- Export Sales administration
- Organising transport/shipment
- Liaising with production and planning to ensure product availability
- Researching competitors' activities, identifying business opportunities for the European sales team
- Developing existing business (building a good relationship with distributors over the telephone).

This is an exciting opportunity to join a fast-growing European sales team in a varied role. This position encompasses many aspects of customer service and sales administration/coordination.

Candidate's profile:
- Fluency in French & English
- Preferably some previous experience in customer service (business-to-business) or export sales administration, and in a manufacturing environment, although not essential
- Excellent communication & interpersonal skills
- Strong commercial/sales acumen
- Good appreciation of international cultures and attitudes
- Will particularly suit recent graduates or 2nd/3rd jobbers

	Export Sales Assistant A well-established Export Management Company is looking for a Bilingual (fluent/native Spanish) candidate to work F/T (no weekends) as an export sales assistant. *Responsibilities:* • *Data entry and documentation* • *Respond to customer requests for pricing, tracking and support* • *Address problems and errors in a timely manner* • *Communicate with suppliers for general support* *Skills/Attributes:* • *Good typing skills* • *Excellent telephone and customer service skills* • *Computer proficiency with Windows, MS Office and email* • *High level of attention to detail. Reliability, punctuality and consistency* • *Ability to handle multiple tasks in a fast past environment* • *Excellent English and Spanish skills (reading, writing and speaking)*
To what extent foreign languages are needed	Unlike other fields, assistants in wholesale or export sales are expected to use the foreign language, mostly English, at least in direct communication situations with customers, co-workers or suppliers. Their company often functions as a subsidiary, regularly reporting to a parent company abroad. Therefore, the foreign language is used on a regular basis. However, it is difficult to determine to what extent, since this depends on the job description of the assistant, the degree of internationalisation of both company and the industry and the type of company.

C.   CONTEXT INFORMATION

	LOCATION	PERSONS, COMMUNITIES, COMPANIES, INSTITUTIONS	COMMUNICATION SITUATIONS	TEXT- AND DISCOURSE-TYPES
Work context	Office, at times at trade fairs, (depending on job and company) in the field, e.g. with customers, suppliers Departments: • Sales • Marketing • Purchasing • Accounts • Warehousing • HR	**Individual:** sales managers, heads of purchasing department, middle managers, HR managers, accountants, co-workers in the same company **Professional:** co-workers in the parent company / headquarters / other subsidiaries, suppliers, customers, insurers, customs officers, forwarding agents in all industries engaged in international trade and companies of varying size	General assistance: • Inform about / confirm / negotiate terms and dates • Check websites, e.g. for suppliers' products • Welcome visitors • Organise events, e.g. workshops or conferences • Draft presentations/reports/minutes/ statistics • Gather information on products, companies, markets, etc. • Man stands at trade fairs Sales/Marketing/Purchasing dept.: • Enquire about goods and services in spoken or written form • Read, write and respond to tenders • Gather information on products, companies, markets, etc. • Deal with problems (suppliers and customers) regarding delivery and payment • Negotiate/communicate terms of delivery (INCOTERMS) and payment • Check and maintain inventory lists	• Telephone conversations • PowerPoint presentations • Reports, memos, minutes • Email communication • Faxes • Business letters • Negotiations (no independent negotiations) / details of negotiations • Tax documents / international tax forms • Freight documents • Certificates of origin • Acknowledgements of order • Offers • Enquiries, also to International Chambers of Commerce or credit agencies • Complaints • Forms for accounting, e.g. P & L account, balance sheet, accounting software • Manuals

- Report to co-workers or superiors
- Deal with general correspondence
- Draft presentations/reports/minutes/contracts
- Arrange for dispatch and procure necessary documents
- Deal with customs and tax authorities
- Draft marketing texts (e.g. website, form letters)

Accounts:
- Write invoices, check invoices, small cases of troubleshooting
- Deal with tax declarations (also international)
- Fill in tax forms (also international)
- Deal with customs, international tax authorities, insurers
- Read P & L accounts, balance sheets, etc.
- Payroll management: check payrolls, make payments
- Check/maintain bank documents
- Deal with minor problems

Human Resources:
- Organise in-company training schemes for staff
- Maintain statistics on staff
- Deal with problems concerning HR (payroll, further education, etc.)

Study context	Vocational college and workplace (dual system for office workers) Foreign language tuition (compulsory) Workplace: (see *Work context* above); trainees usually work in different departments for some months on a rotating basis (only applicable to bigger companies).	• Simulation of business cases in business correspondence • Simulations of work-related communication situations, e.g. receiving a visitor, making travel arrangements, at a trade fair • Simulation of situations on the phone • Class discussions related to economic aspects, based on reading simulations of meetings and discussions, e.g. with role cards • Computer-mediated projects, e.g. video conferences [not typical yet] or simulation on how to run a business • Mediation (oral/written), e.g. based on a few notes in German, write an offer in English • The choice of the communication situation largely depends on the curricula and/or on the type of exam the trainees are preparing for (e.g. CEF-based certificate in vocational English (KMK-Zertifikat, http://www.kmkfsz-hamburg.de/), certificate offered by the German/local Chamber of Commerce and Industry). • An action-oriented approach / task-based language learning is called for by the curricula.	• Telephone conversations • Commercial correspondence • Emails • Role cards for simulations • Textbook texts or more current texts e.g. from the Internet, pieces of news, etc. • Descriptions of situations for mediation • Class discussions (as discourse-type) • The choice of texts largely depends on the curricula and/or on the type of exam the trainees are preparing for (e.g. CEF-based certificate in vocational English (KMK-Zertifikat), certificate offered by the German/local Chamber of Commerce and Industry). • Real-life situations and text that would simulate them are preferred.

D.   THE MOST FREQUENT ROUTINE SITUATIONS

Situation 1. Summing up the deal

Communication situation: written summary of negotiation on the phone

Location: office

Persons: assistant

Critical success factors: First of all, the assistant has to follow the conversation on the telephone and has to stand her ground during the negotiation phase on the phone. She must have the communicative, intercultural and social skills to arrive at a result that is acceptable for both parties. The assistant must also have the linguistic ability to make a concise summary of the results.

Details: The export sales assistant is on the phone to a customer or supplier. They negotiate terms of delivery and terms of payment for a particular case but also talk about other things, not only small talk but also about competitors in the field, recent developments on the market. After the telephone conversation, the assistant writes an email to sum up the contents and results of the negotiation (which INCOTERM, delivery details, etc.) and sends it to her interlocutor. (About INCOTERMS: http://en.wikipedia.org/wiki/Incoterm)

Situation 2. Internet research

Communication situation: summary of information available on markets and/or competitors, internal information gathering

Location: office

Persons: assistant, head of department

Critical success factors: The assistant needs to have sufficient reading skills in order to find and understand the relevant information on filters in the foreign language. She also has to apply her strategic knowledge to skim through the available texts to find out which text is relevant and which is not (skimming). Then the assistant has to summarise the texts and decide on which parts to translate for her superior. The assistant then needs the linguistic skills (mediation/translation) to compile an outline of the information that was sought after.

Details: The head of the department asks the assistant (in German) to gather information on the market for filters, more particularly the suppliers of filters. The assistant uses several channels of information available to her, for example the Internet. The information is mostly in English so the assistant has to skim through the websites and databases available, put together the information and then draft an outline in German for her head of department. She then reports back to him or her in German.

E.   THE MOST DEMANDING SITUATIONS

Situation 1. Unpleasant news

Communication situation: breaking unpleasant news to a customer

Location: office / on the phone or by email

Persons: assistant, customer (via telephone or email)

Challenge factors: The situation is demanding in several ways. Firstly, the assistant has to try to use language that attenuates the bad news and the ensuing trouble and potential costs for the customer. She needs to calm down feelings and also has to outline her arguments in a professional and firm but not arrogant or unfriendly way. She also has to appear cooperative, offering other solutions to accommodate the customer or some sort of compensation so that the company will not lose business in the future. Intercultural and social skills are relevant too since the customer might come from a different business culture. The assistant needs to sound convincing but at the same time has to try and win over the customer in this unfortunate situation.

Details: The assistant is on the phone to a customer from France. The conversation takes place in English. The customer has purchased some steel but would need the steel to be formed before it is delivered. The bend radius for this type of steel, however, cannot be more than seven times its sheet thickness. The forming die in this particular facility is not equipped to form this bend radius, so the customer has to choose a different harbour or change the bend radius of the steel, i.e. place a new order. The assistant must break the news to the customer, which might upset her and might entail further costs which were not planned for the customer. Therefore the assistant has to build up an argument that convinces the customer and does not scare her off for next time.

Situation 2. Bankrupt customer

Communication situation: establishing information on a bankrupt customer, trying to recover outstanding debts

Location: office / on the phone or by email

Persons: assistant, someone from the legal department or lawyer representing the company

Challenge factors: The situation is made demanding by the level of complexity of the situation. The assistant needs some background knowledge (current affairs knowledge, professional skills) in order to accurately judge the situation and gather the information needed by maintaining the conversation, asking appropriate questions, etc. Here, she needs linguistic competence, legal knowledge as well as social and intercultural skills. Intercultural competence would here refer to cultural knowledge, e.g. about the different ways of winding up a business when the owners have filed for bankruptcy (GB vs. US, etc. or other legal systems as opposed to the assistant's own system). She also needs intercultural competence in terms of skills in order to assess the situation correctly and react accordingly since she talks to a member of a different culture. In addition, she needs linguistic skills in the next phase in order to summarise the contents of the conversation with the liquidator / supervisor in English and relate them to the member of the legal department or the lawyer in German. Mediation competence is particularly called for in this situation. Only a highly experienced person would be asked to perform this task.

Details: The international customer that the assistant has attended to in the past has filed for bankruptcy. However, there are outstanding debts, and the assistant's company was regularly engaged in business with the bankrupt customer. Now it is the assistant's turn to contact the liquidator/supervisor in order to find out about the bankrupt's remaining property. She also has to establish which rank the company holds in the whole procedure, in other words estimate the probability of recovering part of the outstanding debts. She needs to process the information and pass it on to the legal department of the company and/or a lawyer who is in charge of representing the company. To do this, the information received, which the customer's liquidator/supervisor provides, has to be mediated for the German-speaking legal department, and so sufficient accuracy is vital.

F. SNAPSHOT

Background

My name is Marcus. Nationality: German. I work in the sales department of a large metal working company in northern Germany, where I'm an assistant in export sales. I'm 29 years of age, and I've been working for this company for almost five years. Before that I worked for a car company, also in sales. I studied engineering science, including electronics, mechanical engineering, and materials at a polytechnic in Germany, but only for one year.

A working day

To explain what I do, I'll just describe what I've done today. The first thing I always do when I come in (after getting myself a cup of coffee, of course) is check my mail. Two of the messages required me to do something, but before I could start on that I got a phone call (at 8.36 am!) from one of our customers who enquired about copper tubes. They wanted to have them as soon as possible since they had run out of tubes on the construction sites they are currently supplying. An emergency – again! I said I'd check and get back to them as soon as possible. So I asked my colleague in warehousing if there were still any in stock, but got an answer in the negative. Consequently, I had to get the stuff elsewhere, so I called up several suppliers.

I also sent some emails to them with a more accurate enquiry but only got an answer from one of them, so I had to do some more phoning around after lunchtime. In between, I got a phone call from a rather angry customer about a delivery that was supposed to have come in two days ago. I contacted the supplier and was told that the delivery would be arriving in the next two days. The customer was not too happy when I told her – they are trying to implement a just-in-time approach, so four days late is a long time – but there wasn't anything I could do about it.

Just before lunchtime I got an email classified as urgent. It was from a customer who is notorious for last-minute orders, but the company frequently places orders – in fact, it's one of our biggest clients - so I had to take care of the order at once. It meant spending an hour trying to get hold of the goods, and even then I had to tell the customer she had to make concessions because the specialised material is produced only on demand. So I phoned her and related the options to her – she has to find a creative solution to problems in situations like these. Fortunately, she proved to be understanding and since I could accommodate her by way of a reduced price, she got a good deal in the end. Lunch at 12.30 in the canteen. Unfortunately, the food is dreadful but going to a restaurant every day would take too much time – and be too expensive. After lunch I went through the mail again – there were a few messages I had not got round to yesterday - and took care of some complaints. One retailer complained that some tubes that we had delivered were of the wrong type – they say they were not insulated. I checked the order and the acknowledgement of order again as well as the delivery note. There did seem to be a discrepancy, so I called up distribution. They double-checked and then we found the mistake: I had confused orders. A simple mix-up, but always very annoying. Especially if you cannot blame anybody else :-) I thought about the various options and how to apologise to the customer. Together we'll have to find a solution that accommodates everyone. I'll do that first thing tomorrow morning.

There was also a problem with a potential Chinese customer. In fact, our first one in China. Our company would like to increase their market share so our first Chinese customer – if she places her first order - just has to be satisfied! The contact with the Chinese company started when, about two months ago, I was asked to search the Internet for new markets. I found several databases for companies on the Chinese market that we could sell our new insulated pipes to. It meant that I spent quite some time on researching legal and insurance questions, together with someone in our legal department. Customs law is also a huge problem sometimes because it depends on the goods, and it can be very difficult from country to country. And I find trading with China can be very difficult sometimes. There are complex registration requirements, for example. Also, I find the English they use is sometimes hard for me to understand. In fact, I think that the problem is a language problem, rather than anything else. We'll have to discuss this at our staff meeting tomorrow. Too big an issue to deal with right now! It's almost 5 pm: time to go.

In all I spent a lot of my time today on correspondence, by email or letter, and also on the phone. Just an ordinary day. In our department we have to take care of enquiries and write offers, check on stocks, communicate with co-workers in the purchasing department and in warehousing, discuss the availability of goods, negotiate terms of delivery and terms of payment. We sometimes negotiate the details of contracts with customers, which usually means that we have to ask our superior for final decisions. Invoices also have to be written and checked, and passed on to the accounting department. Quite often customers complain about a delivery, or the amount of money that they have to pay, and at times invoices are not paid at all. In that case our accounting department often comes back to us, and that usually means a lot of hassle.

Language

I would estimate that 25% of my correspondence (email, letters) is done in English, the language which is used in virtually all correspondence with foreign companies (even with French ones!). Typically, I have some four or five telephone conversations in English each week, often about complaints with deliveries. They sometimes present problems, but, especially when the partner at the other end of the telephone line is also using English as a foreign language, it's not always clear what exactly the problem is! Sometimes there are legal problems, with contracts and the like, and then I'm happy to pass them on to my superior or to the legal department. But on the whole we manage, especially because there is one chap here who has lived in the UK for a number of years. If things are really difficult, we ask her to take over, and she acts as an interpreter.

HEALTHCARE AND SOCIAL SERVICES – REGISTERED NURSE – HIGHER EDUCATION (TERTIARY)

CEF PROFESSIONAL PROFILE

A.   BACKGROUND INFORMATION

Field	Healthcare and social services (nursing)
Education/Programme	Degree Programme in Healthcare and Social Services/Nursing and Healthcare
Specialisation(s)	Registered nurse (RN)
Degree/Qualification	Bachelor of Healthcare and Social Services
Language	English
Drawn up by	Katja Hämäläinen, MA, lecturer, and Mirja Järvinen, MA, lecturer Helsinki Polytechnic Stadia (currently Metropolia University of Applied Sciences)
Date / City and country / Organisation	4 January 2006, Helsinki, Finland Faculty of Healthcare and Social Services, Helsinki Polytechnic Stadia (currently Metropolia University of Applied Sciences)
Methods used for collecting the information (methods, persons, dates)	**Sources:** questionnaires and interviews 7 March 2006: A questionnaire with open questions given to a group of nursing students (N=34) at the Helsinki Polytechnic Stadia to be filled in. Most of the students had studied four or more semesters. The questions dealt with the places and nursing procedures they have taken care of during their on-the-job training periods. Moreover, the oral and spoken communication situations, in which the English language was needed, were discussed and analysed as well as the most frequent and demanding situations at the hospital wards and departments. 22 March 2006: A very similar questionnaire was given to a group of registered nurses (N=23) who study at the Helsinki Polytechnic Stadia. All of them were adults, and they had updated their education to become public health nurses. However, they were registered nurses with 10-20 years' working experience, which was one of the requirements for starting the current training. 23 March 2006: An interview with a registered nurse with 35 years' experience working in the field of nursing and healthcare. For the moment, she works on a long-stay ward at a hospital in Helsinki, Finland.

27 March 2006: An interview with a registered nurse with 15 years' working experience. Earlier she worked at different hospital wards and home service units, but now she works at a nursing home in Helsinki, Finland.

12 April 2006: An interview with a registered nurse with 15 years' experience working in the field of nursing and healthcare. Today, she works on a geriatric long-stay ward at a hospital in Turku, Finland.

Internet:

http://www.mol.fi/english (The home page of the Finnish Ministry of Labour)
http://www.metropolia.fi/en/degree-programmes/health-care-and-nursing/>English (The curriculum is for registered nurses at the Helsinki Metropolia University of Applied Sciences)

Other useful web pages for students and teachers (for new language teachers and instructors, especially): http://www.nmc-uk.org/aDefault.aspx (The Nursing and Midwifery Council in the UK)
http://www.nursefindersuk.com/index.cfm (Online requirements service for nurses and allied healthcare professionals in the UK)
http://www.careerplanner.com/Job-Descriptions/Registered-Nurses.cfm and
http://www.studentdoc.com/nursing-job-description.html (Description and career opportunities for registered nurses)

B.   OCCUPATIONAL INFORMATION

Typical examples of professions/ occupations/jobs	**Hospital:** registered nurse (RN); ward sister / nurse in charge; assistant ward manager **Other:** project manager; special coordinator; nursing and healthcare teacher
Typical organisations, companies, communities to be employed in	Hospital wards and departments; private clinics; health clinics; medical centres; healthcare centres; home service; home nursing unit Social Insurance Institution of Finland (KELA) http://www.kela.fi/in/internet/english.nsf National Institute for Welfare and Health (STAKES) http://www.stakes.fi/EN/index.htm Institute of Occupational Health http://www.iosh.co.uk/ The International Red Cross http://www.icrc.org/WHO http://www.who.int/en/

Typical job descriptions	Treating and educating patients next-of-kin and the public about various medical conditions and self-administration of medicines Recording patients' medical histories and symptoms Helping to perform medical tests Operating medical machinery Helping with patients' follow-ups and rehabilitation as well as diet and exercise programmes. Helping the patient to manage diseases or injury Giving post-treatment home care instructions Giving psychological support and grief counselling to patients and their family members Teaching self-administration of medication and physical therapy as well as general health promotion. **NB:** Registered nurses may also specialise in one or more patient care specialities; by work setting or by the type of work provided; in a particular disease, ailment or condition; in treatment of a particular organ or body system; or by providing preventive and acute care in all healthcare settings. Thus, the job title may vary, although the degree programme and education remain the same.
To what extent foreign languages are needed	The need for English (or other foreign languages) varies according to where the nurse works. Foreign language skills may be unnecessary or only be of limited use in some local/regional contexts. Nurses working for organisations at a national and international level need good language skills in oral and writtencommunication. Languages are needed on hospital wards and in departments, although more in spoken communication situations than in written ones. Most of them are discussions and admission interviews with the patients and their next-of-kin.

C. CONTEXT INFORMATION

	LOCATION	PERSONS, COMMUNITIES, COMPANIES, INSTITUTIONS	COMMUNICATION SITUATIONS	TEXT- AND DISCOURSE-TYPES
Work context	Hospital wards and departments National healthcare organisations and institutions International organisations, such as the Red Cross and the World Health Organisation (WHO)	**Individual:** patient/client, next-of-kin / family member, registered nurses, practical nurses, doctors, social workers, psychologists, therapists **Professional:** pharmaceutical representative **Public:** Royal College of Nursing http://www.rcn.org.uk/ American Nurses Association http://www.nursingworld.org/	Nursing procedures, such as taking a patient's blood pressure, temperature, pulse, blood test, haemoglobin test, giving injections/shots, giving instructions how to treat a particular disease or what to do at home after staying at hospital (post-treatment home care) Following the state of patients and evaluation Patient Case Report to the healthcare team and the family members of the patient Giving instructions face to face or on the phone Discussing the changes and development in nursing and healthcare in society Non-verbal communication and body language play an extremely important role in all communication situations that RNs face at work	• Writing and updating Care and Service Plans (CSP) • Patient reports and documents • Prescriptions • Referrals • Patient data systems • Reports and summaries

Study context			Texts:
Teaching premises	Educational: English teachers, other teachers, visiting lecturers, exchange students, patients of foreign origin during the on-the-job training periods	Following lectures / teaching presentations, giving feedback	Authentic copies
Exchange student placements and short courses abroad		Discussions based on professional literature and articles	Material on the Internet
Different study environments		Small talk	Vocabularies
On-the-job training period		Written assignments (e.g. Patient Case Reports)	Essays
Exchange student activities at school		Emails	Summaries
		Essays	Reports
		Final project	Emails
		Other teaching situations that simulate real-life situations	CVs, portfolios
			Professional literature of the field (articles, papers, Internet)

D.   THE MOST FREQUENT ROUTINE SITUATIONS

Situation 1. A nursing procedure: taking a patient's blood pressure

Communication situation: guiding and advising a patient on health matters after taking their blood pressure (BP)

Location: at patient's home. A registered nurse visits the patient every week.

Persons: the patient and the registered nurse

Critical success factors: giving advice firmly but politely; striking up a rapport with patient.

Details: A registered nurse takes a 70-year-old patient's BP. Last week, the BP was a little high at 145/90. There will be a check-up every week until the BP reduces. After taking the BP, she advises how to lower BP (e.g. exercise more, cut salt intake and drink more fluids).

Taking BP is an easy nursing procedure to perform. The RN has the training and equipment for it. Guiding and advising the patient is harder; the aim is that the patient should be without BP medication as long as possible. The patient must rely on the RN and follow her advice. Changing habits is always a demanding task.

Situation 2. A nursing procedure: giving medicine to a child patient

Communication situation: persuading a reluctant child patient to accept medicine

Location: a paediatric ward at a public hospital

Persons: the patient, the registered nurse, (the parents of the child)

Critical success factors: using language and tone that is appropriate for the patient's age and comprehension of the situation.

Details: On a paediatric ward, a registered nurse (RN) gives medicine to a six-year-old child. The child suffers from high temperature and diarrhoea. Although the child is quite weak, she does not want to swallow the medicine. Thus, the nurse has to explain the importance of taking the medicine and persuade the patient to take it. The interviewed healthcare professionals were of different opinions regarding the effects this might have on the situation: some thought that it would make the situation worse, whereas others saw it as a positive factor.

Key points:
1) The RN has to know the medicine and disease in question.
2) The RN has to know what kinds of differences there are between adults and children as patients, and based on that give the reason for taking the medicine. Moreover, every patient is an individual, and to find out the right way of dealing with each patient, an RN needs both conceptual and tacit knowledge.
3) If the parents are present, the RN has a third dimension as well: concerned adults.

Situation 3. A nursing procedure: preparing a patient for laboratory tests

Communication situation: explaining the purpose and process of a medical test procedure
Location: a patient room at the hospital
Critical success factors: clarity of questions in admission interview; checking ambiguities in patient's answers; clarity and accuracy of explanations of procedures; giving clear instructions.

Details: A 40-year-old man has been taken in for some laboratory tests. He has suffered from constipation and stomach pain without any specific reason for a week. Now, he has a referral for laboratory tests and an appointment with a doctor afterwards. A registered nurse makes an (pre)admission interview to evaluate the current situation and enter the personal information into a patient register system. Then she explains the test procedure, as well as why and how the tests are taken. She explains whether the patient may or may not eat or drink anything, whether he has to stay in overnight and whether driving a car is allowed, or whether there are any other restrictions or not after the laboratory tests. Even though the patient has been informed of these things earlier, in many cases the patient remembers and understands them only when informed repeatedly.

Key points:
1) A quiet room. The room has to be quiet, since according to the interviewees, noise and other people's talking make the communication worse and gives the impression that the healthcare professional is not concerned about the patient.
2) As in all communication situations, the registered nurses have to have the conceptual knowledge (information on the diseases, and in this case, the laboratory tests) and read between the lines and understand the patient and how he or she may react (intuitive information). In the communication, they are dealing with the embodied information, and when they communicate, they produce the information together, that is the nested information.

E.   THE MOST DEMANDING SITUATIONS

The most important situations are discussing the different illnesses, disabilities, injuries and trauma with patients and their next-of-kin and other family members. This is especially important if the client is on her deathbed, or his or her condition is very severe. Other demanding situations may include giving home care instructions. Section E describes the reasons why different places, persons present and situations may involve a high degree of difficulty. In the following fictitious situations, based on the interviews and questionnaires, a foreign language is used as the means of communication.

Situation 1. Taking care of a dying patient

Communication situation: counselling the family members of a dying patient

Location: a long-stay ward

Persons: the patient suffering from prolonged cancer, the next-of-kin of the patients, the registered nurse (RN), the doctors

Challenge factors: dealing with family members; emotional and psychological reactions to death; correctly interpreting mood and emotion; expressing sympathy and understanding.

Details: At a long-stay hospital ward, a 57-year-old RN with 25 years' working experience is taking care of a dying patient, a 72-year-old man with a different native language and cultural background from that of the care team. The patient is suffering from a prolonged cancer that has spread metastases into the whole body. His doctors have estimated that he has 2–4 weeks to live. The patient receives the basic care and normal pain relief, but he does not want any intensive or special care, since that is what the patient's doctors think is best as well.

Most of the family members agree with the doctors and the nursing staff. However, one of the next-of-kin of the dying patient questions it. She is a 27-year-old woman who is very fluent in the native language of the care team, and she cannot bear losing her grandfather. She thinks that the registered nurses and doctors have misunderstood her grandfather. Now, she demands that the patient should be moved to an intensive therapy unit immediately, and the hospital staff should do all they can, if not to save the patient's life, then to give him as many days as possible to live.

Key points:

1) Family members are always a consideration in healthcare provision. In this case, one of them disagrees as to what kind of pain relief the patient should receive: this is sometimes contrary to what the patient asks for.

2) The imminence of approaching death. In many cases nowadays, people are afraid of death. Death is no longer natural, because people are not dying at home, but in hospital wards and nursing homes. Death is not part of our everyday life, which makes it alarming and frightening.

3) At work, the RN has to be empathetic and professional as well as able to read between the lines, since she (probably) has to discuss and explain the situation to the family members more than once.

4) The whole care team has to be unanimous and follow the Care and Service Plan made for the dying patient in the care meetings. No single member of the care team can make decisions to increase the amount of treatment given to the patient.

5) The language and culture. Although the patient has lived many years in his new home country, he has never learned the major language of the country properly. Thus, he cannot express himself very well. He is in pain, which makes it even more difficult for him to speak. He can show where the pain is and make some gestures, but that is all. No one in the hospital ward can speak the first language of the patient. Moreover, the culture is not familiar to the nursing staff.

Situation 2. Guiding a young patient suffering from diabetes

Communication situation: counselling a young patient and the young patient's parents

Location: the office of the primary nurse at a children's hospital

Persons: the primary nurse (registered nurse), the doctors, psychologist, the client/patient, his parents (at a later stage: nutritionist, psychologist, social worker)

Challenge factors: health professionals may have difficulties understanding the source of a patient's anxieties; counselling the parents of a young patient; expressing complex medical concepts in plain (non-technical) English; overcoming cultural and linguistic differences.

Details: Doctors have found out that a 13-year-old boy has diabetes. He has had the typical symptoms of the disease (thirst, tiredness, a frequent need to urinate) for a couple of months, and now he has been diagnosed as a diabetic. He is having a meeting with his primary nurse,' who explains the situation to him and gives information on the disease and treatment. The primary nurse, an educated registered nurse, is the first to give the information on the disease. Later, other healthcare professionals explain the physiological, psychological and social effects of diabetes. The adolescent patient listens to his primary nurse, but nevertheless has difficulties in understanding as he is still in a little shock from hearing the news of having diabetes. Thus, he can perceive neither the information on eating healthily and regularly nor the importance of exercise and taking his medicines on time. He refuses to accept the disease and thinks that he can still live as he used to before the condition was diagnosed. He is of foreign origin and cannot properly understand the language the nurse is speaking. He has lived in his new home country only six months. In a case like this, the parents are taking part in the counselling as well, although the registered nurse thinks that it would be best that they wait for the boy outside. The parents feel that they have failed or done something wrong for the boy to have become diabetic. The primary nurse acts calmly and explains the situation again and what changes in lifestyle the whole family has to make, using all her knowledge of healthcare and cross-cultural communication.

Key points:

1) The information a healthcare professional considers straightforward may in contrast be hard for the patient to understand and accept.

2) The parents and their reactions make the situation difficult; to accept a life-long disease is sometimes challenging for the next-of-kin. The situation is even more demanding since the language skills of the persons present may vary considerably. In many cases, the English language is used as a language of communication, not as the first language. In this case, one parent's language skills in English may be limited and the other may not speak the language at all.

3) For the primary nurse, the work-related vocabulary concerning diabetes, or other diseases, may cause difficulties, although she may otherwise speak English fluently. There may also be difficulties in understanding the pronunciation of the patient and his parents.

4) The cultural framework: both the primary nurse and the patient, as well as his next-of-kin, have to accept the fact that they are dealing with cultures that are different from their own. However, it is important to understand that not all of the differences or problems are due to cultures (personality is a separate factor).

Situation 3. A patient with an acute mental illness behaves violently towards the nursing staff

Communication situation: responding to a patient's violent episode and counselling the patient afterwards

Location: student healthcare centre

Persons: The exchange student, the staff at the healthcare centre, other patients

Challenge factors: remaining calm and professional under difficult circumstances; overcoming linguistic and cultural obstacles.

Details: An exchange student from South America has been studying at a polytechnic in Helsinki, Finland, for the last five months. It will take 3.5 years to complete her bachelor degree programme. In the beginning, everything was fine, but recently she has not been attending lectures or completing assignments. She has not been eating properly or going out. She realises that something is wrong. Right now, she is sitting in the waiting area at the student healthcare centre. She looks at the other patients and experiences a terrible sensation of breathlessness. The nursing staff notice and come to her assistance. The sound of running and loud voices exacerbate the situation, and she hits one of the nurses. The patient is taken into another room with the help of guards, where she is pacified with a tranquiliser. She falls asleep and wakes up some hours later. A registered nurse sitting next to her bed explains what has happened and conducts an admissions interview. The patient feels embarrassed and is drowsy (from the tranquiliser), but the discussion ensues satisfactorily.

Key points:

1) The patient was there for the first time, so the nursing staff could not anticipate her violent behaviour. Staying calm in a situation when a patient behaves violently requires great professionalism.

2) Language was a problem: English was used, but it was the first language of none of the persons involved. Thus, there was much shouting and abusive language (learnt from TV series and films).

3) The situation developed suddenly.

F.   SNAPSHOT

Background

I am a registered nurse. My education took 3.5 years, and after I finished my studies, I spent three years working in an intensive care unit. The pace there was very fast and I worked many night shifts. The night shifts were especially hard for me, and I wanted to change wards. I currently work in a geriatric ward at the same hospital.

A working day

I work in three shifts. My working day (morning shift) begins at 7.00 am. We wake up the patients; help them to wash, dress, eat and take their medication. Then the patients can stay in bed, or if they wish, they can join a hobby club in the day room or the day centre nearby. At the same time, we have a change-of-shift report and coffee. The patients eat lunch at 11.00 am and dinner at 4.00 pm. Visiting hours are between 4.30 pm and 6.00 pm. During the morning shift, blood tests and laboratory samples are taken by laboratory nurses. We work in teams of registered nurses, and I am the primary nurse for two patients.

A registered nurse's work

I assist elderly people in washing, getting dressed, eating, taking medicine and other elements of basic care. My work consists of explaining the situation of these elderly patients to their next-of-kin, observing the state of health of the patient, reporting the events of my shift to the next shift, dealing with other members of the healthcare team (for instance, laboratory nurses, physiotherapists, podiatrists) and doctors. I take care of, help and counsel patients at hospital wards and departments and other healthcare clinics and centres. Nursing procedures and reporting are a big part of my daily work, and I administer medicines prescribed by doctors. In addition, I deal with the next-of-kin of the patients by discussing and comforting them. In the admissions department, I schedule appointments with doctors and, when a patient arrives at hospital, I take care of the patient and do an admission interview. Sometimes, I give other, non-medical information, such as giving directions to hospital wards and departments.

Language

How much language I need depends on where I work. There are hospital wards and departments where I only need English in rare cases. Mostly, I need English during discussions with patients and their next-of-kin. The discussions concern medication, patient instruction, symptoms, diseases and diagnoses, patient information and nursing procedures and treatment. In most cases, English is the common language of communication but not the first language of the participants. Written communication skills are needed when I read about medicines and how to use them and when there is no translation at hand. Sometimes I want to read more about one particular disease or cure on the Internet. Most of the research and scientific articles are published in English. Nowadays I have many colleagues from other countries, and we use English since we don't share a common first language.

I have noticed that in many communicative situations, the patient/client is often in a weaker position than the registered nurse since the former may be physically or psychologically ill, or suffering from a certain disease, or there is a crisis or a turning point in his or her life at the moment. These situations may be highly emotional and the patients may be unable to control themselves. Changes in the patient's circumstances may arise spontaneously and may be particular to the patient. The patient may have limited comprehension of both the situation and the language required to explain it. Child patients may even have difficulties in understanding their own first language (source language) and thus their skills in the foreign language (target language) may be extremely limited. Therefore the communication is comprehensive, and it is important to listen to the patient/client attentively and to empathise. The quality of the client–nurse communication is more important than the specific words uttered in the communication situation.

LAW – LLM LAW – HIGHER EDUCATION (TERTIARY)

CEF PROFESSIONAL PROFILE

A.   BACKGROUND INFORMATION

Field	
Education/Programme	Higher Education / University A five-year LLM degree programme (LLB programmes are not offered by Polish universities)
Specialisation(s)	• Master degree seminars in Polish offered to fourth- and fifth-year students: Civil Law, Criminal Law, Administrative Law, Constitutional Law, International Law • Additional professional qualification courses in foreign languages, offered to students and non-students for extra tuition
Degree/Qualification	LLM Master of Law
Language	English, German (secondary focus)
Drawn up by	Bożena Górska-Poręcka
Date / City and country / Organisation	First version: January–February 2006 Second version: March–April 2006 at the Center for Foreign Language Teaching, the University of Warsaw (http://www.szjo.uw.edu.pl/EN/)

Methods used for collecting the information (methods, persons, dates)	**Sources:** written survey and oral interviews conducted by the author as follows: 19 January 2006 – interviews with three associates at law firm A, Warsaw, Poland 24 January 2006 – interviews with an associate and a partner at law firm B, Warsaw, Poland 25 January 2006 – interviews with two associates at law firm C, Warsaw, Poland 27 January 2006 – interviews with two junior associates at law firm D, Warsaw, Poland 13 March 2006 – interview with a senior associate at law firm E, Warsaw, Poland

B.   OCCUPATIONAL INFORMATION

Typical examples of professions/ occupations/jobs	Attorneys (solicitors) employed by international law firms with practise in various areas of business and civil law, working as: junior associates, associates, senior associates and partners Attorneys (solicitors) employed by Polish law firms with practice in business, civil and criminal law, working as: associates and partners Company lawyers on permanent contracts working for commercial and non-profit organisations, such as: Polish state-owned and private companies; Polish and global banks, insurance companies and other financial institutions; Polish subsidiaries of global companies; charities, foundations and other non-profit organisations Freelance lawyers providing legal services to two or three companies or working as non-salaried associates for a law firm Government lawyers on permanent employment with institutions of state administration working for ministries, government agencies, regional, municipal and county administration; prosecutors in criminal cases, judges in criminal and civil cases, justices of the Supreme Court, the Supreme Administrative Court and the Constitutional Tribunal; parliamentary lawyers, army and police lawyers Academic teachers of law at public universities and private law schools Journalists with law papers and journals

Typical organisations, companies, communities to be employed in	Large international business law firms, represented by Wierzbowski Eversheds, Salans Oleszczuk and Dewey Ballantine Grzesiak, all based in prestigious Warsaw locations
	Small and medium-sized Polish law firms with 2–12 attorneys, represented by Dziedzic Kielmans and Gornicki 'Koncept', based in downtown Warsaw
	Multinational and Polish commercial companies
	Non-profit organisations
	State administration institutions, including national and local legislatures
	Law and arbitration courts and tribunals
	Law enforcement institutions
	Law departments of state universities and private law schools
	Law papers and journals, e.g. *Gazeta Prawna*
Typical job descriptions	**Junior associates** Helping more senior lawyers with case preparation, administrative, technical and language work Providing legal advice and representation to corporate clients (e.g. banks, telecoms, pharmaceuticals) in practice areas (e.g. M&A, employment law, intellectual property, litigation), often collaborating with foreign counterparts or business consultants and reporting to higher-ranking lawyers **Senior associates** Reporting to partners Working independently Specialising in complex and difficult cases from one or two practice areas Acting as mentors and supervisors to junior associates Providing legal advice and representation to both companies and individuals in selected practice areas (i.e. branches of law and/or client types) Organising the work of associates by allocating clients or cases Providing supervision and monitoring and personally handling legal affairs of the firm's most important client(s)

Partners:	Supervising work done by associates in their area of expertise Personally handling the firm's most important cases involving state institutions or blue chip companies and falling under both Polish and international (EU) jurisdiction Taking responsibility for the strategy of the Polish office, acting as its board members
To what extent foreign languages are needed	English is used extensively by all ten of the professionals interviewed, from several times a day for associates with international firms to several times a week for the others. It is routinely used to conduct legal business (i.e. counselling and representation) with foreign corporate clients, consultants and counterparts of all nationalities, as well as for socialising with them. Polish is prevalent in day-to-day office business, although in international law firms some office communication, both oral and written (memos, minutes, reports), is handled in English. German is used by only 40% of those interviewed and much less frequently: from once or twice a week for a lawyer with a German-client division of an international firm to once or twice a month or even once or twice a year for lawyers with Polish firms. Other languages, especially Russian and French are used sporadically, from one to several times a year.

C.   CONTEXT INFORMATION

	LOCATION	PERSONS, COMMUNITIES, COMPANIES, INSTITUTIONS	COMMUNICATION SITUATIONS	TEXT- AND DISCOURSE-TYPES
Work context	Law firm's or client's premises Government institutions Law courts Arbitration chambers Restaurants	**Individual:** business lawyers, individual clients **Professional:** corporate clients, government officials, business consultants	Advising corporate and individual clients on legal issues in the area of business and civil law Drawing up legal documents at the clients' request Representing and coaching clients in trade talks and negotiations regarding major business deals	• Law codes, acts and statutes • Company deeds and bylaws • Business contracts and agreements • Letters of advice and legal opinions • Statements and writs used in court proceedings • Emails, memos and reports • Law publications and articles • Professional, business and informal exchanges

			Representing clients in court and arbitration proceedings (litigation)	
			Dealing with office communication	
			Case preparatory work	
			Socialising with clients outside the office (business lunches, etc.)	
			Small talk	
Study context	Law school premises	**Educational:** foreign professors, international students	Participating in lectures and classes	• Foreign language lectures, talks and presentations
	Exchange student placements		Giving in-class presentations	• Authentic legal texts from printed sources
	On-the-job training programmes		Writing term papers and other assignments (essays, contract drafts)	• Audio and visual material
	Other training and study environments		Receiving feedback on assignments	• Essays and term papers
			Participating in case studies and other simulations	• In-class discussions
			Participating in international conferences organised by the school	• Conference plenary and working sessions
			Team-working and socialising with foreign students	• Study-related and informal communication

D. THE MOST FREQUENT ROUTINE SITUATIONS

Situation 1: Responding to a client's request for legal assistance

Communication situation: responding to the client's request for legal advice, representation, or a legal document to be procured
Location: the lawyer's office
Persons: the lawyer, a foreign national representing the client (usually a multinational corporation or its Polish subsidiary)
Critical success factors: good listening and identification of client problem, good formulation of the situation; meeting client needs with a well-formulated solution.

Details: The lawyer needs to analyse the client's request before consulting the relevant legislation and documents. She may need to translate the most relevant extracts for the client. The lawyer also needs to phrase an appropriate reply to the request or arrange a meeting in order to instruct the client as to the documents needed. This situation calls for an exchange of emails or telephone calls and the use of legal documents in both Polish and English.

Situation 2: Consultation with a foreign counterpart

Communication situation: consulting a foreign counterpart or a business consultant about some aspects of the case
Location: the lawyer's office
Persons: the lawyer, his or her foreign counterpart at another office of the same law firm, or a business consultant (e.g. on fiscal regulations)
Critical success factors: communicating one's expertise to a peer with clarity and integrity; levelling with peer expert on equal terms; collaborating on win-win basis.

Details: A (series of) face-to-face meeting(s) or phone conversation(s) in which the lawyer must define the problem / request for consultation, ask for suggestions and collaborate in working out a solution. The lawyer needs the relevant Polish and foreign legislation documentation. The situation calls for not only the resolution of the problem but also the building of rapport and the exchange of small talk to make a good impression and maintain good relations with the counterpart.

Situation 3: A business lunch

Communication situation: a business lunch held in place of a standard working meeting
Location: a restaurant
Persons: the lawyer, the client's party including a foreign national

Critical success factors: being able to maintain a pleasant, constructive atmosphere over a longer session; knowing food terminology in English and being able to explain the menu items; being able to bind a lasting relationship with connection to mutual acquaintances and new faces.

Details: The lawyer needs to engage in small talk and to be able to describe the contents of the menu (and make recommendations). Discussion of case issues will take place during the meal, and the lawyer should also be prepared to contribute to informal group discussion as well as dialogue.

Situation 4. Attending professional training

Communication situation: a professional training session, workshop or seminar on aspects of international/EU law

Location: a conference room at the firm or an outside facility such as a conference centre

Persons: a group of Polish lawyers (often representing one employer), one or two trainers or consultants (usually foreign nationals)

Critical success factors: functioning as a constructively contributing member by active listening, expertise input, solution search and creation of innovative solutions.

Details: A talk or presentation is delivered by the trainer or expert followed by a question-and-answer session. Break-out sessions may include practical activities in which the new knowledge is utilised (e.g. a case study done in a small groups of participants). Follow-up group discussions may also be included. Participants may be expected to contribute to feedback on the performance/presentations of others on the course.

Such seminars typically involve presentation on some aspect of EU legislation, practice or procedure, and case studies are supported with documents of the relevant legal acts.

E. THE MOST DEMANDING SITUATIONS

Situation 1: A case orientation meeting

Communication situation: a case orientation meeting

Location: a conference room at the law firm

Persons: a senior associate or a partner in charge of a given client or case type, an attorney (solicitor) directly responsible for the case, usually an associate, a senior local executive of the client corporation, usually the general manager of its Polish subsidiary, a senior executive from the client's headquarters and/or a board member responsible for the relevant business area

Challenge factors: participating in lengthy discussion in the foreign language, expressing complex ideas concisely and clearly; fast and accurate reading skills; understanding of business and finance as well as legal issues; understanding the contrast between Polish and non-Polish legal systems.

Details: A large, international law firm has been asked by their client, a global company from the telecommunications, energy or pharmaceutical sector for legal advice on a problem connected with their operation in Poland. Typically, these problems involve aspects of employment law, company law, merger and acquisitions law, anti-trust law, copyright law, law covering public bids and tenders, law covering securities or real estate law. A meeting has been scheduled to clarify the details of the lawyer's task and to gather and briefly examine the documents relevant to the case.

Stages of the meeting:

1. greetings and introductions
2. a brief presentation by the senior lawyer concerning the legal background of the case
3. an overview of relevant documents brought by the client with questions for clarification
4. a brief presentation by the lawyer responsible for the case about what needs to be done, how and according to what schedule
5. deciding on a channel of further communication (email, telephone), or setting up a working meeting to clarify issues

This situation requires good foreign language speaking and listening skills to effectively participate in the discussion, express opinions and present ideas. Selective reading skills, especially reading for gist and scanning the text to find relevant information and to quickly evaluate the documents provided by the client, are also required. The lawyer has to demonstrate sufficient knowledge of legal as well as business and financial terminology, which adds to the challenge as the latter is rarely taught in university FL courses for law students. In addition, the situation calls for considerable interpersonal and general oral communication skills, including elements of public speaking in order that the lawyer can present the procedure to follow and offer advice on how best to handle the case. Finally, a non-linguistic factor that contributes to the overall difficulty of the situation is differences between the two legal systems involved, Polish and foreign.

Situation 2: A case working meeting

Communication situation: a case working meeting

Location: a conference room at the law firm

Persons: the lawyer responsible for the case, usually a senior associate (sometimes accompanied by a junior associate), two–three managers representing the client (e.g. a senior executive representing the company's head office, his or her local counterpart, and (optionally) the general manager of the Polish subsidiary)

Challenge factors: chairing the meeting; reporting on the case, active listening, asking clarifying questions and summarising the information received; the type of documents and/or the subject matter of the meeting.

Details: Such meetings occur in all cases, regardless of the actual nature of the lawyer's task – counselling or representation. The purpose of a working meeting is to clarify details and collect specific information about the corporate client's business processes or financial situation, or else to agree on the content and phrasing of a document being procured by the lawyer. A typical working meeting will be held by a group of four–five persons, each representing a different area of expertise, and will last an hour or two. For instance, a lawyer specialising in merges and acquisition has called a meeting to obtain additional information on the client's company ownership structure and its financial standing in order to assess whether a planned global acquisition in a sensitive sector (e.g. insurance) will conform to Polish anti-trust law.

Stages of the meeting:

1. The lawyer opens the meeting by reporting on the current status of the case and then asks for additional information.
2. One of the client's representatives gives the information required by the lawyer in a brief presentation (e.g. the foreign senior executive or the Polish country manager discusses the company's ownership structure, making reference to its consolidated balance sheet).
3. The lawyer asks questions to make sure he or she understood the information correctly and moves on to another topic.
4. Another client's representative talks about his or her area of expertise (e.g. the client's financial director describes the company's precise financial situation before a planned acquisition and illustrates it by reference to the company's income statement and a current cash flow statement).
5. Again, the lawyer asks questions for qualification and summarises the information presented.
6. The meeting ends with the lawyer's information on how the new facts will bear on the case (here: what the financial information provided means for the proposed acquisition in the light of Polish M&A and anti-trust legislation).

From the purely linguistic point of view, the challenge derives from the wide range of tasks that have to be performed. The challenge is increased by the type of documents and/or the subject matter of the meeting – company finance, which is hardly a typical lawyer's area of expertise, especially at the beginning of his or her career. Another source of difficulty is that the lawyer is faced with the task of assessing the relevance of financial and legal documents in English against Polish regulations, which calls for high mediation skills in order to switch codes without losing the semantics. This can be coupled with cultural problems when the two legal systems involved differ in some significant respect, such as different company types, forms of capitalisation or corporate governance.

Situation 3: A negotiation session

Communication situation: a negotiation session

Location: a conference room of one of the negotiating parties

Persons: a group of two–three managers representing the client (including a foreign executive with considerable decision-making prerogatives), the lawyer representing the client's legal interests, the other side (two–three trade union's activists) accompanied by their lawyer, a professional English/Polish interpreter hired by the other (Polish) side

Challenge factors: negotiation skills; representing the client's interests within the law; language switching and giving translations.

Details: As it is fashionable in the global corporate world to outsource legal services at the time of writing, lawyers are increasingly asked to represent their clients' legal interests in all sorts of negotiations with the Polish government, with other global or local companies or, for instance, with trade unions operating in a factory that the client wishes to acquire.

Typically, the trade unions want the prospective investor to sign an agreement that there will be no layoffs for a certain period of time, which is often against the best interests of the investor, who would prefer to reduce the workforce and is willing to pay some compensation in order to achieve that. The task of the lawyer, with expertise in the area of employment law, is to see to it that the client signs an agreement that complies with the Polish law and does not constitute any more of a constraint and financial burden than necessary.

Stages of the meeting:

1. The senior executive/activist representing the hosting party opens the meeting.
2. The hosting party states what concession they are ready to make and on what terms.
3. The other party responds with their proposal and the bargaining continues until an agreement is reached or the negotiation is adjourned.
4. Throughout the session the lawyer sits by the most senior representative of the client (often a foreign national), commenting on legal aspects, coaching the negotiators and making objections if necessary.
5. At any time, the lawyer may be asked for a legal opinion about a proposed solution, or to present the procedure to follow.

According to those interviewed, negotiations constitute the most difficult of all professional situations, especially if conducted in English. However, the difficulty lies largely outside the purely linguistic domain, in the perceived lack of general negotiation skills, in the mere type of situation which is focused on a conflict between the two sides, and on the duality of the lawyer's task – to protect the client's interests while seeing to it that the nation's law is not breached. As in all other group interactive situations, during most negotiation sessions there is a constant need to switch languages and to translate, mainly orally, which most respondents find difficult, particularly in a larger group.

Situation 4: A court hearing in a civil litigation case

Communication situation: a court hearing in a civil litigation case

Location: a courtroom in a civil court

Persons: a lawyer with expertise in civil and company law, the client, represented by one–two senior executives (including at least one foreign national), the plaintiff or defendant, the plaintiff/defendant's lawyer, the judge, experts, witnesses, an official interpreter to translate into Polish (the hearings are always in Polish)

Challenge factors: the lawyer and the law firm's reputation is at stake if the case is lost, leading to added stress; strong public speaking skills; interpreting the proceedings for the (English-speaking) client.

Details: The lawyer represents the client in a Polish civil court, where the client is suing or is being sued by another company for breaching a contract and/or causing loss to the other party. Depending on the size and scale of the lawsuit in terms of the money involved and the number of operations affected, the corporate client will be represented only by their most senior local executive (country or general manager) or additionally by a vice-president responsible for the Polish market.

Stages of the court hearing:

1. Prior to the hearing the lawyer has to develop a strategy and obtain her client's approval, as well as prepare all the procedural writs and statements that will be used in court, usually in two language versions: in Polish for the court and in English for the client.
2. At the beginning of the hearing, the lawyer often reads a statement on behalf of his or her client.
3. Throughout the hearing the lawyer comments on the proceedings, translates relevant statements by other parties and speaks on behalf of the client, which may include longer speeches.

Litigation is a win/lose situation, which contributes to its considerable stressfulness. In addition, representing the client in court requires considerable public speaking skills, which many professionals lack due to the fact that in Poland these skills are not formally taught at either secondary or higher level. Also contributing to the challenge is the need to interpret for the foreign client in a situation where every word counts and misinterpretations are frequent as Polish and English legal terminology does not always correspond. Finally, at issue are the lawyer's own and the law firm's reputation, which may suffer greatly if a relatively simple case is lost.

Situation 5: Procurement of legal documents at the client's request

Communication situation: procurement of legal documents at the client's request

Location: the lawyer's office

Persons: the client who requested the document, the lawyer assigned to the task (according to the area of expertise), the supervising partner, (possibly also a fellow lawyer or a foreign counterpart)

Challenge factors: finding appropriate English legal terms; dealing with client's (unrealistic) expectations and assumptions about Polish legal practice; negotiating revisions and adjustments to draft documents.

Details: A law firm has been requested to draw up a contract or agreement to protect their foreign/global corporate client's interests in dealing with a third party. In most cases, the third party is another company (customer, supplier or subcontractor), with which the client company collaborates or wishes to collaborate, but it may also be an individual (e.g. an employee or landlord) or a non-governmental organization (e.g. local environmentalists). The type of documents drawn up by the lawyers vary from relatively simple contracts of lease or employment, to lengthy agreements of cooperation, joint venture or acquisition.

Stages:

1. The lawyer sits down to work on the contract or agreement following an orientation meeting at which the client specifies what kind of document is needed and for what purposes, as well as providing all the necessary information and a model agreement (such as may have been used previously in a similar situation).

2. The lawyer checks whether the model agreement/contract conforms to Polish law and proceeds to modify it to ensure full compliance *or* the lawyer uses the client's model document to revise a Polish standard agreement/contract used in similar situations. Either way, the client works on two documents, one in Polish and the other in English, and refers to relevant Polish and sometimes also international legislation.

3. The lawyer presents a draft version of the agreement/contract to the client, which is then discussed and revised following some working meetings and an exchange of correspondence.

4. The final version of the document is presented to the client, usually in two language versions, English and Polish.

Writing legal contracts and agreements in English is generally seen as a challenge due to the specific language ('legalese') used for the purpose: formal, somewhat archaic and very conventional, unlike the language used for any kind of general or business writing. The task is rendered even more difficult by the differences existing between the Polish and English foreign legal systems and professional practices, which global corporate clients often find confusing and refuse to understand that an agreement that works perfectly well in Hungary or Slovakia does not comply with the Polish law and therefore needs to be amended. Also, adjusting and revising the document being procured requires a lot of interaction with the client in order to agree on the content and phrasing of each clause, which again calls for considerable communication and linguistic skills, particularly if done in face-to-face meetings rather than by email or letter.

F.   SNAPSHOT

A working day

A typical day in the life of a law professional begins around 9 am with checking email, which usually contains some office correspondence (memos) and some correspondence about cases in progress from clients, supervisors, foreign counterparts and business consultants involved. Considering that an average lawyer handles three–four cases simultaneously, the number of emails to write and answer is considerable. Communication with clients can also be conducted by phone or traditional mail, especially at local Polish law firms.

The next item on the professional's agenda may be an internal meeting with one of the firm's partners, during which the associate reports on the progress made on the cases he or she is currently working on or is assigned a new task. Alternatively, the lawyer may meet with a junior associate who is handling some aspects of the case to receive a report on the research or fact-finding conducted. Obviously, such meetings do not take place every single day, but they are quite frequent in international law firms, which provide legal services to major global corporations, especially telecoms, pharmaceuticals, chemical companies, retailers, banks and insurance companies. Conversely, in smaller Polish law firms attorneys enjoy a greater degree of independence and their work is less closely supervised by partners, but they have to handle all case work single-handedly.

After the staff meeting, it is time for the lawyer to sit down to work on the case: read relevant documents and legislation, draft agreements or contract, write formal legal opinions, statements or procedural writs, etc., which takes up most of the working day. If not working on the case in the privacy of his or her office, the professional may have to go out to handle some administrative formalities for a client.

Another frequent activity is meeting with the client to discuss case-related issues, develop a strategy, report on the progress made, present and discuss a draft of a document requested, etc. Just as frequently, the lawyer assists the client in business talks or negotiations with another company, a governmental or non-governmental organisation or, rarely, an individual (e.g. a present or former employee), representing their legal interests. Lawyers who specialise in civil litigation will additionally take part in court and arbitration hearings as their client's legal representatives. Such hearings may be scheduled at any time within the court's or chamber's working hours (9 am– 5pm)

All the above activities can be conducted in Polish or in English, depending on the nationality of individuals participating and interacting in a given situation. Statistically, most foreign language communication, both professional and social, is exchanged with foreign nationals representing corporate clients (usually senior executives or board members), foreign business consultants working for the same client or on another aspect of the same case, and with foreign co-workers employed with the same firm but in a different office.

TECHNOLOGY – INFORMATION TECHNOLOGY – TERTIARY EDUCATION

CEF PROFESSIONAL PROFILE

A.   BACKGROUND INFORMATION

Field	Information Technology
Education/Programme	Bachelor's Degree Programme in Computer Science Master's Degree Programme in Computer Science and Software Technologies
Specialisation(s)	Computer Science, Education in Computer Science and Information Technologies at School, Software Technologies, Business Computer Science and English
Degree/Qualification	BSc/MSc Computer Science BSc/MSc Computer Science and Information Technologies
Language	English
Drawn up by	Vanya Ivanova
Date / City and country / Organisation	3 March 2006, University of Plovdiv 'Paisii Hilendarski' Plovdiv, Bulgaria
Methods used for collecting the information (methods, persons, dates)	Written surveys and oral interviews conducted by Vanya Ivanova as follows: 15 February 2006 Interview with QA (Quality Assurance) leader at a software production company for mobile devices, Sofia 18 February 2006 Interview with system administrator at an international fair in Bulgaria March 2006 Interview and email correspondence with a programmer at a software producing company, Varna

B.   OCCUPATIONAL INFORMATION

Typical examples of professions/ occupations/jobs	(C++/ Java) Developers (Helpdesk) consultants (IT Field / Software licence) sales executives Database/System administrators Oracle/SQL administrators Programmers Project managers Software engineers System analysts System testers Teachers / University lecturers of computer science Team leaders Technical support representatives Web designers
Typical organisations, companies, communities to be employed in	Software production companies Internet communications companies Publishing companies Banks Insurance companies IT sectors of schools/universities/companies/institutions
Typical job descriptions	**Database administrator (DBA)** Planning, maintenance and development of a database Setting up disaster recovery (backups and testing of backups) Conducting performance analysis and tuning Assisting in aspects of database design Establishing the needs of database users

Planning data flows for a new or revised database

Mapping out the 'conceptual design' for a planned database in outline

Testing new systems

Maintaining data standards

Writing database documentation

Controlling access permissions and privileges

Training users in database functionality

Meeting users' access requirements and resolving their problems

Ensuring that storage, archiving, backup and recovery procedures are functioning correctly

Developing capacity planning

Working closely with IT project managers, database programmers and web developers

Providing technical support for outdated 'legacy' systems

Communicating regularly with technical, applications and operational staff to ensure the database integrity and security

Commissioning and installing new applications

Programmer

Following clear-cut and complete specifications to perform a variety of programming assignments requiring knowledge of established programming procedures and data processing requirements under general supervision:

Maintaining and modifying programs

Making approved changes by amending flowcharts

Developing processing logic and coding changes

Modifying tests and documents

Writing operational instructions for end users

Performing routine programming assignments requiring knowledge of established programming procedures and data processing requirements

Refining data and formats final product which is very similar to the input or is well defined when significantly different

Maintaining and modifying routine programs

Writing a new program code using prescribed specifications, as appropriate

Evaluating simple interrelationships between programs, e.g. whether a contemplated change in one part of a program would cause unwanted results in a related part

Analysing performance of programs and taking action to correct deficiencies based on consultation with users and approval of supervisor

Conferring with users to gain understanding of needed changes or modifications of existing programs

Providing on-call support and problem resolution for computer applications

Using judgement in selecting among authorised procedures and seeking assistance when guidelines are inadequate, significant deviations are proposed, or when unanticipated problems arise

Maintaining currency of knowledge with respect to relevant state-of-the-art technology, equipment, and/or systems

Performing miscellaneous job-related duties as assigned

Web designer

Developing and maintaining websites for a department, college, or programme

Creating content and/or adapting existing content to a web-friendly format

Creating and maintaining the logical structure of the content

Working with a variety of departments, colleges and others as appropriate

Developing and maintaining a plan for the organisation's internet presence, based on management priorities, policy directions and goals

Creating enhancements and modifications to websites

Organising and maintaining the sites

Assessing new standards, technologies and trends, and formulating strategies and plans for future enhancement of websites

Programming HTML and uploading pages to the websites

Ensuring that websites are accessible from a variety of different environments

Producing a consistent visual image on the websites, including maintenance of templates and image archives

Ensuring that images are delivered to the viewer at sufficiently high speed and quality

Creating image links, and ensuring that links are up to date; updating information on pages and databases so that the content is current

	Troubleshooting and repairing bugs and problems Responding to web designer mail; provides and analyses traffic statistics and reports Writing/Editing and creating layout for new sections/features Performing miscellaneous job-related duties as assigned
To what extent foreign languages are needed	English is used every day by all IT specialists in their work because it is the most common language in information technologies. The operating systems, applications, books and materials for keeping up with professional developments are in English. For this reason reading comprehension skills are the most important ones for IT people, as well as writing skills for communication purposes.

C.   CONTEXT INFORMATION

	LOCATION	PERSONS, COMMUNITIES, COMPANIES, INSTITUTIONS	COMMUNICATION SITUATIONS	TEXT- AND DISCOURSE-TYPES
Work context	The company's conference room The IT person's office The company cafeteria / a restaurant outside the building Conference rooms abroad	**Individual:** system administrator, quality assurer (QA), programmer; other members of the team, members of the company's personnel, the management staff **Professional:** English-speaking visitors from a subsidiary company, IT project partners of different nationalities	Making a weekly report in English about the work done during that period. Includes: • presenting information about the accomplishment of tasks set the previous week • informing the other members of the team of the types of problems they have had to solve, procedures they have taken and their effectiveness • answering related questions afterwards	• Acting in accordance with messages on the computer screen • An exchange of emails • Conducting telephone conversations • Giving/Attending presentations • Participation in net meetings and video conferences • Contribution to forum • Discussions/Chat online (individually or in groups) • Writing faxes, memos, reports • Lectures/presentations by teachers / fellow students / visiting lecturers

Hosting visitors from a subsidiary company:
- Introducing oneself to the visitor(s), small talk
- Taking them around the company to meet members of the personnel
- Having lunch with the visitor(s)
- Optional – taking the visitor(s) on a short trip to do some sightseeing

Working as part of a team on an international project with partners from different nationalities:
- Writing software programs, fault analysis and solving problems in the course of work
- Online communication with project partners
- Meeting project partners (which involves explaining work methods and procedures, and demonstrating the product(s))

- Working with textbooks/dictionaries
- Writing/Reading essays
- Making own webpages
- Using authentic texts
- Reading textbooks, dictionaries, reference books
- Exercise materials
- Advertisements
- Public announcements and notices
- Instructional material
- Tickets, timetables

Study context	Educational: exchange students from foreign countries, foreign university lecturers, the teaching/ assistant staff at university: pro- fessors, lecturers, fellow students, library staff, secretaries, local people	Listening to lectures Participating in class discussions/ conversations/dialogues (role play) Preparing and making presenta- tions of course projects Taking notes Writing home assignments Essay writing Library work Participation in seminars and tutorials Getting relevant information (e.g. when travelling: finding accom- modation, having meals, etc.)
	At university – lecture halls, seminar rooms At a foreign university in Europe (as part of foreign exchange programmes) – lecture halls, seminar rooms, halls of residence Public spaces	

D.   THE MOST FREQUENT ROUTINE SITUATIONS

Situation 1: Induction for a new employee

Communication situation: introducing a new employee to his or her work

Location: the company's new employee's office

Persons: a computer specialist and an IT person

Critical success factors: introducing oneself, using small talk, reading databases, providing instructions, discussing procedures / stages in completing a task / deadlines

Details: An IT company has employed an English-speaking IT person, and a computer specialist working there is expected to introduce himself/herself to the new person, explain their responsibilities, routines and ways of doing things in their job, demonstrate software products and set tasks to complete in order to put the new knowledge into practice.

Situation 2: Dealing with telephone queries

Communication situation: redirecting telephone calls from clients or employees of the company to an IT specialist

Location: the IT person's office

Persons: IT person (Help Desk assistant), company employees, company clients

Critical success factors: conducting telephone conversations, being able to ask general/specific questions in order to select the exact person to deal with the problem that has arisen

Details: A client or employee of the company telephones the IT Help Desk because he or she has encountered a computer problem. The assistant asks detailed questions in order to determine the exact nature of the problem. He or she then redirects the call to the person responsible for handling those specific issues.

E.   THE MOST DEMANDING SITUATIONS

Situation 1: Negotiating the details of a project

Communication situation: a negotiation meeting with international company managers

Location: a conference room in the company branch

Persons: an international manager of the company, computer programmers, representative(s) of a subsidiary company

Challenge factors: communication using various styles and modes (informal, formal, specialist programming knowledge, drawings and diagrams); coping with different cultural expectations of the participants.

Details: A large software producing company has been assigned the demanding project of making bank cards for a bank (Postbank). The international managers of the company have scheduled a meeting to examine the data submitted by their client, negotiate the details and set deadlines for the separate stages of the project. They also need to come to an agreement about testing the final product.

Stages of the negotiation:

1. Greetings and introductions
2. A brief presentation of the project by an international manager
3. A more detailed consideration of relevant data concerning the project
4. Dividing the work to be done into modules
5. Negotiating the form and content of the work (e.g. discussing the format of the product (to be made in Windows/DOS, etc.))
6. Distributing the work to be done among company subsidiaries
7. Setting deadlines for completing the separate stages of work
8. Ensuring adherence to a common standard

This situation requires very good foreign language skills from all participants in the meeting. It is crucial for them to understand the details of the talks in order to reach an agreement. For that reason the meeting participants need to communicate effectively using both general language and key programming terms, and to make sure that everyone is following the discussions they draw diagrams and write down explanations, dates, contact information, etc. The situation is demanding for another reason too, which is presented by the diverse nationalities of the participants in the meeting. Sometimes non-linguistic factors interfere with the process of communication, such as cultural difference between participants, willingness to make concessions, etc.

Situation 2: Finding solutions to the problem of a dissatisfied client

Communication situation: a meeting with unhappy company clients in order to solve problems

Location: the system administrator's office or the exhibiting hall where the computer(s) of the company is (are) located

Persons: the system administrator of the International Fair, representative(s) of the company exhibiting at the Fair

Challenge factors: acknowledging the client's frustration and stress, using appropriate polite and sympathetic language; identifying and explaining the cause of a problem and offering a solution; coping with different cultural expectations of the participants.

Details: Twice a year an International Fair is held in Bulgaria. Companies from all over the world send their representatives to it to introduce their specialised products/services. In order to do that adequately, most of them need to rent certain hardware and software from the internet provider on the premises of the fair. Sometimes problems arise because of assumptions people make on the basis of their experience with types of services and providers in their own countries, for example related to the speed of the connection or services available. Thus discrepancies occur between expectations and actual results, which need to be clarified and sorted out. The company representative goes to the system administrator of the Fair and they discuss the problem(s).

Stages of the meeting:

1. Greetings
2. A brief introduction to the problem by the person from the exhibiting company
3. Determining the exact nature of the problem by the system administrator's asking detailed questions
4. Finding a plausible solution to the problem

The situation is demanding because communicating effectively with an unhappy customer is always a difficult and challenging task. The system administrator of the Fair has to possess excellent communication skills to deal with unhappy clients. He or she is required to determine the nature of the problem by asking questions, answering enquiries and giving satisfactory explanations to them, and also offering plausible solutions. Sometimes the clients cannot explain the problem well, especially under stressful circumstances, and they slip into their own language, which can make the situation rather delicate. The situation needs to be discussed while taking into consideration the cultural differences between the participants in the conversation as well, remaining polite and efficient at all times.

Sometimes the solution to the problem requires the system administrator to act as a mediator between the client of the Fair and another IT person (for example, a hardware engineer who has very limited knowledge of the foreign language), interpreting things without any preparation in advance for as long as it takes to have the problem solved, and that can prove quite a challenging task.

Situation 3: Stage completion review meeting

Communication situation: a partner meeting at the end of a project stage

Location: a conference room

Persons: programmers, programmers and management of the client company

Challenge factors: all the participants are communicating in a second language (English); discussion and agreement on precise details (knowledge of specific programming terminology required).

Details: A Bulgarian software producing company is set the project task of writing some software by an international company (Greece). Normally, the work is done in three stages: first, negotiating the task, second, implementation of the project, and third comes the testing, including the acceptance tests. The participants of the project meet at the end of each stage for a detailed discussion of what has been achieved until then and what remains to be done. At the end of the implementation stage, the project partners meet in Greece to present the pieces of work each of them has completed and put it all together in order to start the tests. Communication is carried out in English.

Stages of the meeting:

1. Greetings and introductions
2. Presenting the work done by the Bulgarian programmers
3. Presenting the work done by the Greek programmers
4. Putting their pieces of work together and finding solutions to a possible lack of consistency
5. Reaching an agreement about test procedures and deadlines

The situation is demanding, first of all because of the linguistic factor: the communication is taking place in a foreign setting and language for the Bulgarian IT specialists. Secondly, the completion of the implementation stage is very important because the work has to be put together well in order to ensure the success of the testing process. Comprehension and speaking skills are very important for the participants in the discussions, as well as content-related knowledge and the necessary terminology, in order that they are able to justify the solutions and choices they have made in their work.

F.   SNAPSHOT

Background

I am a quality assurance engineer working in Bulgaria. I have two main fields of interest, which are connected with the specific nature of my post. As a quality assurance leader, I work with various people, so I take a professional interest in effective communication with people. I read about how to behave with different people and I study ways and techniques of organising their work. The other sphere of interest for me is connected with programming – I keep up with new developments on a regular basis. I study the specifications of certain devices and write Java C. In my work I make test cases, which need to cover most of the functionality of the product we are working with at the moment, and I run the tests.

I currently work in Quality Assurance (QA) for a software production company for mobile devices. The company is located in the USA but has subsidiaries all over the world, for example in Japan, India, Italy, Romania and of course Bulgaria, where I work full time five days a week. Sometimes colleagues from the different subsidiaries visit our company to meet and discuss our work, but usually we communicate via the Internet. Occasionally I attend some further professional training or an English language course.

A working day

I normally start work about 30 minutes or an hour earlier than my colleagues. The very first thing I do when I get into the office is to sit down and check my email. I sort all the messages I have received by their subjects, according to their level of importance, and I flag the most imperative ones. Then I read them and take notes about current problems described in them, or tasks to do. If there are set tasks to carry out during the day, I prioritise them and develop an initial plan of action. Some emails require specific explanations concerning certain problems or products we are working with, so I gather additional information and/or materials in order to write an adequate and accurate reply to the messages. After I have finished reading my emails, I go to the development team and we discuss the current situation of the project we are working on, as well as problems that have arisen by the end of the previous working day, or issues from the morning emails. We also talk about possible tasks that could be conferred to the QA people in order to help the development team in their work. Then I lay down a detailed plan for the day including all that needs to be done. Later on I arrange a meeting for the QA team and we make an analysis of the work done the day before, based on which the team members' tasks for the day are set. Having allocated the responsibilities for the day, I go back to my emails and write the replies. As a member of the QA team, I share my colleagues' work. Whatever problems arise in the course of work, I have to make decisions and find ways of solving them. At the end of the working day, I collect information about the implementation of the tasks and use it to make a report, which I send to my superiors.

Language

Although the nationality of all of my colleagues at work is Bulgarian, our entire official correspondence is in English because the company owners are American. That means that tasks are set, discussed and reported on in English, as well as all the reports and presentations we make and attend. It is easier to stick to one language (even a foreign one) than to switch from English into Bulgarian and then back into English. Besides, the information and materials we use, and the applications and messages on the computer screen, are all in English. I use my communication skills in English on a daily basis, but I also have to be able to talk to people face to face and via chat programs too.

References

Aho, R. (2003). *Systematic Language-in-Education Planning: The Finnish Defence Forces in Focus.* Jyväskylä: Centre for Applied Language Studies, University of Jyväskylä.

Albrecht, L. (1995). *Textual Analysis: The Production of Text.* Frederiksberg: Samfundslitteratur.

Argyris, C. (2002). Double-loop learning, teaching, and research, *Academy of Management Learning and Education*, 1 (2), 206–18.

Argyris, C. & Schön, D. (1996). *Organizational Learning II: Theory, Method, and Practice.* Reading, MA: Addison-Wesley.

Baldauf, R. & Kaplan, R. (2005). Language-in-education planning. In E. Hinkel (ed.), *Handbook of Research in Second Language Teaching and Learning.* Mahwah, NJ: Lawrence Erlbaum, 1013–34.

Barton, D. & Tusting, K. (2005). *Beyond Communities of Practice.* Cambridge: Cambridge University Press.

Basturkmen, H. (1999). Discourse in MBA seminars: towards a description for pedagogical purposes, *English for Specific Purposes*, 18, 63–80.

Bazerman, C, and Russell, D. (2003). *Writing Selves/Writing Societies: Research from Activity Perspectives.* Fort Collins, CO: The WAC Clearinghouse and Mind, Culture, and Activity. Available at http://wac.colostate.edu/books/selves_societies/. Retrieved 15 August 2012.

Belcher, D. D. (2006). English for specific purposes: teaching to perceived needs and imagined futures in worlds of work, study, and everyday life, *TESOL Quarterly*, 40, 1, 133–56.

Benson, P. (2000). *Teaching and Researching Learner Autonomy.* Harlow: Longman.

Benson, P. (2011). *Teaching and Researching Autonomy in Language Learning*, 2nd edn. Harlow: Longman.

Berkenkotter, C. & Huckin, T. N. (1995). *Genre Knowledge in Disciplinary Communication: Cognition/Culture/Power.* Hillsdale, NJ: Lawrence Erlbaum.

Bernat, E. & Gvozdenko, I. (2005). Beliefs about language learning: current knowledge, pedagogical implications, and new research directions, *TESL-EJ* 9 (1). Available at http://tesl-ej.org/ej33/a1.html. Retrieved 5 May, 2010.

Berwick, R. (1989). Needs assessment in language programming: from theory to practice. In R. K. Johnson (ed.), *The Second Language Curriculum.* Cambridge: Cambridge University Press, 48–62.

Bhatia, V. K. [1993] (1998). *Analysing Genre: Language Use in Professional Settings*, 2nd edn. London and New York: Longman.

Bhatia, V. K. (2000). Genres in conflict. In A. Trosborg (ed.), *Analysing Professional Genres.* Pragmatics and Beyond. Amsterdam and Philadelphia: Benjamins, 147–62.

Bhatia, V. K. (2002). Applied genre analysis: a multi-perspective model, *IBÉRICA*, 4, 3–19.

Bhatia, V. K. (2004). *Worlds of Written Discourse: A Genre-Based View.* Advances in Applied Linguistics. London and New York: Continuum.

Bhatia, V. K. & Candlin, C. N. (eds.) (2001). Teaching English to meet the needs of business education in Hong Kong. A project report published by the Centre for English Language Education and Communication Research, City University of Hong Kong.

Blackledge, A. (2005). *Discourse and Power in a Multilingual World*. Amsterdam and Philadelphia: John Benjamins.

Boswood, T. (1999). Redefining the professional in international professional communication. In C. R. Lovitt and D. Goswami (eds.), *Exploring the Rhetoric of International Professional Communication: An Agenda for Teachers and Researchers*. Amityville, NY: Baywood Publishing, 111–36.

Breen, M. P. & Candlin, C. N. (1980). The essentials of a *communicative* curriculum in language teaching, *Applied Linguistics*, 1 (2), 89–112.

Brindley, G. (1989). The role of needs analysis in adult ESL programme design. In R. K. Johnson (ed.), *The Second Language Curriculum*. Cambridge: Cambridge University Press, 63–78.

Broekstra, G. (1998). An organization is a conversation. In D. Grant, T. Keenoy and C. Oswick (eds.), *Discourse and Organization*. London, Thousand Oaks, CA and New Delhi: Sage Publications, 152–76.

Brown, J. D. [2004] (2006). Research methods for applied linguistics: scope, characteristics and standards. In A. Davies and C. Elder (eds.), *The Handbook of Applied Linguistics*. Malden, MA: Blackwell Publishing, 476–500.

Brown, J. D. (2006). Second language studies: curriculum development. In K. Brown (ed.), *Encyclopedia of Language and Linguistics*, 2nd edn. Oxford: Elsevier, 102–10.

Candlin, C. N. (1987). Towards task-based language learning. In C. N. Candlin and D. F. Murphy (eds.), *Language Learning Tasks*. London: Prentice Hall, 5–22.

Candlin, C.N. (ed.) (2002). *Research and Practice in Professional Discourse*. Hong Kong: City University of Hong Kong Press.

Candlin, C. N. (2005). *Researching and Teaching for a Living Curriculum: Australia's Critical Contribution to Praxis in Language Teaching and Learning*. Available at http://www.immi.gov.au/amep/reports/pubs/papers/candlin.htm. Retrieved 4 April 2006.

Candlin, C. N. (2006). Accounting for interdiscursivity: challenges to professional expertise. In M. Gotti and D. Giannone (eds.), *New Trends in Specialized Discourse*. Bern: Peter Lang, 1–25.

Candlin, C. N. & Crichton, J. (eds.) (2010). *Discourses of Deficit*. Basingstoke: Palgrave Macmillan.

Candlin, C. N. & Maley, Y. (1997). Intertextuality and interdiscursivity in the discourse of alternative dispute resolution. In B.-L. Gunnarsson, P. Linell and B. Nordberg (eds.), *The Construction of Professional Discourse*. London: Longman, 201–22.

Candlin, C. N. & Plum, G. A. (1999). Engaging with challenges of interdiscursivity in academic writing: researchers, students and tutors. In C. N. Candlin & K. Hyland (eds.), *Writing: Texts, Processes and Practices*. London: Longman, 193–217.

Cicourel, A. V. (1992). The interpenetration of communicative contexts: examples from medical encounters. In A. Duranti and C. Goodwin (eds.), *Rethinking Context: Language as an Interactive Phenomenon*. Cambridge: Cambridge University Press, 291–310.

Cicourel, A. V. (2007). A personal, retrospective view of ecological validity, *Text & Talk*, 27 (5/6), 735–52.

Clarke, R. J. (2002). Intertextuality at work: large-scale organisation of workpractices. In K. C. Liu, R. J. Clarke, P. B. Anderson and R. K. Stamper (eds.), *Coordination and Communication*

Using Signs: Studies in Organisational Semiotics. Boston, Dordrecht and London: Kluwer Academic Publishers, 59–83.

Council of Europe. (2001). *Common European Framework of Reference for Languages: Learning, Teaching, Assessment.* Cambridge: Cambridge University Press.

Creswell, J. (2003). *Research Design. Qualitative, Quantitative and Mixed Methods Approaches.* Thousand Oaks, CA: Sage Publications.

Crichton, J. (2010). *The Discourse of Commercialization: A Multi-Perspectived Analysis.* Basingstoke: Palgrave Macmillan.

Dam, L. (1995). *Autonomy from Theory to Classroom Practice.* Dublin: Authentik.

Denzin, N. K. (1978). *The Research Act: A Theoretical Introduction to Sociological Methods.* Englewood Cliffs, NJ: Prentice Hall.

Di Pietro, R. J. (1987). *Strategic Interaction: Learning Languages through Scenarios.* Cambridge: Cambridge University Press.

Dörnyei, Z. (2003). *Questionnaires in Second Language Research: Construction, Administration, and Processing.* Mahwah, NJ: Lawrence Erlbaum.

Dörnyei, Z. (2007). *Research Methods in Applied Linguistics.* Oxford: Oxford University Press.

Douglas, D. (2000). *Assessing Languages for Specific Purposes.* Cambridge: Cambridge University Press.

Dudley-Evans, T. (1994). Genre analysis: an approach to text analysis for ESP. In M. Coulthard (ed.), *Advances in Written Text Analysis.* London: Routledge, 219–28.

Dudley-Evans, T. & St. John, M. (1998). *Developments in English for Specific Purposes.* Cambridge: Cambridge University Press.

Dudley-Evans, T. & St John, M. [1998] (2002). *Developments in ESP: A Multidisciplinary Approach,* 4th edn. Cambridge: Cambridge University Press.

Ellis, R. (2003). *Task-Based Language Learning and Teaching.* Oxford: Oxford University Press.

Ewer, J. R. & Latorre, G. (1969). *A Course in Basic Scientific English.* London: Longman.

Fairclough, N. (1995). *Discourse and Social Change.* Cambridge: Polity Press.

Fairclough, N. (2001). *Language and Power,* 2nd edn. Harlow: Longman.

Fiske, J. (1990). *Introduction to Communication Studies,* 2nd edn. London and New York: Routledge.

Foucault, M. (1982). *Power/Knowledge: Selected Interviews and Other Writings by Michel Foucault, 1972–1977.* New York: Pantheon.

Freedman, A. & Medway, P. (eds.) (1994). *Genre and the New Rhetoric.* London: Taylor & Francis.

Freeman, R. E. & Reed, D. L. (1983). Stockholders and stakeholders: a new perspective on corporate governance, *California Management Review,* 25 (3), 88–105.

Gee, J. P. (1996). *Social Linguistics and Literacies: Ideology in Discourses,* 2nd edn. London: Taylor & Francis.

Glowacz, R. (2004). A language audit in a Polish financial and legal consultancy. In C. Koster (ed.), *Language Auditing.* Amsterdam: de Werelt, 201–19.

Goffman, E. (1959). *The Presentation of Self in Everyday Life.* Garden City, NY: Doubleday.

Grant, D., Keenoy, T. and Oswick, C. (2001). Organizational discourse, *International Studies of Management and Organization,* 31 (3), 5–24.

Gunnarsson, B.-L. (2000). Discourse, organizations and national cultures, *Discourse Studies,* 2 (1), 5–33.

Hagen, S. (ed.) (1999). *Business Communication across Borders: A Study of Language Use and Practice in European Companies.* London: Languages National Training Organization.

Hall, A. (2007). Fremdsprachenkenntnisse im Beruf – Anforderungen an Erwerbstätige, *Berufsbildung in Wissenschaft und Praxis,* 36 (3), 48–9.

Hall, D. R. (2001a). Materials writing: theory and practice. In D. R. Hall and A. Hewings (eds.), *Innovation in Language Teaching*. London: Routledge, 229–39.

Hall, D. R. (2001b). Relinquishing teacher control: learners as generators of course content. In I. Leki (ed.), *Academic Writing Programs*. Washington: TESOL: Case Studies in TESOL Practice, 147–57.

Halliday, M. A. K. (1978). *Language as a Social Semiotic*. London: Edward Arnold.

Halliday, M. A. K. (1985). *An Introduction to Functional Grammar*. London: Edward Arnold.

Hatch, M. J. (1997). *Organization Theory: Modern, Symbolic and Postmodern Perspectives*. Oxford: Oxford University Press.

Hecker, U. (2000). Berufswechsel – Chancen und Risiken. Ergebnisse der BIBB/ IAB-Erhebung 1998/99, *Berufsbildung in Wissenschaft und Praxis*, 29 (4), 12–17.

Herbert, A. J. (1965).*The Structure of Technical English*. Harlow: Longman.

Hirokawa, R. Y. & Poole, M. S. (eds.) (2004). *Communication and Group Decision Making*, 2nd edn. Thousand Oaks, CA: Sage Publications.

Hirokawa, R. Y., Erbert, L. & Hurst, A. (2004). Communication and group decision-making effectiveness. In R. Y. Hirokawa and M. S. Poole (eds.), *Communication and Group Decision Making*, 2nd edn. Thousand Oaks, CA: Sage Publications, 269–300.

Holec, H. (1981). *Autonomy and Foreign Language Learning*. Oxford: Pergamon.

Holme, R. & Chalauisaeng, B. (2006). The learner as needs analyst: the use of participatory appraisal in the EAP reading classroom, *English for Specific Purposes*, 25, 403–19.

Huckin, T. (2003). Specificity in LSP, *IBÉRICA*, 5, 3–17.

Huhta, M. (1997). *The Dynamics of Language Training: From an Element of Cost into an Investment in Communication*. Helsinki: Opetushallitus. Tutkimus/Research 1.

Huhta, M. (1999). *Language/Communication Skills in Industry and Business: Report for Prolang, Finland*. Helsinki: Opetushallitus. Available at http://www.oph.fi/download/47735_skills42.pdf. Retrieved 15 August 2012.

Huhta, M. (2002a). *Tools for Planning Language Training: Language Policy Division Directorate of School, Out-of-School and Higher Education*, DG IV. Strasbourg: Council of Europe. Available at http://www.coe.int/t/dg4/linguistic/Source/HuhtaEN.pdf. Retrieved 15 August 2012.

Huhta, M. [2000] (2002b). *Connections: Communication Guidelines for Engineers*. Helsinki: Edita.

Huhta, M. (2007). CEF Professional Project: developing a CEF-based design method for professional purposes. In S. Schöpper-Grabe and K. Vogt (eds.), *Fremdsprachen in der Berufswelt: Foreign Languages in the World of Work*. Frankfurt am Main: Peter Lang, 33–46.

Huhta, M. (2010). *Language and Communication for Professional Purposes: Needs Analysis Methods in Industry and Business and their Yield to Stakeholders*. Espoo: Yliopistopaino. Helsinki University of Technology. Doctoral dissertation. Available at: http://lib.tkk.fi/Diss/2010/isbn9789522482273/isbn9789522482273.pdf.

Huhta, M., Jaatinen, R. & Johnson, E. (2006). Työelämään valmentavan kieltenopetuksen perusteet (The fundamentals of Language and Communication for Professional Purposes). In M. Huhta, E. Johnson, U. Lax and S. Hantula (eds.), *Työelämän kieli- ja viestintätaito* (Language and Communication Skills in the Workplace). Helsinki: Yliopistopaino. Helsingin ammattikorkeakoulu Stadian julkaisuja Sarja A. Tutkimukset ja raportit 8, 32–57.

Hutchinson, T. & Waters, A. (1980). ESP at the crossroads. Reprinted in J. Swales, *Episodes in ESP*. Oxford: Pergamon, 1985.

Hutchinson, T. & Waters, A. (1987). *English for Specific Purposes: A Learner-Centred Approach*. Cambridge: Cambridge University Press.

Hyland, K. (2000). *Disciplinary Discourses: Social Interactions in Academic Writing.* London: Longman.

Hyland, K. (2002). Specificity revisited: how far should we go now? *English for Specific Purposes*, 21 (4), 385–95.

Jaatinen, R. (2001). Autobiographical knowledge of foreign language education and teacher development. In V. Kohonen, R. Jaatinen, P. Kaikkonen and J. Lehtovaara (eds.), *Experiential Learning in Foreign Language Education.* London: Longman, 106–40.

Jackson, M. [2003] (2007). *Systems Thinking: Creative Holism for Managers.* Chichester: Wiley.

Jasso-Aguilar, R. (1999). Sources, methods and triangulation in needs analysis: a critical perspective in a case study of Waikiki hotel maids. *English for Specific Purposes*, 18, 27–46.

Johns, A. M. (1997). *Text, Role and Context: Developing Academic Literacies.* Cambridge: Cambridge University Press.

Johns, A. M. (ed.) (2002). *Genre in the Classroom: Multiple Perspectives.* Mahwah, NJ: Lawrence Erlbaum.

Johnson, E. (2006). Kieli- ja viestintäosaamisen kehittämismalli (Model for Developing Language and Communication Competences). In E. Johnson (ed.), *Kieli ja viestintä ICT-alan arjessa (Language and Communication in the Everyday Life of the ICT Sector).* Keski-Pohjanmaan ammattikorkeakoulu. Sarja A: Tutkimusraportteja – Forskningsrapporter. Kokkola: Keski-Pohjanmaan, 22–58.

Kankaanranta, A. (2005). *'Hej, Seppo, could you pls comment on this?' Internal Email Communication in Lingua Franca English in a Multinational Company.* Centre for Applied Language Studies. Jyväskylä: University of Jyväskylä Printing House.

Kersten, A. (1986). A critical-interpretive approach to the study of organizational communication: bringing communication back to the field. In L. Thayer (ed.), *Organization to Communication: Emerging Perspectives I.* Norwood, NJ: Ablex Publishing Corporation, 133–50.

Kiely, R., Rea-Dickins, P., Woodfield, H. and Clibbon, G. (2006). *Language, Culture and Identity in Applied Linguistics.* London: BAAL/Equinox.

Killoran, J. B. (2006). Self-published web résumés: their purpose and their genre system, *Journal of Business and Technical Communication*, 20 (4), 425–59.

Kohonen, V. (2001). Towards experiential foreign language education. In V. Kohonen, R. Jaatinen, P. Kaikkonen and J. Lehtovaara (eds.), *Experiential Learning in Foreign Language Education.* London: Longman, 8–60.

Kohonen, V. (2005). The Common European Framework of Reference and the Language Portfolio as a challenge for developing FL education. *Panorama* (Schola Europea, Brussels), 1/2005, 18–27.

Koster, C. (2004a). Areas of competence of a language auditor. In C. Koster (ed.), *A Handbook on Language Auditing.* Amsterdam: Editions 'de Werelt', 32–62.

Koster, C. (2004b). Language auditing: an introduction. In C. Koster (ed.), *A Handbook on Language Auditing.* Amsterdam: Editions 'de Werelt', 5–13.

Koster, C. (ed.) (2004c). *A Handbook of Language Auditing.* Amsterdam: Editions 'de Werelt'.

Kragh, B. & Basballe, T. (2000). *Analysing Professional and Academic Texts.* Copenhagen: Copenhagen Business School.

Lave, J. & Wenger, E. (1991). *Situated Learning: Legitimate Peripheral Participation.* Cambridge: Cambridge University Press.

Layder, D. (1993). *New Strategies of Social Research.* Cambridge: Polity Press.

Layder, D. (1997). *Modern Social Theory: Key Debates and New Directions.* London: UCL Press.

Little, D. (1991). *Learner Autonomy: Definitions, Issues and Problems*. Dublin: Authentik.

Long, M. (1985). A role for instruction in second language acquisition: task-based language training. In K. Hylenstam and M. Pienemann (eds.), *Modelling and Assessing Second Language Acquisition*. Clevedon: Multilingual Matters, 77–99.

Long, M. (2005). Methodological issues in language needs analysis. In M. Long (ed.), *Second Language Needs Analysis*. Cambridge: Cambridge University Press, 19–76.

Louhiala-Salminen, L. (1999). 'Was there life before them?' Fax and email in business communication, *The Journal of Language for International Business*, 10, 24–42.

Louhiala-Salminen, L. (2002). The fly's perspective: discourse in the daily routine of a business manager, *English for Specific Purposes*, 21, 211–31.

Louhiala-Salminen, L. & Kankaanranta, A. (2005). 'Hello Monica – kindly change your arrangements': business genres in a state of flux. In P. Gillaerts and M. Gotti (eds.), *Genre Variation in Business Letters: Linguistic Insights*. Bern: Peter Lang, 55–84.

Luoma, M. (2000). *Human Resource Development as a Strategic Activity: A Single Component View of Strategic Human Resource Management*. Vaasa: University of Vaasa.

Mackay, R. & Mountford, A. (eds.) (1978). *English for Specific Purposes: A Case Study Approach*. London: Longman.

Martin, J. (1993). Life as a noun. In M. A. K. Halliday and J. R. Martin (eds.), *Writing Science: Literacy as Discursive Power*. London: Falmer Press, 221–67.

Matthes, C.-Y. & Wordelmann, P. (1995). *Fachkräfte, Fremdsprachen und Mobilität*. Bielefeld: Bertelsmann.

Mauranen, A. (2003). The corpus of English as a lingua franca in academic settings. *TESOL Quarterly*, 37, 513–27.

Mead, R. (1982). Review of Munby 1978, *Applied Linguistics*, 3 (1): 70–8.

Mendelow, A. L. (1987). Stakeholder analysis of strategic planning and implementation. In W. R. King and D. I. Cleland (eds.), *Strategic Planning and Management Handbook*. New York: Van Nostrand Reinhold, 176–91.

Miller, C. & Shepherd, D. (2004). Blogging as social action: a genre analysis of the weblog. In L. J. Gurak, S. Antonijevic, L. Johnson, C. Ratcliff and J. Reyman (eds.), *Into the Blogosphere: Rhetoric, Community and Culture of Weblogs*. Available online at http://blog.lib.umn.edu/blogosphere/. Retrieved 15 August 2012.

Munby, J. (1978). *Communicative Syllabus Design*. Cambridge: Cambridge University Press.

Norton, B. (2000). *Identity and Language Learning: Gender, Ethnicity and Educational Change*. Harlow: Pearson Education.

Nunan, D. (1989). *Designing Tasks for the Communicative Classroom*. Cambridge: Cambridge University Press.

Nunan, D. (2004). *Task-Based Language Teaching*. Cambridge: Cambridge University Press.

O'Halloran, K. L., ed. (2004). *Multimodal Discourse Analysis: Systemic-Functional Perspectives*. London: Continuum.

Orlikowski, W. J. and Yates, J. (1994). Genre repertoire: the structuring of communicative practices in organizations, *Administrative Science Quarterly*, 39 (4), 541–74.

Patton, M. (1990). *Qualitative Evaluation and Research Methods*, 2nd edn. Newbury Park, CA: Sage Publications.

Patton, M. (2002). *Qualitative Research and Evaluation Methods*, 3rd edn. Thousand Oaks, CA: Sage Publications.

Poncini, G. (2002). Business relationships and roles in a multicultural group: an investigation of discourse at an Italian company's meetings of its international distributors. Doctoral dissertation, University of Birmingham, UK.

Reeves, N. & Wright, C. (1996). *Linguistic Auditing: A Guide to Identifying Foreign Language Communication Needs in Corporations*. Clevedon: Multilingual Matters.

Richards, J. C. (1989). *The Context of Language Teaching*. Cambridge: Cambridge University Press.

Risager, K. (2006). *Language and Culture: Global Flaws and Local Complexity*. Clevedon: Multilingual Matters.

Risager, K. (2007). *Language and Culture Pedagogy: From a National to a Transnational Paradigm*. Clevedon: Multilingual Matters.

Roberts, C., Byram, M., Barro, A., Jordan, S. & Street, B. (2001). *Language Learners as Ethnographers*. Clevedon: Multilingual Matters.

Robinson, P. (1991). *ESP Today: A Practitioner's Guide*. New York: Prentice Hall.

Samuda, V. & Bygate, M. (2008). *Tasks in Second Language Learning*. Basingstoke: Palgrave Macmillan.

Sarangi, S. (2005). The conditions and consequences of professional discourse studies, *Journal of Applied Linguistics*, 2 (3), 371–94.

Sarangi, S. & Candlin, C. N. (2001). 'Motivational relevancies': some methodological reflections on social theoretical and sociolinguistic practice. In N. Coupland, S. Sarangi and C. N. Candlin (eds.), *Sociolinguistics and Social Theory*. London: Longman, 350–88.

Sarangi, S. & Candlin, C. N. (2011). Professional and organisational practice: a discourse/communication perspective. In C. N. Candlin and S. Sarangi (eds.), *Handbook of Applied Linguistics: Communication in Organisations and Professions*. Berlin: Mouton de Gruyter, 3–48.

Sarangi, S. & Roberts, C. (eds.) (1999). *Talk, Work and Institutional Order. Discourse in Medical and Management Settings*. Berlin: Mouton de Gruyter.

Savage, W. & Storer, G. (1992). An emergent language program framework: actively involving learners in needs analysis, *System*, 20 (2), 187–99.

Saville-Troike, M. [1982] (1989). *The Ethnography of Communication: An Introduction*, 2nd edn. Oxford: Blackwell Publishing.

Schöpper-Grabe, S. & Weiß, R. (1998). *Vorsprung durch Fremdsprachentraining*. Cologne: Deutscher Institutsverlag (=Kölner Texte und Thesen 43).

Schröder, K. (1984). Fremdsprachenbedarf bei Schering: 183 Arbeitsplatzanalysen (unteres und mittleres Management), *Die Neueren Sprachen*, 83, 78–103.

Scollon, R. (2001). *Mediated Discourse: The Nexus of Practice*. London: Routledge.

Scollon, R. & Scollon, S.W. [1995] (2001). *Intercultural Communication: A Discourse Approach*. Oxford: Blackwell Publishing.

Senge, P. M. (1990). *The Fifth Discipline: The Art and Practice of the Learning Organization*. New York: Doubleday.

Sešek, U. (2007). English for teachers of EFL: toward a holistic description, *English for Specific Purposes*, 26, 411–25.

Skehan, P. (1998). *A Cognitive Approach to Language Learning*. Oxford: Oxford University Press.

Strevens, P. (1988a). The learner and teacher of ESP. In D. Chamberlain and R. J. Baumgardner (eds.), *ESP in the Classroom: Practice and Evaluation*. Hong Kong: Modern English Publications and the British Council, 39–44.

Strevens, P. (1988b). ESP after twenty years: a re-appraisal. In M. Tickoo (ed.), *ESP: State of the Art*. Singapore: SEAMEO Regional Language Centre, 1–13.

Swales, J. M. (1971). *Writing Scientific English*. London: Nelson.

Swales, J. M. (1980). ESP: the textbook problem. *The ESP Journal*, 1 (1), 11–23.

Swales, J. M. (1981). *Aspects of Article Introductions*. University of Aston Language Studies Unit.

Swales, J. M. (1990). *Genre Analysis: English in Academic and Research Settings*. Cambridge: Cambridge University Press.

Swales, J. M. (1998). *Other Floors, Other Voices: A Textography of a Small University Building*. Mahwah, NJ: Lawrence Erlbaum.

Talbot, M., Atkinson, K. and Atkinson, D. (eds.) (2003). *Language and Power in the Modern World*. Tuscaloosa: The University of Alabama Press.

Tashakkori, A. & Teddlie, C. (1998). *Mixed Methodology: Combining Qualitative and Quantitative Approaches*. Thousand Oaks, CA: Sage Publications.

van Els, T. (2005). Status planning for learning and teaching. In E. Hinkel (ed.), *Handbook of Research in Second Language Teaching and Learning*. Mahwah, NJ: Lawrence Erlbaum, 957–91.

van Lier, L. (1996). *Interaction in the Language Curriculum: Awareness, Autonomy & Authenticity*. London: Longman.

Vandermeeren, S. (2005). Foreign language need of business firms. In M. Long (ed.), *Second Language Needs Analysis*. Cambridge: Cambridge University Press, 159–81.

Ventola, E., Shalom, C. & Thompson, E. (eds.) (2002). *The Language of Conferencing*. Frankfurt am Main: Peter Lang.

Weiß, R. (1992). Fremdsprachen in der Wirtschaft: Bedarf und Qualifizierung. In W. Kramer and R. Weiß (eds.), *Fremdsprachen in der Wirtschaft: Ein Beitrag zu interkultureller Kompetenz*. Cologne: Deutscher Institutsverlag, 10–46.

Widdowson, H. G. [1978] (1981). *Teaching Language as Communication*. Oxford: Oxford University Press.

Widdowson, H. G. (1990). *Aspects of Language Teaching*. Oxford: Oxford University Press.

Wilkins, D. (1976). *Notional Syllabuses*. Oxford: Oxford University Press.

Willis, J. (1996). *A Framework for Task-Based Learning*. London: Longman.

Wodak, R. (1996). *Disorders of Discourse*. Harlow: Longman.

Wodak, R., Muntigl, P. & Weiss, G. (2000). *EU Discourses on Un/employment: An Interdisciplinary Approach to Employment Policy-Making and Organizational Change*. Amsterdam: Benjamins.

Yates, J., Orlikowski, W. J., Rennecker, J. (1997). Collaborative genres for collaboration: genre systems in digital media. *Proceedings of the 30th Annual Hawaii International Conference on System Sciences: Digital Documents, Vol. VI (HICSS-27)*, IEEE Computer Society, Washington, DC, 50–9.

Yli-Jokipii, H. M. (2001). The local and the global: an exploration into the Finnish and English websites of a Finnish company. *Professional Communication, IEEE Transactions*, 44 (2), June, 104–13.

Index

Note: Page numbers in *italic* indicate Glossary entries.